Scott Foresman

CALIFORNIA
MATHEMATICS

Authors and Advisors

Jennie Bennett	Charles Calhoun	Mary Cavanagh
Lucille Croom	Stephen Krulik	Robert A. Laing
Donna J. Long	Stuart J. Murphy	Jesse A Rudnick
Clementine Sherman	Marian Small	William Tate
Randall I. Charles	Alma B. Ramirez	Jeanne F. Ramos

Scott
Foresman

Editorial Offices: Glenview, Illinois • Parsippany, New Jersey • New York, New York
Sales Offices: Reading, Massachusetts • Duluth, Georgia • Glenview, Illinois
Carrollton, Texas • Ontario, California

ISBN: 0-328-00465-0

23-V064-12 11 10

Mathematician Content Reviewers

Roger Howe *Grades K–2*
Professor of Mathematics
Yale University
New Haven, Connecticut

Edward Barbeau *Grades 3–4*
Professor of Mathematics
University of Toronto
Toronto, Ontario, Canada

Gary Lippman *Grades 3–6*
Professor of Mathematics and
Computer Science
California State University Hayward
Hayward, California

David M. Bressoud *Grades 5–6*
DeWitt Wallace Professor of
Mathematics
Macalester College
Saint Paul, Minnesota

California Content Standards Reviewers

Damien Jacotin *Kindergarten*
Los Angeles, California

Donna M. Kopenski *Grade 3*
Poway, California

Jennifer Lozo *Kindergarten*
Lodi, California

Armine Aghajani *Grade 4*
Tujunga, California

Sharon Frost *Grade 1*
Burbank, California

Floyd Flack *Grade 4*
Westminster, California

Beth Gould-Golland *Grade 1*
Encinitas, California

Donna Crist *Grade 5*
Turlock, California

Linda Newland *Grade 2*
Santa Clarita, California

Jimmy C. Jordan *Grade 5*
La Crescenta, California

Wendy York *Grade 2*
Merced, California

Felicia Clark *Grade 6*
Compton, California

Shakeh Balmanoukian *Grade 3*
Glendale, California

Vahe Tcharkhoutian *Grade 6*
Pasadena, California

Contents

CHAPTER 2 — Understanding Addition

CHAPTER

3

Understanding Subtraction

5 Geometry and Fractions

CHAPTER 6

Patterns and Numbers to 100

CHAPTER 7

Relating Addition and Subtraction

CHAPTER

8

Addition and Subtraction to 20

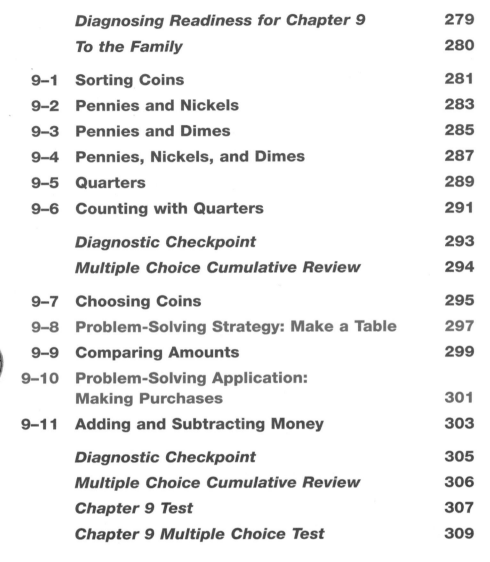

Time and Probability

CHAPTER 11

Measurement

Two-Digit Addition and Subtraction

California Mathematics Content Standards

Grade 1

Reproduced from the Mathematics Content Standards for California Public Schools. The symbol () indicates a key standard as designated by a green oval in the Mathematics Framework for California Public Schools.

By the end of grade one, students understand and use the concept of ones and tens in the place value number system. Students add and subtract small numbers with ease. They measure with simple units and locate objects in space. They describe data and analyze and solve simple problems.

Number Sense

1.0 Students understand and use numbers up to 100:

   1.1 (🗝) Count, read, and write whole numbers to 100.

   1.2 (🗝) Compare and order whole numbers to 100 by using the symbols for less than, equal to, or greater than ($<, =, >$).

   1.3 Represent equivalent forms of the same number through the use of physical models, diagrams, and number expressions (to 20) (e.g., 8 may be represented as $4 + 4, 5 + 3, 2 + 2 + 2 + 2, 10 - 2, 11 - 3$).

   1.4 Count and group objects in ones and tens (e.g., three groups of 10 and 4 equals 34, or $30 + 4$).

   1.5 Identify and know the value of coins and show different combinations of coins that equal the same value.

2.0 Students demonstrate the meaning of addition and subtraction and use these operations to solve problems:

   2.1 (🗝) Know the addition facts (sums to 20) and the corresponding subtraction facts and commit them to memory.

   2.2 (🗝) Use the inverse relationship between addition and subtraction to solve problems.

   2.3 (🗝) Identify one more than, one less than, 10 more than, and 10 less than a given number.

   2.4 (🗝) Count by 2s, 5s, and 10s to 100.

   2.5 (🗝) Show the meaning of addition (putting together, increasing) and subtraction (taking away, comparing, finding the difference).

   2.6 Solve addition and subtraction problems with one- and two-digit numbers (e.g., $5 + 58 = \_\_$).

   2.7 Find the sum of three one-digit numbers.

3.0 Students use estimation strategies in computation and problem solving that involve numbers that use the ones, tens, and hundreds places:

   3.1 Make reasonable estimates when comparing larger or smaller numbers.

Algebra and Functions

1.0 Students use number sentences with operational symbols and expressions to solve problems:

   1.1 Write and solve number sentences from problem situations that express relationships involving addition and subtraction.

   1.2 Understand the meaning of the symbols $+, -, =$.

   1.3 Create problem situations that might lead to given number sentences involving addition and subtraction.

Measurement and Geometry

1.0 Students use direct comparison and nonstandard units to describe the measurements of objects:

   1.1 Compare the length, weight, and volume of two or more objects by using direct comparison or a non-standard unit.

   1.2 Tell time to the nearest half hour and relate time to events (e.g., before/after, shorter/longer).

2.0 Students identify common geometric figures, classify them by common attributes, and describe their relative position or their location in space:

   2.1 Identify, describe, and compare triangles, rectangles, squares, and circles, including the faces of three-dimensional objects.

   2.2 Classify familiar plane and solid objects by common attributes, such as color, position, shape, size, roundness, or number of corners, and explain which attributes are being used for classification.

   2.3 Give and follow directions about location.

   2.4 Arrange and describe objects in space by proximity, position, and direction (e.g., near, far, below, above, up, down, behind, in front of, next to, left or right of).

Statistics, Data Analysis, and Probability

1.0 Students organize, represent, and compare data by category on simple graphs and charts:

   1.1 Sort objects and data by common attributes and describe the categories.

   1.2 Represent and compare data (e.g., largest, smallest, most often, least often) by using pictures, bar graphs, tally charts, and picture graphs.

2.0 Students sort objects and create and describe patterns by numbers, shapes, sizes, rhythms, or colors:

   2.1 (🗝) Describe, extend, and explain ways to get to a next element in simple repeating patterns (e.g., rhythmic, numeric, color, and shape).

Mathematical Reasoning

1.0 Students make decisions about how to set up a problem:

   1.1 Determine the approach, materials, and strategies to be used.

   1.2 Use tools, such as manipulatives or sketches, to model problems.

2.0 Students solve problems and justify their reasoning:

   2.1 Explain the reasoning used and justify the procedures selected.

   2.2 Make precise calculations and check the validity of the results from the context of the problem.

3.0 Students note connections between one problem and another.

Diagnosing Readiness
for Chapter 1

Count the objects.
Draw a line to match.

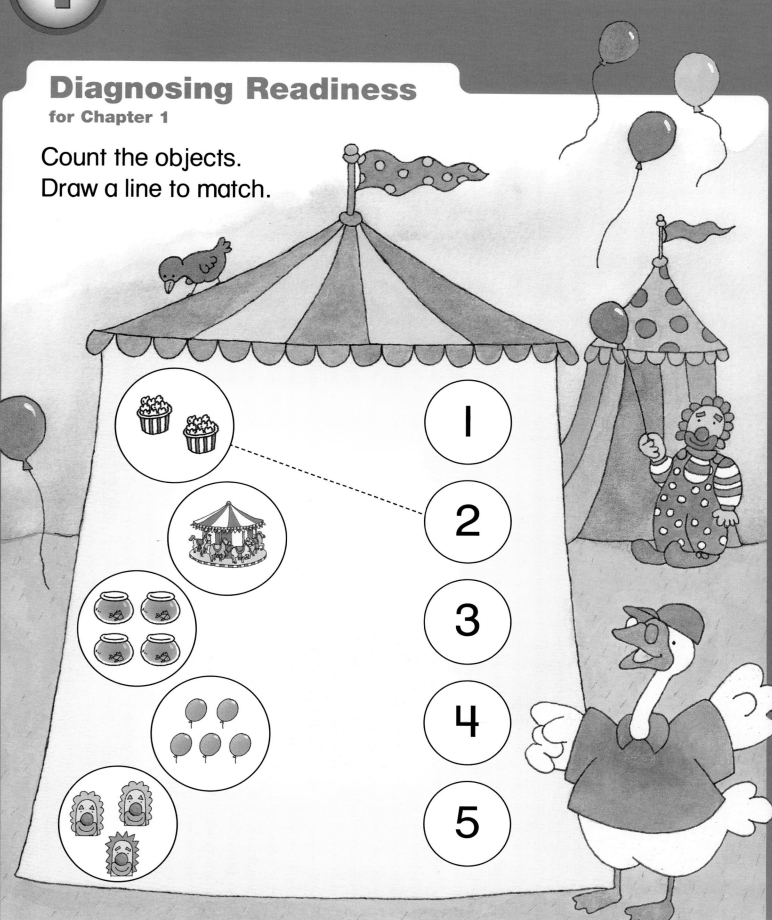

To the Family

| Looking Back | Chapter 1 | Looking Ahead |

In Kindergarten children learned to identify numbers to 100. They also compared groups of objects to determine which has more or fewer.

Children review counting numbers to 20 and learn to read and write them. They also work with place value, symbols for comparing numbers, and pictographs.

Later in Grade 1 children will use numbers to 100 and will group objects in ones and tens. They will count when learning basic facts, evaluating groups of coins, and measuring.

Page 1 Your child solved problems that review math skills from Kindergarten and will help your child with the skills in Chapter 1.

Math at Home Have your child count toys on a shelf or items in a grocery bag (up to 20). Practice comparing numbers (greater than, less than) such as two numbers on a calendar or two soccer team scores.

Math Literature Read counting stories with your child. Look for the following books in your local library.
One, Two, Three Count With Me by Catherine and Laurence Anholt (Puffin Books, 1996)
Ten Black Dots by Donald Crews (William Morrow & Company, 1986)

California Content Standards in Chapter 1 Lessons*

Number Sense	Teach and Practice	Practice
1.0 Students understand and use numbers up to 100.		12
1.1 (🔑) Count, read, and write whole numbers.	1–3, 7, 8	4–6, 9, 10
1.2 (🔑) Compare and order whole numbers by using the symbols for less than, equal to, or greater than (<, =, >).	4, 5, 9, 10	
1.3 Represent equivalent forms of the same number through the use of physical models, diagrams, and number expressions (to 20).	7	3, 8
1.4 Count and group objects in ones and tens.	7, 8	
2.3 (🔑) Identify one more than, one less than, 10 more than, and 10 less than a given number.	8	3

Measurement and Geometry	Teach and Practice	Practice
2.3 Give and follow directions about location.		11
2.4 Arrange and describe objects in space by position.	11	

Statistics, Data Analysis, and Probability	Teach and Practice	Practice
1.0 Students organize, represent, and compare data by category on simple graphs.	6	
2.0 Students sort objects and create and describe patterns by numbers, shapes, sizes, rhythms, or colors.	12	
2.1 (🔑) Describe, extend, and explain ways to get to a next element in simple repeating patterns.	13	

Mathematical Reasoning	Teach and Practice	Practice
1.0 Students make decisions about how to set up a problem.		9, 11, 13
1.2 Use tools, such as manipulatives or sketches, to model problems.		10, 12
2.0 Students solve problems and justify their reasoning.		1–3, 5–7

* The symbol (🔑) indicates a key standard as designated in the Mathematics Framework for California Public Schools.
Full statements of the California Content Standards are found at the beginning of this book following the Table of Contents.

Name_____

Numbers to 9

  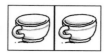 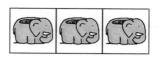 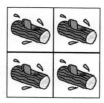 

1	2	3	4	5
one	two	three	four	five

Write the numbers.

1. one

2. two

3. three

4. four

5. five

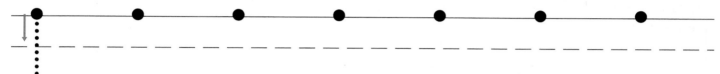

California Content Standards *Number Sense 1.1 (🔑) Count, read, and write whole numbers. Also Mathematical Reasoning 2.0.*

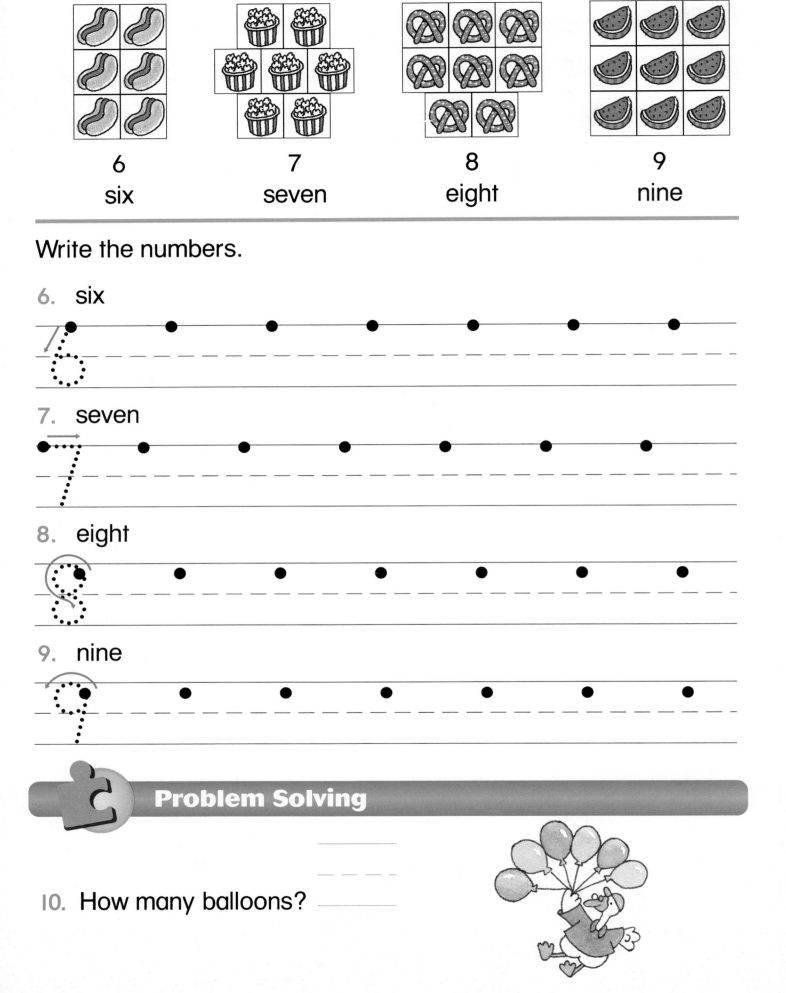

6	7	8	9
six	seven	eight	nine

Write the numbers.

6. six

7. seven

8. eight

9. nine

Problem Solving

10. How many balloons? _____

Home Activity Give your child groups containing between 1 and 9 objects. Have him or her count to tell you how many.
Homework Workbook 1-1

Name_____ **Zero**

There are zero children.

1. Write the number.

zero

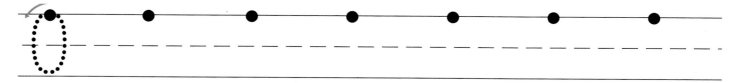

2. Write how many children in each cup.

California Content Standards *Number Sense 1.1 (🔑)*
Count, read, and write whole numbers. Also Number Sense 1.3,
Mathematical Reasoning 2.0.

Write how many riders are in each log.

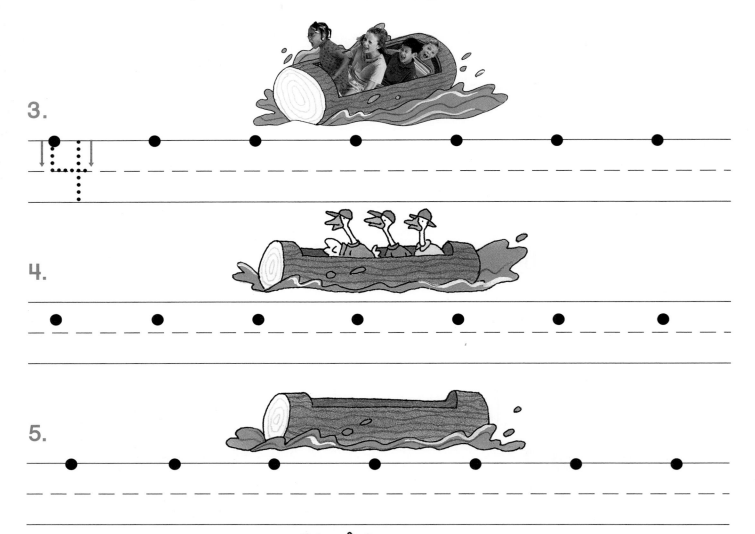

3.

4.

5.

6.

Problem Solving

7. Count.
Circle the two groups with the same number.

🏠 **Home Activity** Ask which teacups show zero children. Then have your child think of zero items in your home, such as lions.
Homework Workbook 1-2

Name_____ **Numbers to 10**

 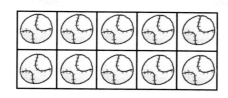

10
ten

Count and write how many.

1.

2.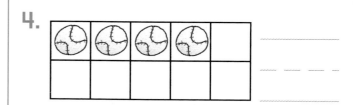

3.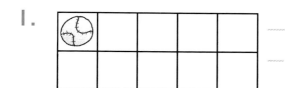

4.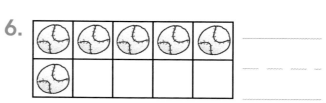

5.

6.

7.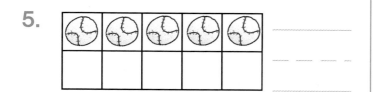

8.

9.

10.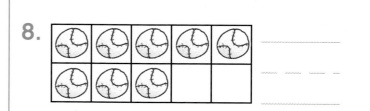

California Content Standards *Number Sense 1.1 (*🗝*)
Count, read, and write whole numbers. Also Number Sense 1.3,
2.3 (*🗝*), Mathematical Reasoning 2.0.*

seven **7**

Draw how many.

11. **3**
three
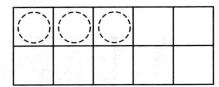

12. **4**
four
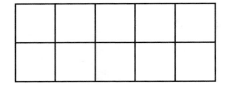

13. **5**
five
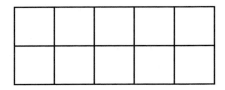

14. **9**
nine
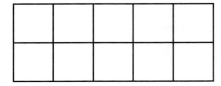

15. **8**
eight
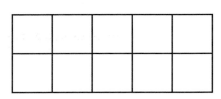

16. **6**
six
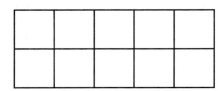

17. **10**
ten
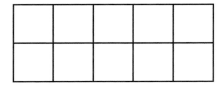

18. **7**
seven

Math Reasoning

19. Draw 1 more.
Then write how many.
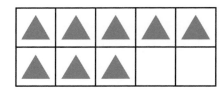

20. Draw 1 more.
Then write how many.
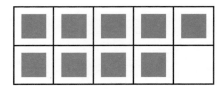

21. What pattern do you see in 19 and 20?

Home Activity Ask, "Which number is one more than 5? than 6?" and so on, for all the numbers your child knows.
Homework Workbook 1-3

Name_____   **Comparing Numbers**

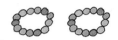

5 is **greater** than **3**

2 is **less** than **4**

Circle the number that is **greater** than the other number.

Word Bank
greater
less

1.

1   or   **2**

2.

3   or   1

3.

2   or   4

4.

6   or   5

5.   5   or   3

6.   7   or   4

7.   8   or   5

8.   1   or   6

9.   9   or   10

10.   8   or   6

California Content Standards Number Sense 1.2 (⚷)
Compare whole numbers. Also Number Sense 1.1 (⚷).

nine   **9**

Circle the number that is **less** than
the other number.

11.

5 or 8

(5 is circled)

12.

7 or 4

13. 2 or 3

14. 6 or 4

15. 3 or 1

16. 9 or 10

Circle the answer.

17. 4 is greater than / (is less than) 5

18. 6 is greater than / is less than 5

19. 3 is greater than / is less than 1

20. 1 is greater than / is less than 2

21. 8 is greater than / is less than 7

22. 10 is greater than / is less than 5

23. 9 is greater than / is less than 10

24. 6 is greater than / is less than 9

10 ten

Home Activity Show two groups of buttons with 12 or fewer in each group. Have your child tell you how many in each group and which number is greater. Homework Workbook 1-4

Name_____

Comparing Numbers to 10

3 is **greater than** 2.	2 is **less than** 3.	2 is **equal to** 2.
3 > 2	2 < 3	2 = 2

Write the numbers.
Write >, <, or = in the .

Word Bank

equal

1.   1, 2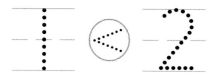

2, 3

5, 4

2.   4, 8

6, 5

9, 10

3.   9, 8

7, 2

3, 3

4.   6, 3

1, 1

4, 5

California Content Standards *Number Sense 1.2 (🔑)*
Compare whole numbers. Also Number Sense 1.1 (🔑),
Mathematical Reasoning 2.0.

eleven   **11**

Compare the numbers.
Write >, <, or = in the ○.

5. 2 ⧀ 4	3 ○ 5	6 ○ 2
6. 5 ○ 5	9 ○ 7	8 ○ 10
7. 2 ○ 1	3 ○ 6	4 ○ 4
8. 7 ○ 8	2 ○ 2	10 ○ 5

 **Problem Solving**

Use numbers between 1 and 10.
Make number statements that are true.

9. _____ ○ _____   _____ ○ _____

10. _____ ○ _____   _____ ○ _____

Home Activity Say any two numbers between 1 and 10 to your child: for example, 6 and 8. Have your child tell which is less. Homework Workbook 1-5

Name_____

How many balloons are in each color?

Understand

You need to find how many , , and .

Plan

You can make a graph.

Word Bank

graph

Solve

Look at the picture.
Color the balloons in the graph.

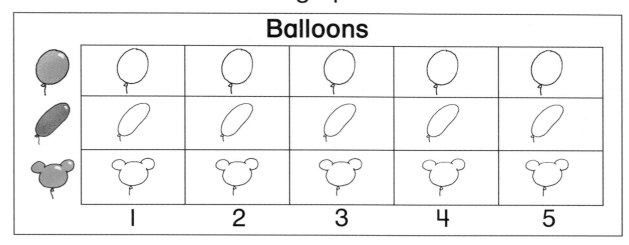

Balloons

| | 1 | 2 | 3 | 4 | 5 |

How many of each are there?

 _____   _____   _____

Look Back

Do your answers make sense?

California Content Standards *Statistics, Data Analysis, and Probability 1.0 Students organize, represent, and compare data by category on simple graphs. Also Number Sense 1.1 ( ), Mathematical Reasoning 2.0.*

1. Use the picture to make a graph.
   Color to show how many.

Prizes

2. How many of each are there?

 _____   _____   _____

Home Activity Pick some simple objects in your house and help your child make a pictograph to show how many.
Homework Workbook 1-6

Name_____

How many children are in each wagon?
Write the number.

1.

_____

_____

_____

2.

_____

_____

_____

Circle the **greater** number.

3. **9** or **6**

Circle the number that is **less**.

4. **3** or **8**

Circle the answer.

5. **4** is greater than **2**
      is less than

6. **5** is greater than **7**
      is less than

Write how many.

7. 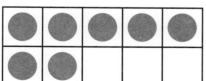 _____

8. 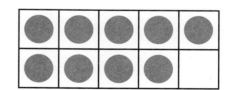 _____

Compare the numbers.
Write >, <, or = in the ◯.

9. 3 ◯ 6   10. 5 ◯ 5   11. 10 ◯ 8

Name_____

1.

   20   10   8   18
   ○   ○   ○   ○

2.

   8   9   10   11
   ○   ○   ○   ○

3.     _____

                     NH

   ○   ○   ○   ○

4. $2 < 4$ $6 > 5$ $8 > 10$ NH

   ○   ○   ○   ○

5. $5 > 2$ $3 = 6$ $10 < 9$ NH

   ○   ○   ○   ○

Oral Directions *Mark the correct answer. NH means "Not here." Mark it whenever the answer is not given.*

#1. How many counters are there?
#2. What is one more than the number in the circle?

#3. Look at the pattern. What fruit is most likely to come next?
#4. Which one is *not* true?
#5. Which one is true?

Name_____ **Numbers to 15**

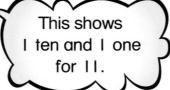

This shows
I ten and I one
for 11.

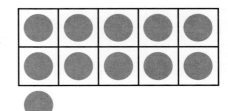

Write the number.

1. ten

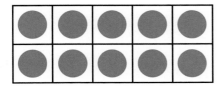

2. eleven

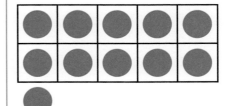

3. twelve

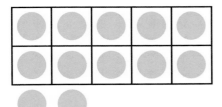

4. thirteen

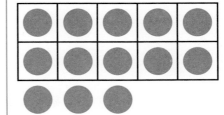

5. fourteen

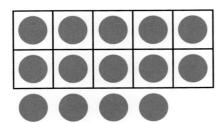

6. fifteen

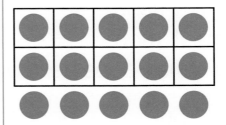

California Content Standards Number Sense 1.4 Count and group objects in ones and tens. Number Sense 1.1 (🔑), 1.3. Also Mathematical Reasoning 2.0.

Write how many.
Use counters and Workmat 2 if you like.

7. 1 ten and 2 ones is 12

8. _____ ten and _____ ones is _____

9. _____ ten and _____ ones is _____

10. _____ ten and _____ ones is _____

11. _____ ten and _____ ones is _____

Problem Solving

12. Sam had 14 fish.
He bought 1 more.
How many fish does he have?

13. Fred gave Sam 10 more fish.
How many fish are there altogether?

Home Activity Help your child find 10, 11, and 12 different objects. Ask: "How many more is 11 than 10? How many more is 12 than 10?" Homework Workbook 1-7

Name_____ **Numbers to 20**

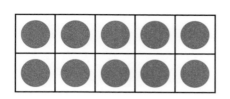 

We have 2 tens and 0 ones for 20!

Tens	Ones
2	0

Write how many tens and ones.
Use counters and Workmat 2 if you like.

1. **15**
fifteen

Tens	Ones

2. **16**
sixteen

Tens	Ones

3. **17**
seventeen

Tens	Ones

4. **18**
eighteen

Tens	Ones

5. **19**
nineteen

Tens	Ones

6. **20**
twenty

Tens	Ones

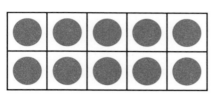

California Content Standards *Number Sense 1.4 Count and group objects in ones and tens. Number Sense 1.1 (🔑), 2.3 (🔑). Also Number Sense 1.3.*

Count. Write how many.
Then write the number that is 1 more.

7.    I more is

8.    _____   I more is   _____

9.    _____   I more is   _____

10.    _____   I more is   _____

Count. Write how many.
Circle the number that is 10 more.

11.   _____   10 more is

0   I5   25

12.   _____   10 more is

3   23   33

Home Activity Write several numbers between 10 and 20 on a sheet of paper. Ask your child how many tens and how many ones are in each number. Homework Workbook 1-8

Name_____ **Comparing Numbers**

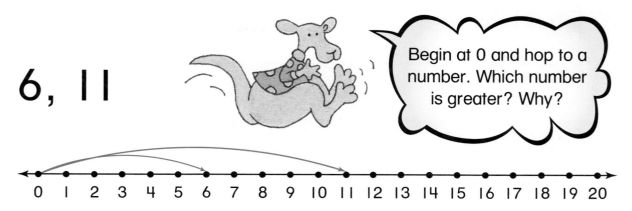

6, 11

Begin at 0 and hop to a number. Which number is greater? Why?

Hop to each number on the number line.
Then circle the greater number.

Word Bank

number line

1. 8, 10

2. 15, 12

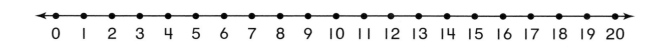

3. 6, 14

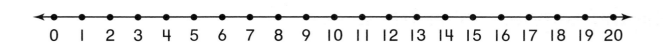

4. 20, 15

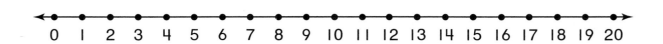

California Content Standards *Number Sense 1.2 (🔑)*
Compare whole numbers by using symbols. Also Number Sense
1.1 (🔑), Mathematical Reasoning 1.0.

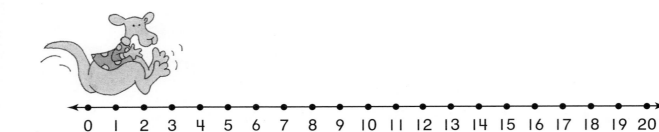

0 1 2 3 4 5 6 7 8 9 10 11 12 13 14 15 16 17 18 19 20

Use the number line to compare numbers.
Write >, <, or = in the ◯.

5. 10 ◯< 11   12 ◯ 3   7 ◯ 2

6. 15 ◯ 13   19 ◯ 20   15 ◯ 15

7. 8 ◯ 18   14 ◯ 16   17 ◯ 11

8. 1 ◯ 1   1 ◯ 4   19 ◯ 16

Problem Solving

Use numbers between 0 and 20.

Write >, <, or = in the ◯.

9. _____ ◯   10. _____ ◯

Home Activity Say a number bween 10 and 20. Have your child tell you a number that is greater or less than yours. Repeat. Homework Workbook 1-9

Name_____ **Ordering Numbers to 20**

17 comes just **before** 18.
18 is **between** 17 and 19.
19 comes just **after** 18.

Word Bank

before
after
between

Write each number that comes just **after**.

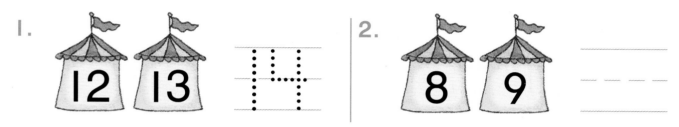

1. 12 13 14

2. 8 9 ____

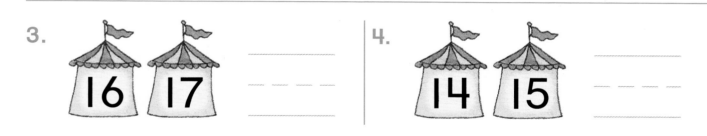

3. 16 17 ____

4. 14 15 ____

Write each number that comes just **before**.

5. ____ 8 9

6. ____ 10 11

7. ____ 12 13

8. ____ 19 20

California Content Standards *Number Sense 1.2 (◉—)* *Compare and order whole numbers. Also Number Sense 1.1 (◉—), Mathematical Reasoning 1.2.*

twenty-three **23**

Write each number that comes **between**.

9. 5, 6, 7

10. 10, ____, 12

11. 15, ____, 17

12. 18, ____, 20

Write each number that comes just **before** and **after**.

13. ____, 11, ____

14. ____, 4, ____

15. ____, 15, ____

16. ____, 17, ____

Problem Solving

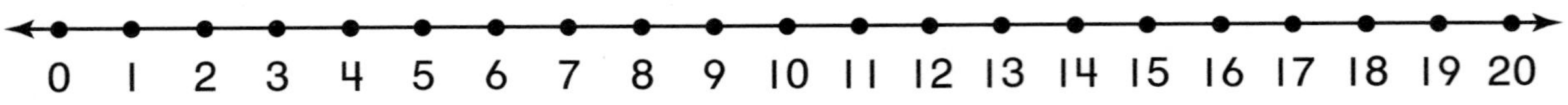

0 1 2 3 4 5 6 7 8 9 10 11 12 13 14 15 16 17 18 19 20

Count backwards.
Use the number line if you need to.

17. 20, 19, 18, ____, ____, ____,

Home Activity Invite your child to count with you from 1 to 20. Talk about numbers that come before, after, or between other numbers. Homework Workbook 1-10

Name_____ **Ordinals**

first   second   third   fourth   fifth   sixth   seventh   eighth   ninth   tenth

Circle the correct place.

1.

second
~~third~~
fourth

2.

third
fourth
fifth

3.

first
fifth
seventh

4.

ninth
seventh
sixth

5.

tenth
first
fourth

6.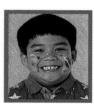

eighth
sixth
fourth

7.

sixth
ninth
third

8.

second
tenth
seventh

9.

eighth
third
second

California Content Standards *Measurement and Geometry 2.4 Arrange and describe objects in space by position. Also Measurement and Geometry 2.3, Mathematical Reasoning 1.0.*

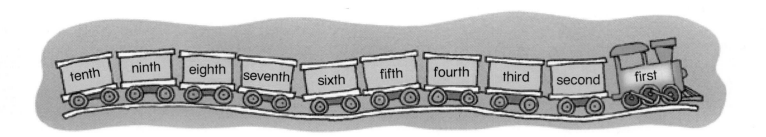

tenth | ninth | eighth | seventh | sixth | fifth | fourth | third | second | first

Color.

10. third (blue)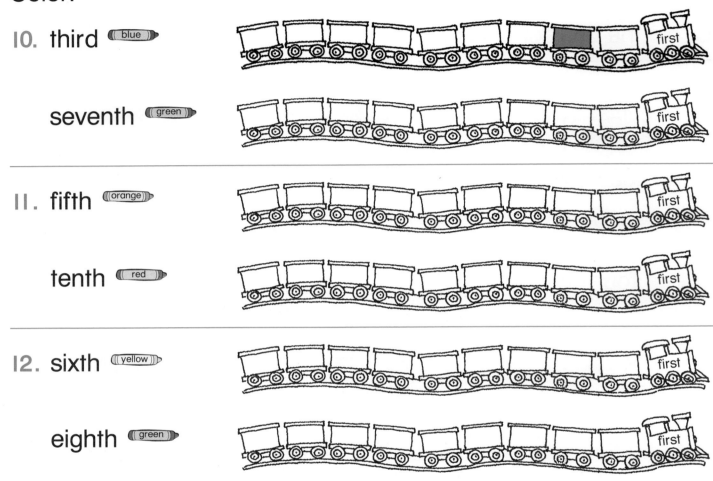

seventh (green)

first

11. fifth (orange)

first

tenth (red)

first

12. sixth (yellow)

first

eighth (green)

first

Problem Solving

13. Bob is first in line.
Tina is farthest from Bob.
Brian is next to Tina.
Jane is between Brian and Bob.
Name the children in order.

 Home Activity Discuss with your child the order in which tasks are done. For example, say: "First, I put on my socks. Second, I put on my shoes. Third, I tie my laces." Homework Workbook 1-11

Name_____ **Patterns in Numbers**

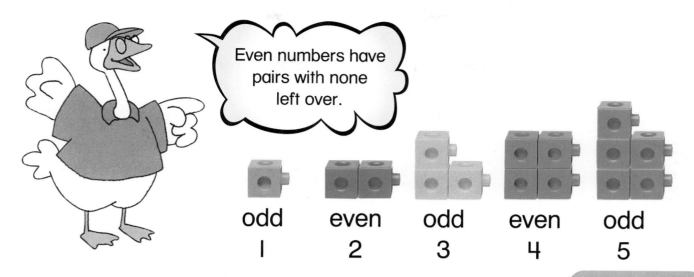

Even numbers have pairs with none left over.

odd 1　even 2　odd 3　even 4　odd 5

Circle **even** or **odd**.
Use cubes if you like.

1.
3
even　(odd)

2.
5
even　odd

3.
6
even　odd

4.
7
even　odd

5.
2
even　odd

6.
10
even　odd

7.
11
even　odd

8.
12
even　odd

California Content Standards *Statistics, Data Analysis, and Probability 2.0 Students sort objects and describe patterns by numbers. Also Number Sense 1.0, Mathematical Reasoning 1.2.*

twenty-seven **27**

Look at the pattern. What number comes next?

9.
4, 5, 6, _____   7

10.
12, 13, 14, _____

11.
2, 4, 6, _____

12.
1, 3, 5, 7, _____

13.
5, 4, 3, _____

14.
20, 19, 18, _____

15.
5, 10, 15, _____

16.
0, 10, 20, _____

Problem Solving

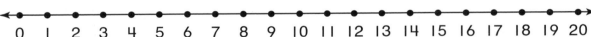

0 1 2 3 4 5 6 7 8 9 10 11 12 13 14 15 16 17 18 19 20

17. Use the number line to count backwards by even numbers.
Write the missing numbers.

20, 18, _____, 14, _____, _____, 8

18. Use the number line to count backwards by odd numbers.
Write the missing numbers.

19, 17, _____, 13, _____, _____, 7

28 twenty-eight

Home Activity Have your child skip count to 20 by even
numbers (0, 2, 4 ,6, etc.) or odd numbers (1, 3, 5, etc.).
Homework Workbook 1-12

Name_____

Think: Color to show the pattern.
What color is most likely to come next?

1.

2.

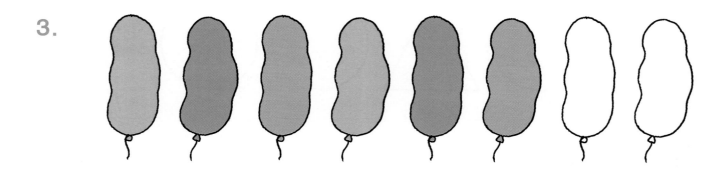

3.

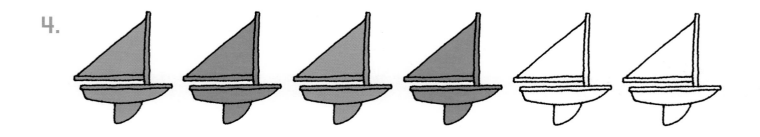

4.

5.

California Content Standards *Statistics, Data Analysis, and Probability 2.1 (🔑) Describe, extend, and explain ways to get to a next element in simple repeating patterns. Also Mathematical Reasoning 1.0.*

Draw and color to show a pattern.

6.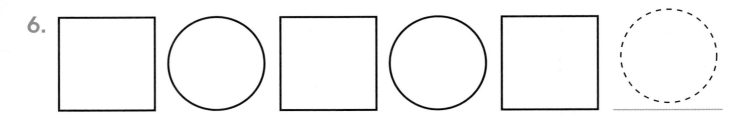

7.

8.

9.

10.

 Math Reasoning

11. What if you have only 1 crayon?
What pattern could you make?
Draw and color a pattern.

🏠 **Home Activity** Ask your child to tell you about each pattern.
Then have your child make a pattern with household objects
such as forks and spoons. Homework Workbook 1-13

1. Write how many ducks.
   Write the number that is 1 more.

   _ _ _ _ _ _ _   _ _ _ _ _ _

   1 more is   _ _ _ _ _ _

---

2. Circle the animal that is most likely
   to come next in the pattern.

Write how many tens and ones.

3. 16
    sixteen

Tens	Ones

4. 20
    twenty

Tens	Ones

Write the missing numbers.

5. _ _ _ _ _ , 10, 11

6. 19, 18, _ _ _ _ _

Use the number line to compare numbers.

Write <, >, or = in the ◯ .

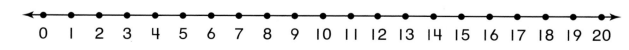

   0 1 2 3 4 5 6 7 8 9 10 11 12 13 14 15 16 17 18 19 20

7. 5 ◯ 1   8. 14 ◯ 17   9. 3 ◯ 13

Name_____

1.    19

9	29	39	20
○	○	○	○

2.

0	2	3	5
○	○	○	○

3.   11, 12, _____

10	14	12	13
○	○	○	○

4.

○   ○   ○   ○   first

5.
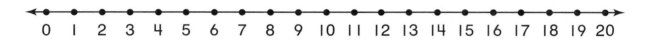

13 < 16	19 < 17	12 > 14	NH
○	○	○	○

6.

1	3	7	NH
○	○	○	○

7.

5	6	8	NH
○	○	○	○

Oral Directions *Mark the correct answer. NH means "Not here." Mark it whenever the answer is not given.*

#1. What is ten more than the number in the circle?
#2. How many flowers are in the third vase?

#3. What number comes just after twelve if you are counting by ones?
#4. Mark under the tenth butterfly.
#5. Which one is true?
#6. Which one is an even number?
#7. Which one is an odd number?

Name_____

Write the number of balloons.

1. 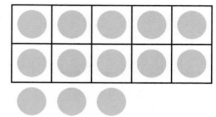 _____

2.  _____

Count.
Write how many.

3.

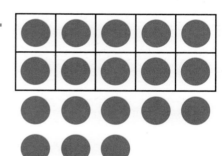

_____ ten and _____ ones is _____

4.

_____ ten and _____ ones is _____

Use the graph.
Write how many there are.

5. _____   6. _____

Circle the even numbers.

7.   1   2   3   4   5   6   7   8   9   10

Circle the answer.

8. 3   is greater than   1
      is less than

9. 12   is greater than   18
      is less than

Write the missing numbers.

10. 7, _____ , 9

11. 11, 12, _____

Use the number line to compare numbers.
Write <, >, or = in the ◯.

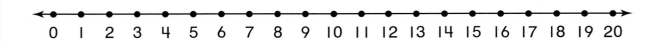

0 1 2 3 4 5 6 7 8 9 10 11 12 13 14 15 16 17 18 19 20

12. 6 ◯ 9   13. 14 ◯ 4   14. 19 ◯ 17

15. Draw and color the shape that is most likely to come next.

        _____

first

16. Color the third bear yellow.

17. Color the seventh bear red.

Name_____ Multiple Choice Test

1.    10 ○   14 ○   15 ○   20 ○

2.   (11)   12 ○   13 ○   10 ○   11 ○

3.   (14)   4 ○   10 ○   24 ○   34 ○

4. 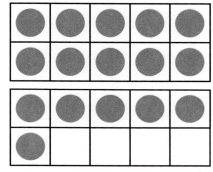   0 ○   1 ○   2 ○   6 ○

5. **Farm Animals**

2 ○   5 ○   0 ○   4 ○

Oral Directions *Mark the correct answer. NH means "Not here." Mark it whenever the answer is not given.*

#1. How many stars are shown?

#2. What is one more than the number in the circle?
#3. What is ten more than the number in the circle?
#4. How many tens are shown?
#5. Look at the graph. How many cows are there?

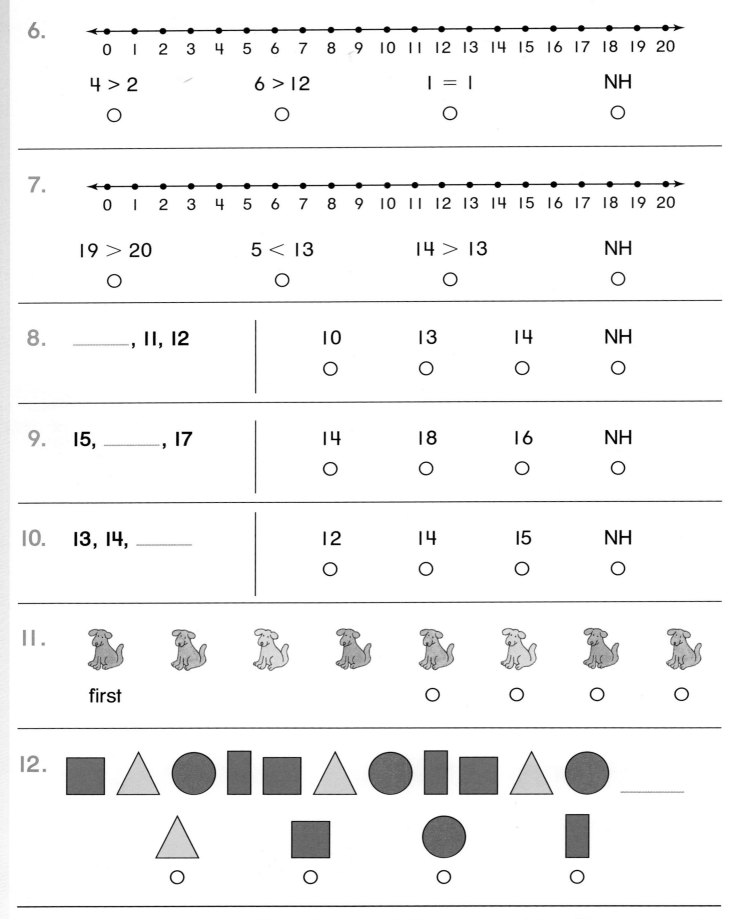

6.

| 0 1 2 3 4 5 6 7 8 9 10 11 12 13 14 15 16 17 18 19 20 |

4 > 2	6 > 12	1 = 1	NH
○	○	○	○

7.

| 0 1 2 3 4 5 6 7 8 9 10 11 12 13 14 15 16 17 18 19 20 |

19 > 20	5 < 13	14 > 13	NH
○	○	○	○

8. _____ , 11, 12

10	13	14	NH
○	○	○	○

9. 15, _____, 17

14	18	16	NH
○	○	○	○

10. 13, 14, _____

12	14	15	NH
○	○	○	○

11.

first   ○   ○   ○   ○

12.

○   ○   ○   ○

Oral Directions *Mark the correct answer. NH means "Not here." Mark it whenever the answer is not given.*

#6–7. Which one is *not* true?
#8. What number comes just before eleven if you are counting by ones?

#9. What number comes between fifteen and seventeen?
#10. What number comes just after fourteen if you are counting by ones?
#11. Mark under the fifth dog.
#12. Look at the pattern. What shape is most likely to come next?

36 thirty-six

CHAPTER 2

Understanding Addition

Diagnosing Readiness

for Chapter 2

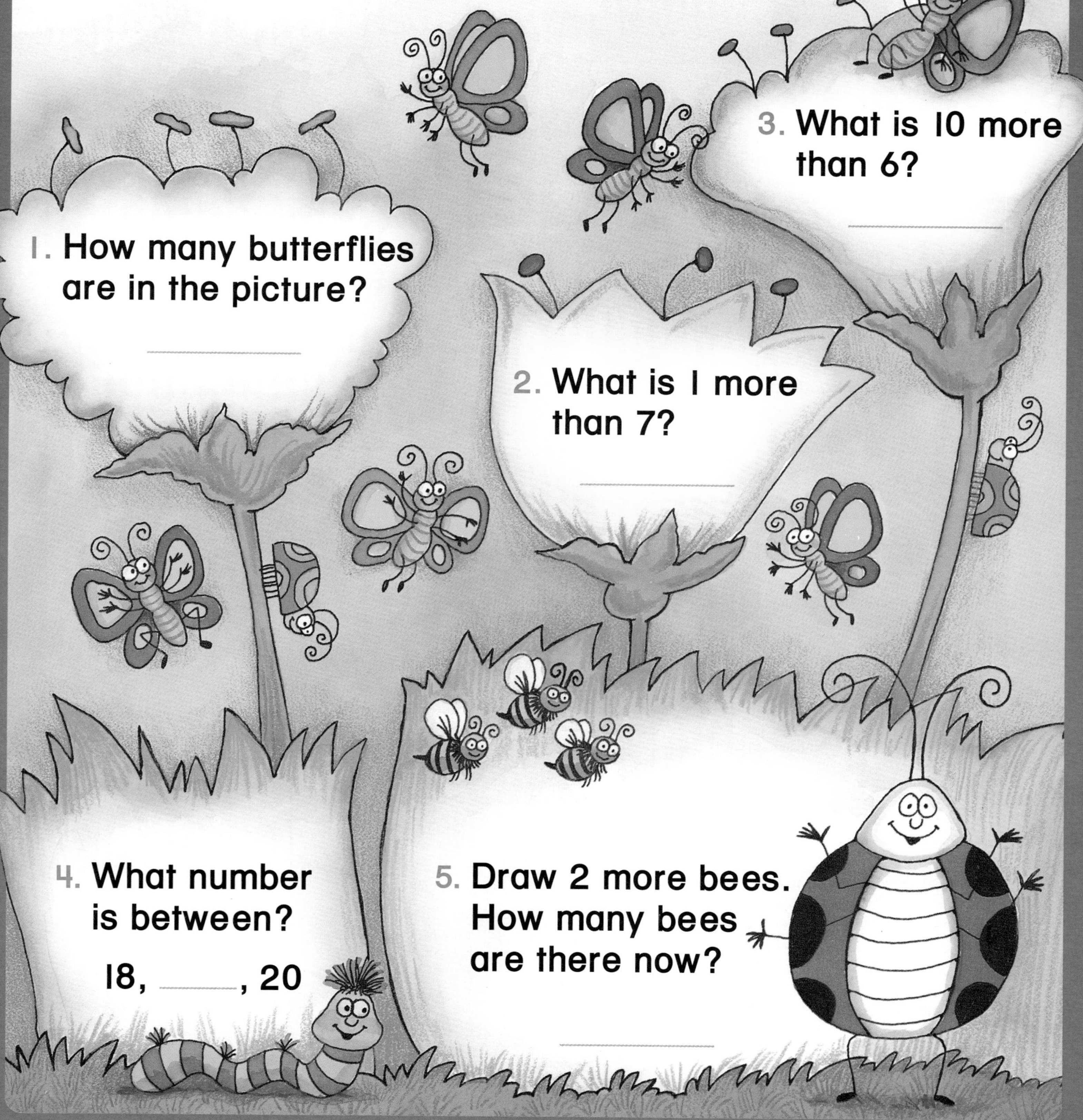

1. How many butterflies are in the picture? ______

2. What is 1 more than 7? ______

3. What is 10 more than 6? ______

4. What number is between?

   18, ______, 20

5. Draw 2 more bees. How many bees are there now? ______

To the Family

In Kindergarten children were introduced to addition through the process of joining two groups. Children learned basic addition facts with sums to ten.	While studying basic facts with sums to eight, children learn two meanings of addition: joining two groups and adding on to a group. Also, they are introduced to the + sign.	In Chapters 4 and 8 children learn basic fact strategies for addition facts with sums to 20. In Chapter 12 they learn to add a one-digit number to a two-digit number.

Page 37 Your child solved problems that review math skills from previous chapters and will help your child with the skills in Chapter 2.

Math at Home Help your child learn and memorize basic facts through experiences that involve joining two groups or adding on to a given quantity. For example, add two separate groups of toys or add toys to an existing group of toys.

Math Literature Read stories about addition with your child. Look for the following books in your local library.
One Gorilla by Atsuko Morozumi (Econo-Clad Books, 1999)
So Many Cats! by Beatrice Schenk De Regniers (Houghton Mifflin Co, 1988)

California Content Standards in Chapter 2 Lessons*

	Teach and Practice	Practice		Teach and Practice	Practice
Number Sense			**Statistics, Data Analysis, and Probablity**		
1.3 Represent equivalent forms of the same number through the use of physical models, diagrams, and number expressions (to 20).	4, 5	10	1.0 Students organize, represent, and compare data by category on simple graphs and charts.	7	
2.1 (🔑) Know the addition facts (sums to 20) and the corresponding subtraction facts and commit them to memory.	4–6, 9, 10	11	**Mathematical Reasoning**		
			1.0 Students make decisions about how to set up a problem.		2
2.5 (🔑) Show the meaning of addition (putting together, increasing).	1, 2, 4, 5, 8	3, 6, 7, 9, 10, 12	1.1 Determine the approach, materials, and strategies to be used.	12	6, 8
Algebra and Functions			1.2 Use tools, such as manipulatives or sketches, to model problems.	8	1–5, 11
1.0 Students use number sentences with operational symbols and expressions to solve problems.	7		2.0 Students solve problems and justify their reasoning.		9
1.1 Write and solve number sentences from problem situations that express relationships involving addition.	11	10	2.1 Explain the reasoning used and justify the procedures selected.		4, 7
1.2 Understand the meaning of +, −, =.	3		3.0 Students note connections between one problem and another.	6	7
1.3 Create problem situations that might lead to given number sentences involving addition and subtraction.		3, 8, 12			

* The symbol (🔑) indicates a key standard as designated in the Mathematics Framework for California Public Schools.
Full statements of the California Content Standards are found at the beginning of this book following the Table of Contents.

Name_____

Using Counters to Add

You can add numbers together to find how many in all.

3 and **2**  in all

Word Bank
in all
altogether

Use counters
Write how many.

1.
   1   and   **3** _____ in all

2.
   4   and   **1** _____ in all

3.
   2   and   **2** _____ in all

4.
   4   and   **2** _____ in all

5.
   2   and   **1** _____ altogether

6.
   2   and   **3** _____ altogether

California Content Standards *Number Sense 2.5* Show the meaning of addition. Also Mathematical Reasoning 1.2.

thirty-nine **39**

Write how many.

7. 	3	2	5 altogether
8. 	_____	_____	_____ in all
9.	_____	_____	_____ in all
10. 	_____	_____	_____ altogether
11. 	_____	_____	_____ in all

 **Problem Solving**

Solve. Use counters if you like.

12. How many bugs are there in all?

_____ bugs

13. I more bug joins them. How many bugs are there now?

_____ bugs

🏠 **Home Activity** Counters can help children add. Use pennies or common household items to help your child show numbers and add. Homework Workbook 2-1

Name_____ **Using Pictures to Add**

Write the numbers.

1.

   2   and   2   are   4   in all

2.

   _____ and _____ are _____ in all

3.

   _____ and _____ are _____ in all

4.

   _____ and _____ are _____ in all

5.

   _____ and _____ are _____ in all

6.

   _____ and _____ are _____ in all

7.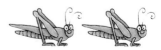

   _____ and _____ are _____ in all

California Content Standards *Number Sense 2.5* (🗝️) *Show the meaning of addition. Also Mathematical Reasoning 1.0, 1.2.*

Draw to show each number.
Write how many.

8.

2   and   3   are   _____ in all

9.

4   and   I   are   _____ altogether

10. Draw 2 groups. Write how many.

_____ and _____ are _____ in all

Home Activity Ask your child to draw simple pictures to make addition stories. Homework Workbook 2-2

Name_____ **Using Symbols to Add**

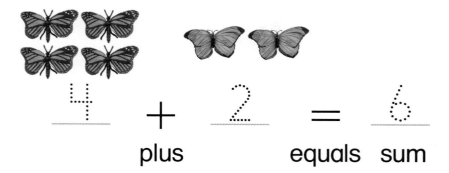

$$\underline{4} \quad + \quad \underline{2} \quad = \quad \underline{6}$$

plus   equals   sum

Word Bank

plus
equals
sum
add

Write the numbers. Add.

1.

____ + ____ = ____

2.

____ + ____ = ____

3.

____ + ____ = ____

4.

____ + ____ = ____

5.

____ + ____ = ____

6.

____ + ____ = ____

7.

____ + ____ = ____

8.

____ + ____ = ____

California Content Standards *Algebra and Functions 1.2
Students understand the meaning of the symbols + and =. Also
Number Sense 2.5 (⬤), Algebra and Functions 1.3,
Mathematical Reasoning 1.2.*

Find each sum.
Use counters if you like.

9. $3 + 1 = $ _____ $4 + 2 = $ _____ $3 + 3 = $ _____

10. $2 + 3 = $ _____ $1 + 1 = $ _____ $4 + 1 = $ _____

11. $2 + 2 = $ _____ $5 + 1 = $ _____ $1 + 3 = $ _____

12. $2 + 4 = $ _____ $3 + 2 = $ _____ $1 + 4 = $ _____

13. $1 + 2 = $ _____ $1 + 5 = $ _____ $2 + 2 = $ _____

Problem Solving

Draw a picture for each number sentence.

14. $4 + 1 = 5$ 15. $2 + 4 = 6$

Home Activity Give your child some buttons or pennies to add. Ask your child to write the problems, using + and =.
Homework Workbook 2-3

Name_____ **Sums to 6**

I can make sums for 3 in many ways.

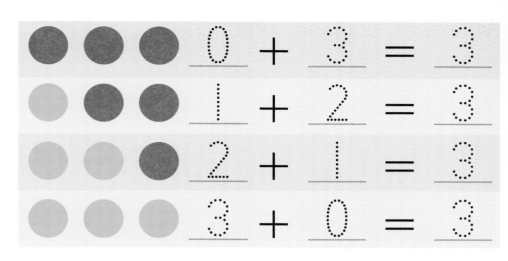

0 + 3 = 3

1 + 2 = 3

2 + 1 = 3

3 + 0 = 3

How many ways can you make sums for 5?
Use counters. Color.
Write each addition sentence.
Look for a pattern.

Word Bank

addition sentence

1. ○○○○○   _____ + _____ = _____

2. ○○○○○   _____ + _____ = _____

3. ○○○○○   _____ + _____ = _____

4. ○○○○○   _____ + _____ = _____

5. ○○○○○   _____ + _____ = _____

6. ○○○○○   _____ + _____ = _____

California Content Standards *Number Sense 1.3 Represent equivalent forms of the same number. Number Sense 2.1 (🔑), 2.5 (🔑). Also Mathematical Reasoning 1.2, 2.1.*

forty-five **45**

How many ways can you make sums for 6?
Use counters. Color.
Write each addition sentence.

7. ◯◯◯◯◯◯   _____ + _____ = _____

8. ◯◯◯◯◯◯   _____ + _____ = _____

9. ◯◯◯◯◯◯   _____ + _____ = _____

10. ◯◯◯◯◯◯   _____ + _____ = _____

11. ◯◯◯◯◯◯   _____ + _____ = _____

12. ◯◯◯◯◯◯   _____ + _____ = _____

13. ◯◯◯◯◯◯   _____ + _____ = _____

Math Reasoning

Number Sense

14. Are there more ways to make
sums for 4 or to make sums for 6?
Tell why. Then try it.

Home Activity Review different ways to show sums for 5
and 6. Encourage your child to write sums for other numbers.
Homework Workbook 2-4

Name_____

Sums to 8

Use counters to show ways to make sums
for 7. Color. Write the addition sentence.

1.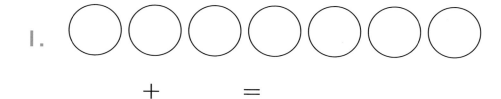

_____ + _____ = _____

2.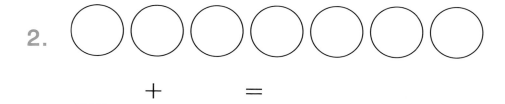

_____ + _____ = _____

3. ○○○○○○○

_____ + _____ = _____

4. ○○○○○○○

_____ + _____ = _____

5. ○○○○○○○

_____ + _____ = _____

6. ○○○○○○○

_____ + _____ = _____

California Content Standards Number Sense 1.3 Represent equivalent forms of the same number. Number Sense 2.1 (🔑), 2.5 (🔑). Also Mathematical Reasoning 1.2.

Use counters to show ways to make sums
for 8. Color. Write the addition sentence.

7.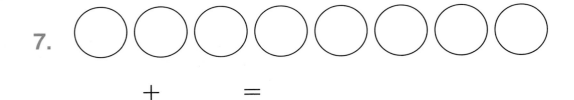

_____ + _____ = _____

8.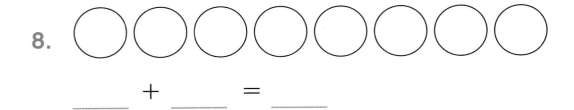

_____ + _____ = _____

9. ⬤⬤⬤⬤⬤⬤⬤⬤

_____ + _____ = _____

10. ⬤⬤⬤⬤⬤⬤⬤⬤

_____ + _____ = _____

11. ⬤⬤⬤⬤⬤⬤⬤⬤

_____ + _____ = _____

12. ⬤⬤⬤⬤⬤⬤⬤⬤

_____ + _____ = _____

Home Activity Review the different ways to show sums for 7
and 8. Encourage your child to write sums for other numbers.
Homework Workbook 2-5

Name_____ **Adding Across and Down**

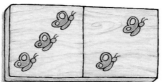

You can add across.
You can add down.

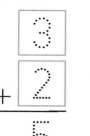

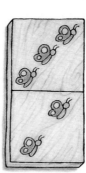

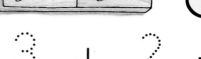

3 + 2 = 5

$+\begin{array}{c}3\\2\\\hline 5\end{array}$

Write the numbers. Add.

1.

_____ + _____ = _____

2.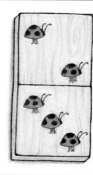

_____ + _____ = _____

3.

_____ + _____ = _____

4.

_____ + _____ = _____

California Content Standards *Number Sense 2.1 (🔑) Know the addition facts. Mathematical Reasoning 3.0. Also Number Sense 2.5 (🔑), Mathematical Reasoning 1.1.*

Add.

Use counters if you like.

5. $1 + 5 = \underline{6}$ $2 + 2 = \underline{}$ $5 + 2 = \underline{}$

6. $4 + 4 = \underline{}$ $3 + 2 = \underline{}$ $1 + 1 = \underline{}$

7. $2 + 4 = \underline{}$ $3 + 5 = \underline{}$ $3 + 4 = \underline{}$

8.
$$
\begin{array}{cccccc}
5 & 1 & 2 & 6 & 5 & 4 \\
+\,1 & +\,3 & +\,5 & +\,1 & +\,3 & +\,1 \\
\hline
\end{array}
$$

9.
$$
\begin{array}{cccccc}
6 & 4 & 2 & 1 & 4 & 3 \\
+\,2 & +\,3 & +\,6 & +\,7 & +\,2 & +\,1 \\
\hline
\end{array}
$$

 Math Reasoning

10. Use only even numbers: 2, 4, 6, and 8.
Write as many addition sentences as you can.

Home Activity Show two groups of buttons. Ask your child to add in horizontal and vertical problems. Discuss similarities and differences. Homework Workbook 2-6

Write the number sentences.

1.

_____ + _____ = _____

2.

_____ + _____ = _____

Write the numbers.

3.

_____ and _____ are _____ altogether

Show 1 way to make a sum for 8.
Color. Write the addition sentence.

4. ◯ ◯ ◯ ◯ ◯ ◯ ◯ ◯

_____ + _____ = _____

Find the sum.
Use counters if you like.

5. 1 + 1 = _____   6. 2 + 3 = _____   7. 5 + 2 = _____

8.   4   9.   7   10.   3
    + 2   + 1   + 3
   _____   _____   _____

1. 13, 14, _____

    12   15   16   17
    ○   ○   ○   ○

2.

    4 + 2 = 6   3 + 2 = 5
        ○   ○

    4 + 1 = 5   3 + 3 = 6
        ○   ○

3.  16

    6   16   26   36
    ○   ○   ○   ○

4.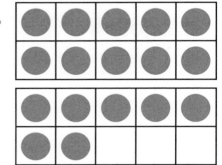

    17   1   7   10
    ○   ○   ○   ○

5. **Weather**
    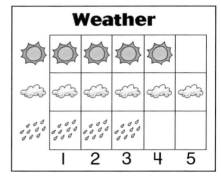

    2   3   4   5
    ○   ○   ○   ○

6.  ★ ★ ★ ★ ★ ★ ★ ★ ★

    first

                    ○   ○   ○   ○

Oral Directions *Mark the correct answer. NH means "Not here." Mark it whenever the answer is not given.*

#1. What number comes just after fourteen if you are counting by ones?

#2. Look at the picture. Mark the addition sentence that tells about the picture.
#3. What number is ten more than the number in the circle?
#4. A box of ten is shown. How many ones are shown?
#5. Look at the graph. How many suns are there?
#6. Mark under the ninth star.

Name_____

Solve.
Draw a picture or write an addition sentence.

1. 2 ants crawl.
    3 more come.
    How many ants are there in all? _____

2. 3 bugs fly.
    4 more join them.
    How many bugs are there altogether? _____

3. 2 bees buzz.
    2 more join them.
    How many bees are there in all? _____

California Content Standards Algebra and Functions 1.0
Students use number sentences to solve problems. Statistics, Data
Analysis, and Probability 1.0. Also Number Sense 2.5 (☞),
Mathematical Reasoning 2.1, 3.0.

4. Ask 5 friends how they like to add.
Color a box to show each friend's way.

How We Like to Add

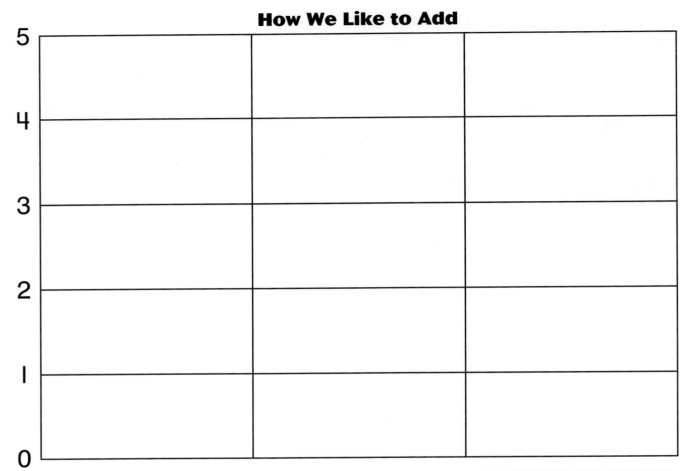

Use counters	Use pictures	Use numbers
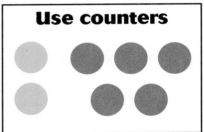  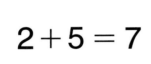

$2 + 5 = 7$

Math Reasoning

Number Sense

5. Share your graph with a friend.
Tell how your graphs are the same.
Tell how they are different.

 Home Activity Encourage your child to talk about the different ways to solve addition problems. Make up some problems for your child to solve. Homework Workbook 2-7

Name_____ **Problem-Solving Strategy**

Act It Out

3 frogs are in the pond. In hop 3 more. How many frogs are there in all?

Understand

You need to find out how many frogs in all.

Plan

You can act out the problem. Use counters and the pond.

Solve

Show 3 counters. Put in 3 more. There are 6 frogs in all.

Look Back

Did you answer the question?

Use counters to solve.

1. On the log are 2 butterflies. 2 more are on the rock. How many butterflies are there altogether?

2. 2 ducks are in the pond. 3 more join them. How many ducks are there now?

   _____

 California Content Standards Mathematical Reasoning 1.2 Use tools, such as manipulatives or sketches, to model problems. Number Sense 2.5 (🔑). Also Algebra and Functions 1.3, Mathematical Reasoning 1.1.

Use counters to act out the story.
Write the number.

3. 2 ladybugs come to the picnic. I bee flies to join them. How many bugs are there?

_____

4. 3 ants play games. 3 butterflies join them. How many bugs play games?

_____

5. 4 bees fly into the jam jar. 3 more bees come. How many bees are in the jar?

_____

6. 5 ladybugs and 3 butterflies eat grapes. How many bugs eat grapes?

_____

7. I butterfly and 4 ants dance. How many bugs dance?

_____

8. 6 ladybugs and 2 ants take a nap. How many bugs take a nap?

_____

 Math Reasoning

Write a number story that tells about the number sentence.

9. $5 + 1 = 6$

_____

_____

Home Activity Children can use counters or common household items to act out a problem. Make up problems for your child to act out. Homework Workbook 2–8

Name_____

Adding with Zero

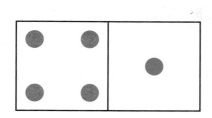

What happens when you add zero?

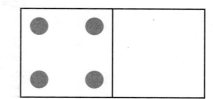

$4 + 1 = \underline{5}$

$4 + 0 = \underline{4}$

Add.

1.

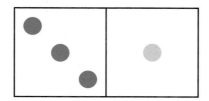

$3 + 1 = \underline{\hspace{1cm}}$

2.

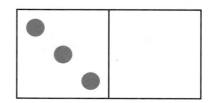

$3 + 0 = \underline{\hspace{1cm}}$

3.

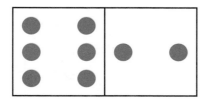

$6 + 2 = \underline{\hspace{1cm}}$

4.

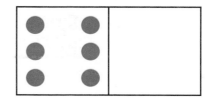

$6 + 0 = \underline{\hspace{1cm}}$

5.

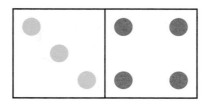

$3 + 4 = \underline{\hspace{1cm}}$

6.

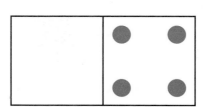

$0 + 4 = \underline{\hspace{1cm}}$

California Content Standards *Number Sense 2.1 (key)*
Know the addition facts. Also Number Sense 2.5 (key),
Mathematical Reasoning 2.0.

fifty-seven **57**

Add. Use counters if you like.
Look for facts with zero.

7. $2 + 0 = 2$ $1 + 3 = \underline{\hspace{1cm}}$ $0 + 0 = \underline{\hspace{1cm}}$

8. $5 + 2 = \underline{\hspace{1cm}}$ $3 + 0 = \underline{\hspace{1cm}}$ $0 + 1 = \underline{\hspace{1cm}}$

9.
$$\begin{array}{c} 3 \\ +\,3 \\ \hline \end{array} \qquad \begin{array}{c} 4 \\ +\,0 \\ \hline \end{array} \qquad \begin{array}{c} 1 \\ +\,4 \\ \hline \end{array} \qquad \begin{array}{c} 0 \\ +\,7 \\ \hline \end{array} \qquad \begin{array}{c} 5 \\ +\,0 \\ \hline \end{array} \qquad \begin{array}{c} 7 \\ +\,1 \\ \hline \end{array}$$

10.
$$\begin{array}{c} 2 \\ +\,6 \\ \hline \end{array} \qquad \begin{array}{c} 0 \\ +\,3 \\ \hline \end{array} \qquad \begin{array}{c} 3 \\ +\,2 \\ \hline \end{array} \qquad \begin{array}{c} 8 \\ +\,0 \\ \hline \end{array} \qquad \begin{array}{c} 4 \\ +\,3 \\ \hline \end{array} \qquad \begin{array}{c} 0 \\ +\,2 \\ \hline \end{array}$$

11.
$$\begin{array}{c} 0 \\ +\,6 \\ \hline \end{array} \qquad \begin{array}{c} 1 \\ +\,2 \\ \hline \end{array} \qquad \begin{array}{c} 7 \\ +\,0 \\ \hline \end{array} \qquad \begin{array}{c} 4 \\ +\,2 \\ \hline \end{array} \qquad \begin{array}{c} 0 \\ +\,5 \\ \hline \end{array} \qquad \begin{array}{c} 4 \\ +\,4 \\ \hline \end{array}$$

Math Reasoning

12. What is the sum of zero and any number?

_____

_____

Home Activity Ask your child "What is one million and one plus zero?" and similiar questions with large numbers.
Homework Workbook 2-9

Name_____

Adding in Any Order

Algebra

$4 + 1 = 5$

I can add in any order.

$1 + 4 = 5$

Use counters.
Write each sum.

1. $4 + 3 = $ _____

   $3 + 4 = $ _____

2. $5 + 1 = $ _____

   $1 + 5 = $ _____

3. $1 + 3 = $ _____

   $3 + 1 = $ _____

4. $6 + 1 = $ _____

   $1 + 6 = $ _____

5. $5 + 2 = $ _____

   $2 + 5 = $ _____

6. $3 + 2 = $ _____

   $2 + 3 = $ _____

7. $5 + 3 = $ _____

   $3 + 5 = $ _____

8. $7 + 1 = $ _____

   $1 + 7 = $ _____

California Content Standards *Number Sense 2.1 (🔑) Know the addition facts. Also Number Sense 1.3, 2.5 (🔑), Algebra and Functions 1.1.*

fifty-nine **59**

Add. Then change the order. Add.
Use counters if you like.

9.
$$\begin{array}{r} 1 \\ + 2 \\ \hline 3 \end{array}$$
$$\begin{array}{r} 2 \\ + 1 \\ \hline 3 \end{array}$$

10.
$$\begin{array}{r} 3 \\ + 2 \\ \hline \end{array}$$
$$\begin{array}{r} \square \\ + \square \\ \hline \end{array}$$

11.
$$\begin{array}{r} 0 \\ + 4 \\ \hline \end{array}$$
$$\begin{array}{r} \square \\ + \square \\ \hline \end{array}$$

12.
$$\begin{array}{r} 6 \\ + 2 \\ \hline \end{array}$$
$$\begin{array}{r} \square \\ + \square \\ \hline \end{array}$$

13.
$$\begin{array}{r} 2 \\ + 4 \\ \hline \end{array}$$
$$\begin{array}{r} \square \\ + \square \\ \hline \end{array}$$

14.
$$\begin{array}{r} 1 \\ + 6 \\ \hline \end{array}$$
$$\begin{array}{r} \square \\ + \square \\ \hline \end{array}$$

Problem Solving  Algebra

15. Look at the picture.
How many bugs are there in all?
Write two addition sentences.

_____ + _____ = _____

_____ + _____ = _____

Home Activity Give your child some addition sentences.
Have him or her change the order of the numbers and find
each answer. Homework Workbook 2-10

Name_____

Missing Parts

6 in all

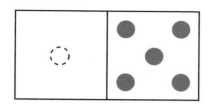

What number is missing?

7 in all

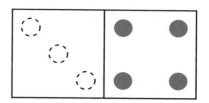

____ + 5 = 6

7 = 3 + 4

Draw how many are missing.
Write the number.
Use counters if you like.

1. 5 in all

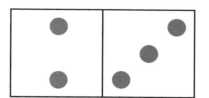

____ + 3 = 5

2. 4 in all

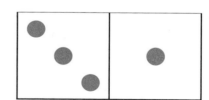

4 = ____ + 1

3. 6 in all

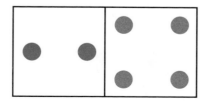

6 = 2 + ____

4. 7 in all

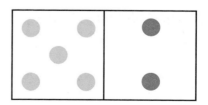

5 + ____ = 7

California Content Standards Algebra and Functions 1.1 Write and solve number sentences that express the relationship of addition and subtraction. Also Number Sense 2.1 (🔑), Mathematical Reasoning 1.2.

Write the missing numbers.
Use counters if you like.

5.   3 in all

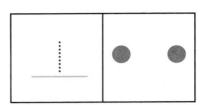

_____ + 2 = 3

6.   5 in all

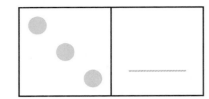

5 = 3 + _____

7. _____ + 2 = 4

8. 8 = _____ + 5

9. 7 = 3 + _____

10. 6 + _____ = 8

11. 5 + _____ = 6

12. 5 = _____ + 5

 Problem Solving

Write the number sentence.
Solve.

13. Mother gave Alex 4 pancakes.
Then she gave him more.
Now Alex has 6 pancakes.
How many more did
she give him?

6 in all

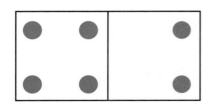

_____ + _____ = _____

Home Activity Tell your child you have eight pencils. Hide some
in a shoe and display the rest. Have him or her guess the number
in the shoe and state the addition fact. Homework Workbook 2-11

Name_____ **Problem-Solving Application**
Use Data from a Picture

Use the picture to solve each problem.
Think: What do you need to find out?

1. There are __2__ bees.
   There are __4__ butterflies.
   How many bugs are there in all? __6__

2. There are _____ ladybugs.
   There is _____ ant.
   How many bugs are there altogether? _____

3. There are _____ turtles.
   There are _____ rabbits.
   How many animals are there in all? _____

4. There are _____ birds.
   There are _____ turtles.
   How many animals are there in all? _____

5. There are _____ butterflies.
   There are _____ ladybugs.
   How many bugs are there in all? _____

6. There is _____ ant.
   There are _____ bees.
   How many bugs are there altogether? _____

California Content Standards *Mathematical Reasoning 1.1 Determine approach, materials, and strategies to be used. Also Number Sense 2.5 ( ), Algebra and Functions 1.3.*

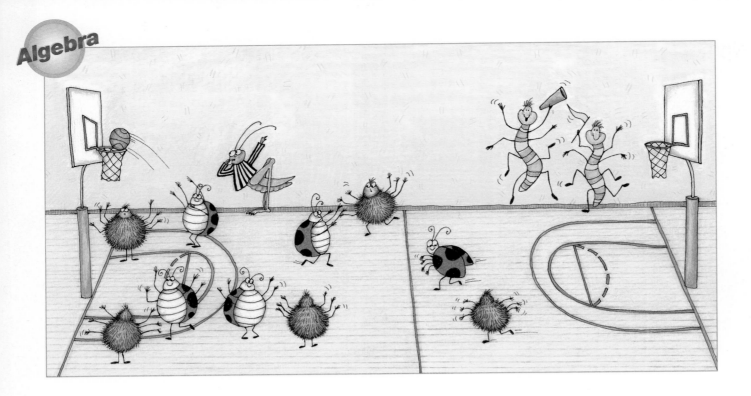

Look at the picture.
Draw or write a story for each number sentence.

7. $2 + 1 = 3$

8. $5 + 2 = 7$

Home Activity Show your child a magazine picture. Help him or her make up and solve addition problems about the scene. Homework Workbook 2-12

Add. Then change the order. Add.
Use counters if you like.

1.
```
    2
  + 3
```
+ ☐/☐

2.
```
    0
  + 4
```
+ ☐/☐

3.
```
    3
  + 4
```
+ ☐/☐

4.
```
    6
  + 2
```
+ ☐/☐

Use the picture to solve.

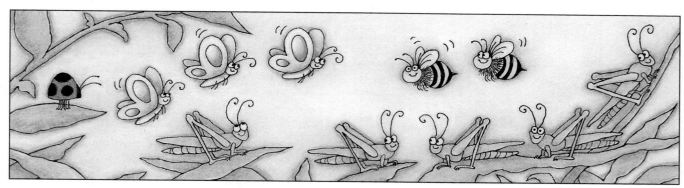

5. There is _____ ladybug and _____ grasshoppers. How many bugs are there in all? _____

6. There are _____ bees. There are _____ butterflies. How many bugs are there in all? _____

1.

$$2 + \boxed{} = 5$$

3   4   5   NH
○   ○   ○   ○

2.

$$\boxed{} + 2 = 6$$

3   4   5   NH
○   ○   ○   ○

3.

$$4 + 0 = \boxed{}$$

0   3   4   NH
○   ○   ○   ○

4.

$$3 + 3 = \boxed{}$$

5   6   9   NH
○   ○   ○   ○

5.

$$\begin{array}{r} 2 \\ + 5 \\ \hline \end{array}$$

5   10   7   NH
○   ○   ○   ○

6.

$$\begin{array}{r} 1 \\ + 7 \\ \hline \end{array}$$

4   7   9   NH
○   ○   ○   ○

7.

1 fish   2 fish   5 fish   NH
○   ○   ○   ○

8.

$1 + 5 = 6$ $2 + 3 = 5$
      ○   ○

$5 + 2 = 7$ NH
      ○   ○

Oral Directions *Mark the correct answer. NH means "Not here." Mark it whenever the answer is not given.*

#1–2. Mark the missing number that makes the number sentence true.

#3–6. Solve.
#7. Three fish are swimming. Two fish join them. How many fish in all?
#8. Look at the picture. Mark the addition sentence that tells about the frogs in the picture.

1. Write how many.

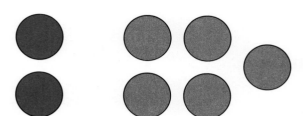

_____ + _____ = _____

2. Show 1 way to make a sum for 7.
   Color. Write the addition sentence.

_____ + _____ = _____

Write the numbers. Add.

3.

_____ + _____ = _____

4.

_____ + _____ = _____

Add.
Then change the order. Add.

5. $\begin{array}{r} 1 \\ + 4 \\ \hline \end{array}$ $\begin{array}{r} \square \\ + \square \\ \hline \end{array}$

6. $\begin{array}{r} 2 \\ + 6 \\ \hline \end{array}$ $\begin{array}{r} \square \\ + \square \\ \hline \end{array}$

Write the missing number.

7. $2 + \underline{\hspace{1cm}} = 3$

8. $7 = \underline{\hspace{1cm}} + 2$

9. $8 = 4 + \underline{\hspace{1cm}}$

10. $\underline{\hspace{1cm}} + 4 = 4$

Add.

11. $5 + 0 = \underline{\hspace{1cm}}$ | $2 + 2 = \underline{\hspace{1cm}}$ | $4 + 3 = \underline{\hspace{1cm}}$

Add.

12.
$$\begin{array}{r} 3 \\ + 3 \\ \hline \end{array} \qquad \begin{array}{r} 0 \\ + 2 \\ \hline \end{array} \qquad \begin{array}{r} 1 \\ + 6 \\ \hline \end{array} \qquad \begin{array}{r} 5 \\ + 3 \\ \hline \end{array} \qquad \begin{array}{r} 3 \\ + 2 \\ \hline \end{array}$$

13. Use the picture to solve.

There are \underline{\hspace{1cm}} ladybugs.

There are \underline{\hspace{1cm}} turtles.

How many animals are there in all? \underline{\hspace{1cm}}

Name_____ **Multiple Choice Test**

1.

2	4	6	8
○	○	○	○

2.

3 + 1 = 4   4 + 1 = 5
   ○   ○

3 + 2 = 5   3 + 3 = 6
   ○   ○

3.   5
   + 2
   ───
     7

5 + 3 = 8   3 + 2 = 5
   ○   ○

1 + 1 = 2   2 + 5 = 7
   ○   ○

4.   3
   + 0

1 + 2 = 3   0 + 1 = 1
   ○   ○

0 + 3 = 3   3 + 3 = 6
   ○   ○

5.   2   4
   + 4   + 2

6	5	4	2
○	○	○	○

6.   4   3
   + 3   + 4

7	6	5	4
○	○	○	○

Oral Directions *Mark the correct answer. NH means "Not here." Mark it whenever the answer is not given.*

#1. How many counters are there in all?
#2. Mark the number sentence that tells how many butter-flies there are in all.

#3. What is another way to write five plus two equals seven?
#4. What is another way to write three plus zero equals three?
#5. Two plus four and four plus two equal what number?
#6. Four plus three and three plus four equal what number?

7.

$$1 + 2 = \boxed{}$$

3	4	1	NH
○	○	○	○

8.

$$2 + 3 = \boxed{}$$

6	4	5	NH
○	○	○	○

9.

$$\begin{array}{r} 5 \\ + 3 \\ \hline \end{array}$$

7	8	10	NH
○	○	○	○

10.

$$\begin{array}{r} 7 \\ + 0 \\ \hline \end{array}$$

9	0	7	NH
○	○	○	○

11.

$$6 = 5 + \boxed{}$$

0	1	2	NH
○	○	○	○

12.

$$\boxed{} + 2 = 8$$

3	4	6	NH
○	○	○	○

13.

5	6	7	8
○	○	○	○

14.

5	6	7	8
○	○	○	○

Oral Directions *Mark the correct answer. NH means "Not here." Mark it whenever the answer is not given.*

#7–10. Add.
#11–12. Mark the missing number that makes the number sentence true.

#13. Look at the picture. There are four butterflies flying in the garden. Two butterflies join them. How many butterflies are there in all?
#14. There are three bees resting on the hive. Five bees fly to join them. How many bees are there altogether?

Understanding Subtraction

Diagnosing Readiness

for Chapter 3

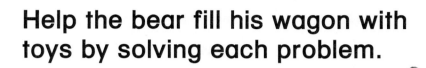

Help the bear fill his wagon with toys by solving each problem.

1. $3 + 1 =$ _____

2. $4 + 2 =$ _____

3. $2 + 0 =$ _____

4. $3 +$ _____ $= 8$

5. $5 - 4 =$ _____

To the Family

Looking Back	Chapter 3	Looking Ahead
In Kindergarten children were introduced to basic subtraction facts up to ten.	While studying basic subtraction facts, children learn two processes of subtraction: taking away and comparing groups. Also they are introduced to the minus sign.	In Chapters 4 and 8 children learn basic fact strategies for subtraction facts up to 20. In Chapter 12 they learn to subtract one- and two-digit numbers.

Page 71 Your child solved problems that review math skills from previous chapters and will help your child with the skills in Chapter 3.

Math at Home Help your child learn and memorize basic subtraction facts by involving them in everyday experiences using subtraction. For example, ask your child how many toys are left when some of the toys have been removed from a group or ask your child how many more books are in one pile than in another pile.

Math Literature Read stories about subtraction with your child. Look for the following books in your local library.
Counting Kids by Annie Kubler (Childs Play International Ltd., 1990)
Ten Tiny Monsters by Sheila White Samton (Crown Publishing, 1997)

California Content Standards in Chapter 3 Lessons*

	Teach and Practice	Practice		Teach and Practice	Practice
Number Sense			**1.2** Understand the meaning of the symbols +, −, =.	3, 11	
2.1 (🔑) Know the addition facts (sums to 20) and the corresponding subtraction facts and commit them to memory.	4, 5, 7, 8	3, 6	**1.3** Create problem situations that might lead to given number sentences involving addition and subtraction.		6, 9, 11
2.2 (🔑) Use the inverse relationship between addition and subtraction to solve problems.	10		**Mathematical Reasoning**		
2.5 (🔑) Show the meaning of addition (putting together, increasing) and subtraction (taking away, comparing, finding the difference).	1–3, 9	4, 5, 7, 8, 11	**1.1** Determine the approach, materials, and strategies to be used.		1, 2, 9–11
			1.2 Use tools, such as manipulatives or sketches, to model problems.		1, 5, 6, 9
Algebra and Functions			**2.1** Explain the reasoning used and justify the procedures selected.		8
1.1 Write and solve number sentences from problem situations that express relationships involving addition and subtraction.	5–7, 9–11	4	**3.0** Students note connections between one problem and another.		3

* The symbol (🔑) indicates a key standard as designated in the Mathematics Framework for California Public Schools.
Full statements of the California Content Standards are found at the beginning of this book following the Table of Contents.

Name_____ **Using Counters to Subtract**

3 take away **2** ⋮____ left

Use counters.
Take away to subtract.

1.

   2   take away   1   _____ left

2.

   5   take away   3   _____ left

3.

   4   take away   2   _____ left

4.

   3   take away   2   _____ left

5.

   4   take away   3   _____ left

6.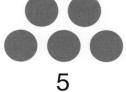

   5   take away   4   _____ left

California Content Standards *Number Sense 2.5 (🔑) Show the meaning of subtraction. Also Mathematical Reasoning 1.1, 1.2.*

Use counters to subtract.
Write how many are left.

	Show	Take Away	Left
7.	4	3	
8.	2	1	
9.	5	2	
10.	3	2	
11.	5	1	
12.	4	1	

 **Problem Solving**

Solve. Use counters if you like.

13. There are 4 counters.
1 counter is blue.
How many counters
are not blue? _____

14. There are 5 counters.
2 counters are red.
How many counters
are not red? _____

Home Activity Use household items such as buttons and paperclips to help your child show numbers and subtract.
Homework Workbook 3-1

Name_____

Using Pictures to Subtract

Word Bank

minus

5 minus **4** ____ left

Write how many are left.

1.

3 minus **1** ____ left

2.

6 minus **2** ____ left

3.

5 minus **3** ____ left

4.

6 minus **1** ____ left

California Content Standards Number Sense 2.5 (🔑) Show the meaning of subtraction. Also Mathematical Reasoning 1.1.

seventy-five **75**

Write the numbers.

5.

4   minus   1   3   left

6.

_____ minus _____ _____ left

7.

_____ minus _____ _____ left

 **Problem Solving**

Solve. Use counters if you like.

8. You have 5 cars.
2 cars drive away.
How many cars are left?

_____

9. You have 4 cars.
3 cars drive away.
How many cars are left?

_____

Home Activity Using the pictures on this page, ask your child to say how many toys are in each picture, how many are leaving, and how many will be left. Homework Workbook 3-2

Name_____

Using Symbols to Subtract
Dolls Around the World

Algebra

$4 - 2 = 2$

minus   difference

Word Bank
difference

Cross out to subtract.

1.
$6 - 2 = \underline{\quad}$

2.
$4 - 1 = \underline{\quad}$

3.
$8 - 2 = \underline{\quad}$

4.
$6 - 1 = \underline{\quad}$

5.
$6 - 3 = \underline{\quad}$

6.
$5 - 1 = \underline{\quad}$

7.
$5 - 2 = \underline{\quad}$

8.
$7 - 3 = \underline{\quad}$

California Content Standards Algebra and Functions 1.2 Students understand the meaning of the symbols − and =. Number Sense 2.5 (🔑). Also Number Sense 2.1 (🔑), Mathematical Reasoning 3.0.

Cross out to subtract.

9.

$3 - 2 =$ _____

10.

$6 - 2 =$ _____

11.

$5 - 4 =$ _____

12.

$2 - 1 =$ _____

13.

$4 - 3 =$ _____

14.

$4 - 2 =$ _____

15.

$8 - 5 =$ _____

16.

$8 - 3 =$ _____

Math Reasoning

Number Sense

17. Look at 15 and 16 above.
How are they alike?
How are they different?

 Home Activity Have your child draw and cross out simple shapes to show subtraction. Homework Workbook 3-3

Name_____ **Subtracting from 5 and 6**

Look at the cube train.
Write how many of each color.
Complete each subtraction sentence.

1.

_2_ and _3_

$5 - 3 = 2$

$5 - 2 = 3$

2.

  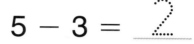

____ and ____

$5 - 4 = $ ____

$5 - 1 = $ ____

3.

____ and ____

$5 - 0 = $ ____

$5 - 5 = $ ____

California Content Standards Number Sense 2.1 Know the subtraction facts. Also Number Sense 2.5, Algebra and Functions 1.1.

Look at the cube train.
Write how many of each color.
Complete each subtraction sentence.

4.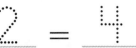

 and

$6 - 2 = 4$

$6 - 4 = 2$

_____ and _____

5.

$6 - \underline{\hspace{1cm}} = \underline{\hspace{1cm}}$

$6 - \underline{\hspace{1cm}} = \underline{\hspace{1cm}}$

_____ and _____

6.

$6 - \underline{\hspace{1cm}} = \underline{\hspace{1cm}}$

_____ and _____

7.

$6 - \underline{\hspace{1cm}} = \underline{\hspace{1cm}}$

$6 - \underline{\hspace{1cm}} = \underline{\hspace{1cm}}$

_____ and _____

Home Activity Show your child 5 or 6 objects in your hand.
Take some out. Ask your child how many are still in your hand.
Then count them together. Homework Workbook 3-4

Name_____

Use two colors of cubes to show
ways to make 7. Color.
Write the subtraction sentences.

Algebra

1.

$7 - 5 = 2$

$\underline{2}$ and $\underline{5}$

$7 - 2 = 5$

2.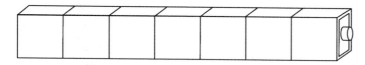

_____ $-$ _____ $=$ _____

_____ and _____

_____ $-$ _____ $=$ _____

3.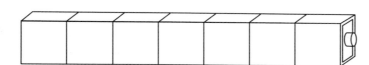

_____ $-$ _____ $=$ _____

_____ and _____

_____ $-$ _____ $=$ _____

4.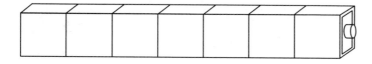

_____ $-$ _____ $=$ _____

_____ and _____

_____ $-$ _____ $=$ _____

California Content Standards *Number Sense 2.1 (☞) Know the subtraction facts. Algebra and Functions 1.1. Also Number Sense 2.5 (☞), Mathematical Reasoning 1.2.*

Use two colors of cubes to show ways
to make 8. Color.
Write the subtraction sentences.

5.
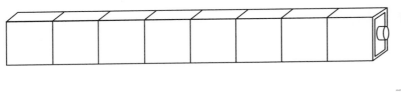

$8 - 7 = 1$

___1___ and ___7___

$8 - 1 = 7$

6.
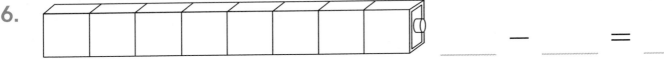

___ $-$ ___ $=$ ___

___ and ___

___ $-$ ___ $=$ ___

7.
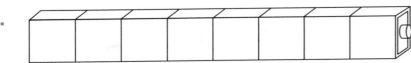

___ $-$ ___ $=$ ___

___ and ___

___ $-$ ___ $=$ ___

8.
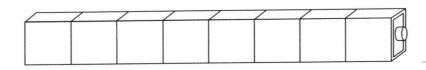

___ $-$ ___ $=$ ___

___ and ___

___ $-$ ___ $=$ ___

9.
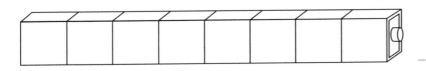

___ $-$ ___ $=$ ___

___ and ___

___ $-$ ___ $=$ ___

Home Activity Challenge your child to name a combination
for 7. Ask your child to write two subtraction sentences to
show the combination. Homework Workbook 3-5

Name_____ **Problem-Solving Strategy**

Write a Number Sentence

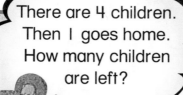

There are 4 children.
Then 1 goes home.
How many children
are left?

Algebra

Understand

You need to find how many children are left.

Plan

You can write a number sentence.

Solve

4 – 1 = 3 children

Look Back

Did you answer the question?

Write each number sentence.

1.

___ – ___ = ___

2.

___ – ___ = ___

California Content Standards *Algebra and Functions 1.1 Write and solve number sentences from problem situations. Also Number Sense 2.1 (🔑), Algebra and Functions 1.3, Mathematical Reasoning 1.2.*

eighty-three **83**

Write each number sentence.

3.

$$3 - 1 = 2$$

4.

___ − ___ = ___

5.

___ − ___ = ___

6.

___ − ___ = ___

7.

___ − ___ = ___

8.

___ − ___ = ___

 Problem Solving

Draw a picture for each number sentence.

9. $6 - 2 = 4$

10. $8 - 5 = 3$

84 eighty-four

Home Activity Act out simple math stories using common household items. Ask your child to write number sentences to go with each story. Homework Workbook 3-6

Use counters to subtract.
Write how many are left.

1.

Show	Take Away	Left
3	2	_____
7	3	_____

Look at the cube train.
Write the subtraction sentences.

2.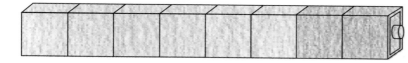

_____ − _____ = _____

_____ and _____   _____ − _____ = _____

Cross out to subtract.

3.

6 − 3 = _____

4.

5 − 4 = _____

Write a number sentence.

5. 2 children leave.

_____ − _____ = _____

1.   7   2   9   5
       ○   ○   ○   ○

2.   18 = 18   20 > 8   17 < 16   3 < 5
       ○   ○   ○   ○

3.

     ○   ○   ○   ○
  8 − 6 = 2   8 − 2 = 6   5 − 3 = 2   8 − 8 = 0

4.   2 + 2 = ☐   6   0   4   2
                      ○   ○   ○   ○

5.   7 − ☐ = 1   6   7   5   NH
                      ○   ○   ○   ○

6.   4   8   5   3   6
      + 2   ○   ○   ○   ○

Oral Directions *Mark the correct answer. NH means "Not here." Mark it whenever the answer is not given.*

#1. Mark the even number.
#2. Mark the statement that is not true.

#3. Mark the subtraction sentence that matches the picture.
#4. Add.
#5. Mark the missing number to make the number sentence true.
#6. Add.

Name_____

Subtracting Across and Down

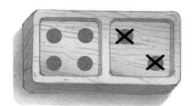

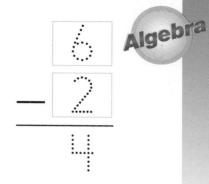

6 − 2 = 4

$$\begin{array}{r} 6 \\ -\ 2 \\ \hline 4 \end{array}$$

Write the numbers. Subtract.

1.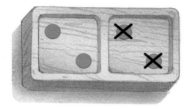

    ___ − ___ = ___

    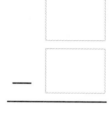

    $$\begin{array}{r} \\ -\ \\ \hline \end{array}$$

2.

    ___ − ___ = ___

    $$\begin{array}{r} \\ -\ \\ \hline \end{array}$$

3.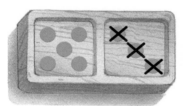

    ___ − ___ = ___

    $$\begin{array}{r} \\ -\ \\ \hline \end{array}$$

4.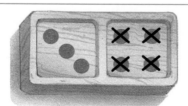

    ___ − ___ = ___

    $$\begin{array}{r} \\ -\ \\ \hline \end{array}$$

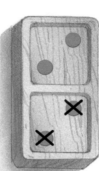

California Content Standards *Number Sense 2.1 (🔑) Know the subtraction facts. Algebra and Functions 1.1. Also Number Sense 2.5 (🔑).*

Find each difference.
Write the matching subtraction sentence.

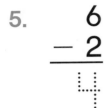

5.
```
  6
- 2
---
  4
```
6 − 2 = 4

6.
```
  5
- 3
```
____ − ____ = ____

7.
```
  4
- 1
```
____ − ____ = ____

8.
```
  7
- 3
```
____ − ____ = ____

9.
```
  5
- 4
```
____ − ____ = ____

10.
```
  8
- 5
```
____ − ____ = ____

11.
```
  6
- 3
```
____ − ____ = ____

Home Activity Ask your child to use some small items such as buttons to make up a subtraction problem, and solve it.
Homework Workbook 3-7

Name_____ **Subtracting with Zero**

What happens when you subtract zero?

$4 - 0 = \underline{4}$

$4 - 4 = \underline{0}$

Subtract.

1.

$5 - 2 = \underline{\hphantom{00}}$ trucks

2.

$5 - 0 = \underline{\hphantom{00}}$ trucks

3.

$3 - 1 = \underline{\hphantom{00}}$ robots

4.

$3 - 3 = \underline{\hphantom{00}}$ robots

5.

$7 - 5 = \underline{\hphantom{00}}$ airplanes

6.

$7 - 7 = \underline{\hphantom{00}}$ airplanes

7.

$8 - 4 = \underline{\hphantom{00}}$ dogs

8.

$8 - 0 = \underline{\hphantom{00}}$ dogs

California Content Standards *Number Sense 2.1 (━) Know the subtraction facts. Also Number Sense 2.5 (━), Mathematical Reasoning 2.1.*

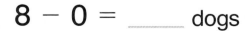

eighty-nine **89**

Subtract.
Use counters if you like.

9. $\begin{array}{r} 1 \\ -\ 0 \\ \hline \end{array}$ $\begin{array}{r} 2 \\ -\ 2 \\ \hline \end{array}$ $\begin{array}{r} 7 \\ -\ 2 \\ \hline \end{array}$ $\begin{array}{r} 4 \\ -\ 0 \\ \hline \end{array}$ $\begin{array}{r} 5 \\ -\ 4 \\ \hline \end{array}$ $\begin{array}{r} 6 \\ -\ 6 \\ \hline \end{array}$

10. $\begin{array}{r} 8 \\ -\ 8 \\ \hline \end{array}$ $\begin{array}{r} 6 \\ -\ 0 \\ \hline \end{array}$ $\begin{array}{r} 4 \\ -\ 4 \\ \hline \end{array}$ $\begin{array}{r} 2 \\ -\ 0 \\ \hline \end{array}$ $\begin{array}{r} 7 \\ -\ 3 \\ \hline \end{array}$ $\begin{array}{r} 1 \\ -\ 1 \\ \hline \end{array}$

11. $\begin{array}{r} 7 \\ -\ 0 \\ \hline \end{array}$ $\begin{array}{r} 8 \\ -\ 3 \\ \hline \end{array}$ $\begin{array}{r} 5 \\ -\ 5 \\ \hline \end{array}$ $\begin{array}{r} 7 \\ -\ 4 \\ \hline \end{array}$ $\begin{array}{r} 3 \\ -\ 0 \\ \hline \end{array}$ $\begin{array}{r} 6 \\ -\ 2 \\ \hline \end{array}$

12. $\begin{array}{r} 3 \\ -\ 3 \\ \hline \end{array}$ $\begin{array}{r} 8 \\ -\ 0 \\ \hline \end{array}$ $\begin{array}{r} 6 \\ -\ 5 \\ \hline \end{array}$ $\begin{array}{r} 5 \\ -\ 0 \\ \hline \end{array}$ $\begin{array}{r} 0 \\ -\ 0 \\ \hline \end{array}$ $\begin{array}{r} 8 \\ -\ 7 \\ \hline \end{array}$

Math Reasoning

Number Sense

13. How is subtracting 0 like adding 0?

Home Activity Have your child use buttons or other house-hold items to solve problems involving taking away zero or taking away all, for example, 5 − 5 and 5 − 0. Homework Workbook 3-8

Name_____

Subtracting to Find How Many More

How many more blue cars than red cars?

It looks like there are 3 more. I can subtract to find out.

Algebra

$$8 - 5 = 3$$

How many more blue cubes than red cubes are there? Write the number sentence. Use cubes if you like.

1. $$\underline{7} - \underline{4} = \underline{3}$$ more

2. _____ − _____ = _____ more

3. _____ − _____ = _____ more

4. _____ − _____ = _____ more

California Content Standards Number Sense 2.5 (🔑) Show the meaning of subtraction. Algebra and Functions 1.1. Also Algebra and Functions 1.3, Mathematical Reasoning 1.1, 1.2.

ninety-one **91**

Write the number sentence. Solve.
Use cubes if you like.

5. Jay has 8 baseballs.
   Ann has 4 baseballs.
   How many more baseballs
   does Jay have?

   _____ — _____ = _____ more

6. Julia saw 6 birds.
   Adam saw 5 birds.
   How many more birds did
   Julia see than Adam?

   _____ — _____ = _____ more

7. 7 butterflies are on the tree.
   3 butterflies are on the
   bush. How many more
   butterflies are on the tree?

   _____ — _____ = _____ more

8. Mary scored 4 points.
   Ann scored 5 points.
   How many more points
   did Ann score?

   _____ — _____ = _____ more

Problem Solving

9. Draw some people on each bus.
   How many more people are on
   one bus than the other?
   Write a number sentence.

   _____ — _____ = _____ more

Home Activity Show your child two groups of objects. Have
your child write a number sentence to find out how many more
are in one group than the other. Homework Workbook 3-9

Name_____ **Missing Numbers**

5 toys in all

How many toys are in the box?

$5 - 3 = 2$

3 toys in the box

**Write the missing numbers.
Use counters if you like.**

1. 7 toys in all

 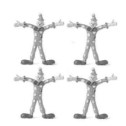

$7 - \underline{} = 4$

_____ toys in the box

2. 4 toys in all

$4 - \underline{} = 2$

_____ toys in the box

3. 6 toys in all

$6 - \underline{} = 5$

_____ toy in the box

4. 8 toys in all

$8 - \underline{} = 3$

_____ toys in the box

California Content Standards Algebra and Functions 1.1 Write and solve number sentences that express the relationship of addition and subtraction. Number Sense 2.2 (🔑). Also Mathematical Reasoning 1.1.

ninety-three **93**

Write the missing numbers.
Use counters if you like.

5. $1 + 3 = 4$

$4 - 3 = 1$

6. $5 + 2 = 7$

$7 - \underline{\quad} = 2$

7. $6 + 0 = 6$

$6 - \underline{\quad} = 6$

8. $1 + 7 = 8$

$8 - \underline{\quad} = 1$

9. $2 + 4 = 6$

$6 - \underline{\quad} = 2$

10. $0 + 4 = 4$

$4 - \underline{\quad} = 4$

11. $1 + 4 = 5$

$5 - \underline{\quad} = 4$

12. $6 + 2 = 8$

$8 - \underline{\quad} = 2$

Problem Solving

Solve. Write the subtraction sentence.
Use counters if you like.

13. There are 8 kites flying in the sky.
Some kites fly away.
5 kites are left.
How many kites fly away?

$8 - \underline{\quad} = 5$

_____ kites fly away

Home Activity Hide some objects under a bowl. Tell your
child how many objects there are in all and have him or her tell
how many are under the bowl and the subtraction fact.
Homework Workbook 3-10

Name_____

Write each number sentence.

Think: Do you need to add or subtract?

1. 2 seahorses leave.

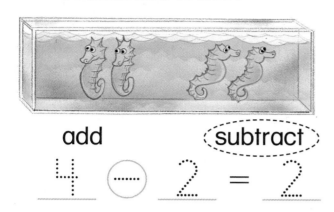

add   (subtract)

$4 - 2 = 2$

2. 2 fish join the others.

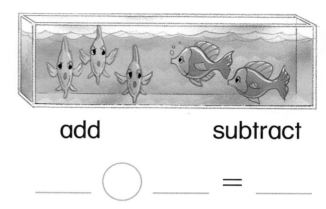

add   subtract

___ ◯ ___ = ___

3. 3 fish come to play.

add   subtract

___ ◯ ___ = ___

4. 2 fish swim away.

add   subtract

___ ◯ ___ = ___

5. 2 fish go away.

add   subtract

___ ◯ ___ = ___

6. 4 fish join the others.

add   subtract

___ ◯ ___ = ___

Would you add or subtract?
Write each number sentence.

7. 2 elephants walk in.

add   subtract

_____ ◯ _____ = _____

8. 3 lions come to play.

add   subtract

_____ ◯ _____ = _____

9. I giraffe goes home.

add   subtract

_____ ◯ _____ = _____

10. 4 hippos leave.

add   subtract

_____ ◯ _____ = _____

 **Problem Solving**

Draw a picture for each number sentence.

11. 2 + 5 = 7

12. 8 − 4 = 4

Home Activity Use favorite toys to make up addition and subtraction problems. Ask your child if he or she would like to add or subtract to solve. Homework Workbook 3-11

Name_____

Subtract.

1.
$$\begin{array}{r} 6 \\ -5 \\ \hline \end{array} \quad \begin{array}{r} 7 \\ -4 \\ \hline \end{array} \quad \begin{array}{r} 1 \\ -0 \\ \hline \end{array} \quad \begin{array}{r} 5 \\ -3 \\ \hline \end{array} \quad \begin{array}{r} 7 \\ -1 \\ \hline \end{array} \quad \begin{array}{r} 8 \\ -3 \\ \hline \end{array}$$

2. $3 - 1 =$ _____ | $8 - 2 =$ _____ | $6 - 0 =$ _____

3. $7 - 5 =$ _____ | $4 - 4 =$ _____ | $8 - 7 =$ _____

Write the missing numbers.

4. $6 -$ _____ $= 2$ | _____ $- 3 = 0$ | $5 -$ _____ $= 4$

Do you need to add or subtract?
Write each number sentence.

5. 2 fish come to play.

add   subtract

_____ ◯ _____ = _____

6. How many more
red balloons are there?

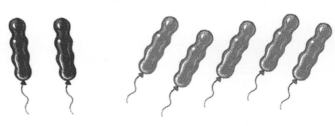

add   subtract

_____ ◯ _____ = _____

Name_____

1. $7 - 3 = \square$

   | 5   4   2   3
   | ○   ○   ○   ○

2.

$3 - 1 = 2$ $1 + 3 = 4$ $4 - 1 = 3$ $3 + 0 = 0$

○   ○   ○   ○

---

3.   Prizes

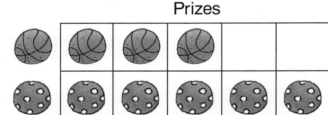

    1   2   3   4   5

   2   5 | 3

   ○   ○   ○   ○

4.

   ○   ○   ○   ○

Oral Directions *Mark the correct answer. NH means "Not here." Mark it whenever the answer is not given.*

#1. Subtract.
#2. One child leaves. Mark the number sentence that tells how many children are left.
#3. How many basketballs are there? Mark your answer.
#4. Look at the pattern. What shape is most likely to come next?

Write the numbers.

1.

_____ minus _____ = _____

Look at the cube train.
Write how many of each color.
Write the subtraction sentences.

2.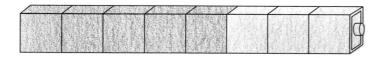

_____ − _____ = _____

_____ and _____   _____ − _____ = _____

Subtract.

3. $3 - 1 =$ _____ | $7 - 6 =$ _____ | $5 - 5 =$ _____

4. $6 - 4 =$ _____ | $2 - 0 =$ _____ | $8 - 7 =$ _____

Cross out to subtract.

5.

$4 - 4 =$ _____

6.

$7 - 3 =$ _____

Subtract.

7.
$$8 - 8$$
$$6 - 5$$
$$8 - 4$$
$$7 - 5$$
$$3 - 0$$
$$7 - 2$$

Write the missing numbers.

8. $2 - \underline{\quad} = 1$ | $\underline{\quad} - 1 = 0$ | $8 - 6 = \underline{\quad}$

9. $\underline{\quad} - 0 = 6$ | $5 - \underline{\quad} = 3$ | $\underline{\quad} - 3 = 1$

Write the number sentence.

10. Sam had 8 frogs.
Mia had 2 frogs.
How many more frogs
did Sam have?

$\underline{\quad} - \underline{\quad} = \underline{\quad}$

11. Kim walked 4 miles.
Lisa walked 7 miles.
How many more miles did
Lisa walk?

$\underline{\quad} - \underline{\quad} = \underline{\quad}$

12. 2 fish leave.

add   subtract

$\underline{\quad} \bigcirc \underline{\quad} = \underline{\quad}$

13. 3 children leave.

$\underline{\quad} - \underline{\quad} = \underline{\quad}$

1. 6 − 4 = 2

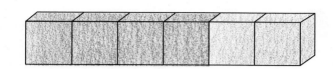

6 − 6 = 0   6 − 2 = 4   6 + 4 = 10   6 + 2 = 8
   ○   ○   ○   ○

---

2. 7 − 4 = ☐   4   2   3   5
                             ○   ○   ○   ○

---

3. 6 − ☐ = 6   6   1   3   0
                             ○   ○   ○   ○

---

4.   8   4   3   0   2
     − 5   ○   ○   ○   ○

5.

5 + 0 = 5   5 + 4 = 9   5 − 4 = 1   5 − 5 = 0
   ○   ○   ○   ○

Oral Directions *Mark the correct answer. NH means "Not here." Mark it whenever the answer is not given.*

#1. The subtraction sentence six minus four equals two tells about the cube train. What is another subtraction sentence that tells about the cube train?

#2. Subtract.
#3. Mark the missing number that makes the number sentence true.
#4. Subtract.
#5. Jeff had five basketballs. He lost four of them. Mark the number sentence that tells how many basketballs there are now.

6.

5 fish	7 fish	I fish	3 fish
○	○	○	○

7.

$8 - 3 = 5$	$3 + 5 = 8$	$8 - 5 = 3$	$5 + 3 = 8$
○	○	○	○

8.

$2 + 2 = 4$	$4 - 2 = 2$	$2 - 2 = 0$	NH
○	○	○	○

---

9.   6
      – 3

6	0	3	2
○	○	○	○

---

10. $4 - 4 = \square$

I	4	0	8
○	○	○	○

II. $\square - 1 = 2$

2	3	8	4
○	○	○	○

Oral Directions *Mark the correct answer. NH means "Not here." Mark it whenever the answer is not given.*

#6. Dan had seven fish. He gave two fish away. How many fish does Dan have left?

#7. Pat had three turtles. Jake had eight turtles. Mark the number sentence that tells how many more turtles Jake had.
#8. Two trains leave. Which number sentence tells how many trains are left?
#9–10. Subtract.
#11. Mark the missing number that makes the number sentence true.

102   one hundred two

CHAPTER 4 Introducing Basic-Fact Strategies

Diagnosing Readiness
for Chapter 4

1. Use >, <, or = to make the statement true.

   8 ◯ 10

2. What number comes just after 4? _____

3. 5 + 2 = _____

4. 7
   − 4
   ———

5. How many monkeys are there? Write a number sentence.

To the Family

Looking Back	**Chapter 4**	**Looking Ahead**
Previously in Grade 1 children used objects, pictures, and symbols to add.	**Introducing Basic-Fact Strategies** Children learn the following addition and subtraction strategies: counting on 1, 2, 3 and using doubles.	By the end of Grade 1 children will learn all the basic addition and subtraction facts.

Page 103 Your child solved problems that review math skills from previous chapters and will help your child with the skills in Chapter 4.

Math at Home Cut out pictures of animals from magazines with your child. Then have your child glue different numbers of animal pictures on several sheets of paper. Work together to think of and write addition and subtraction stories for each sheet of pictures.

Math Literature Read math-related stories with your child. Look for the following books in your local library.
Freight Train by Donald Crews (Mulberry Books, 1992)
Red Fox and His Canoe by Nathaniel Benchly (HarperTrophy, 1985)

California Content Standards in Chapter 4 Lessons*

	Teach and Practice	Practice		Teach and Practice	Practice
Number Sense			**1.2** Understand the meaning of the symbols +, −, =.	11	6, 10
1.2 (🔑) Compare whole numbers.		3	**1.3** Create problem situations that might lead to given number sentences involving addition and subtraction.		4, 11
2.1 (🔑) Know the addition facts and the corresponding subtraction facts and commit them to memory.	1–5, 7, 8, 10	9	**Mathematical Reasoning**		
2.2 (🔑) Use the inverse relationship between addition and subtraction to solve problems.	9, 10		**1.1** Determine the approach, materials, and strategies to be used.		1–5, 8, 9, 11
2.5 (🔑) Show the meaning of addition (putting together, increasing) and subtraction (taking away, comparing, finding the difference).		1–8	**1.2** Use tools, such as sketches, to model problems.	6	
Algebra and Functions			**2.1** Explain the reasoning used and justify the procedures selected.		5, 7
1.1 Write and solve number sentences from problem situations that express relationships involving addition and subtraction.	6, 11	1, 4, 10			

* The symbol (🔑) indicates a key standard as designated in the Mathematics Framework for California Public Schools.
  Full statements of the California Content Standards are found at the beginning of this book following the Table of Contents.

Name_____

There are 3 bananas in the bag.
Count on to find the sum.

Word Bank

count on

4, 5

3   +   2   =   5

Count on to find each sum.

1.

   4   +   1   =   ___

2.

   6   +   2   =   ___

3.

   7   +   1   =   ___

4.

   9   +   2   =   ___

California Content Standards *Number Sense 2.1 (🔑) Know the addition facts. Also Number Sense 2.5 (🔑), Algebra and Functions 1.1, Mathematical Reasoning 1.1.*

one hundred five   **105**

Count on to find each sum.

5.

_____ , _____

$$\begin{array}{r} 8 \\ +\ 2 \\ \hline \end{array}$$

6.

$$\begin{array}{r} 7 \\ +\ 2 \\ \hline \end{array} \qquad \begin{array}{r} 6 \\ +\ 1 \\ \hline \end{array} \qquad \begin{array}{r} 3 \\ +\ 2 \\ \hline \end{array} \qquad \begin{array}{r} 1 \\ +\ 2 \\ \hline \end{array} \qquad \begin{array}{r} 5 \\ +\ 1 \\ \hline \end{array} \qquad \begin{array}{r} 7 \\ +\ 1 \\ \hline \end{array}$$

7.

$$\begin{array}{r} 4 \\ +\ 1 \\ \hline \end{array} \qquad \begin{array}{r} 2 \\ +\ 2 \\ \hline \end{array} \qquad \begin{array}{r} 8 \\ +\ 2 \\ \hline \end{array} \qquad \begin{array}{r} 4 \\ +\ 2 \\ \hline \end{array} \qquad \begin{array}{r} 1 \\ +\ 1 \\ \hline \end{array} \qquad \begin{array}{r} 9 \\ +\ 1 \\ \hline \end{array}$$

8.

$$\begin{array}{r} 9 \\ +\ 2 \\ \hline \end{array} \qquad \begin{array}{r} 5 \\ +\ 2 \\ \hline \end{array} \qquad \begin{array}{r} 8 \\ +\ 1 \\ \hline \end{array} \qquad \begin{array}{r} 6 \\ +\ 2 \\ \hline \end{array} \qquad \begin{array}{r} 2 \\ +\ 1 \\ \hline \end{array} \qquad \begin{array}{r} 3 \\ +\ 1 \\ \hline \end{array}$$

 Math Reasoning **Algebra**

9. You started at 5.
You counted on 2.
Write the addition
sentence.

_____

10. You started at 7.
You ended at 9.
Write the addition
sentence.

_____

 Home Activity Use pennies or buttons to practice counting
on. Help your child see that counting on can be quicker than
counting all. Homework Workbook 4-1

Name _____ **Counting On 1, 2, and 3**

There are 5 people in the bus.
3 people get on the bus.
Count on to find the sum.

 6 , 7 , 8

5 + 3 = 8

Count on to find each sum.

1.

7 + 2 = ____

2. 9
+ 1

3. 6 + 1 = ____   4 + 3 = ____   1 + 2 = ____

4. 7 + 3 = ____   9 + 2 = ____   3 + 3 = ____

5. 9   8   8   4   5   5
  + 3   + 1   + 2   + 1   + 2   + 1

6. 6   3   7   6   8   4
  + 3   + 2   + 1   + 2   + 3   + 2

California Content Standards *Number Sense 2.1 ( ) Know the addition facts. Also Number Sense 2.5 ( ), Mathematical Reasoning 1.1.*

one hundred seven **107**

Follow each rule. Look for patterns.

7.

Count on 1	
1	2
2	
3	
4	

Count on 2	
6	
5	
4	
3	

Count on 3	
7	
8	
9	
10	

8.

Count on 1	
7	
6	
5	
4	

Count on 2	
6	
7	
8	
9	

Count on 3	
4	
6	
8	
10	

Problem Solving

Solve.

9. There are 7 birds.
3 birds join them.
How many birds
are there in all?

_____ birds

10. Tim saw 3 yellow birds.
Sara saw 5 blue birds.
How many birds did
they see in all?

_____ birds

108 one hundred eight

Home Activity Have your child practice counting on 1, 2, and 3 when setting a dinner table or putting clothes away.
Homework Workbook 4-2

Name_____ **Finding Doubles**

Add to find the double.

Algebra

Word Bank

double

$3 + 3 = 6$

Write each addition sentence.
Use cubes if you like.

1.

___ + ___ = ___

2.

___ + ___ = ___

3.

___ + ___ = ___

4.

___ + ___ = ___

5.

___ + ___ = ___

6.

___ + ___ = ___

California Content Standards *Number Sense 2.1 (🔑) Know the addition facts. Also Number Sense 2.5, Algebra and Functions 1.1, 1.3, Mathematical Reasoning 1.1.*

one hundred eleven   **111**

Add. Circle the doubles facts.

7. (2 + 2 = 4)   5 + 2   3 + 8   2 + 4   6 + 6   2 + 8

8. 3 + 1   0 + 0   6 + 2   3 + 9   4 + 3   1 + 1

9. 5 + 3   7 + 3   0 + 7   3 + 3   4 + 0   1 + 8

10. 3 + 2   5 + 5   6 + 1   9 + 2   4 + 4   0 + 6

 **Problem Solving**

11. Add. Create a problem for the number sentence.

5 + 5 = _____

12. Write the missing number that makes the number sentence true.

_____ + 4 = 8

Home Activity Have your child practice making doubles with small objects and then tell you the addition sentence he or she made. Homework Workbook 4-4

Name_____ **Using Doubles to Add**

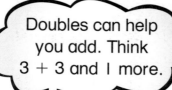
Doubles can help you add. Think 3 + 3 and 1 more.

3 + 3 = 6   3 + 4 = 7

Find each sum.
Use cubes if you like.

1. 2 + 2 = _____

    2 + 3 = _____

2. 5 + 5 = _____

    5 + 6 = _____

3. 4 + 4 = _____

    4 + 5 = _____

4. 3 + 3 = _____

    3 + 4 = _____

5. 1 + 1 = _____

    1 + 2 = _____

6. 6 + 6 = _____

    6 + 7 = _____

California Content Standards *Number Sense 2.1 (☞) Know the addition facts and commit them to memory. Also Number Sense 2.5 (☞), Mathematical Reasoning 1.1, 2.1.*

Find each sum. Think of a double to help you.

7. $1 + 1 = 2$ $1 + 2 = \underline{\quad}$ $2 + 1 = \underline{\quad}$

8. $4 + 4 = \underline{\quad}$ $4 + 5 = \underline{\quad}$ $5 + 4 = \underline{\quad}$

9.
$$\begin{array}{r} 0 \\ + 0 \\ \hline \end{array}$$
$$\begin{array}{r} 6 \\ + 5 \\ \hline \end{array}$$
$$\begin{array}{r} 3 \\ + 3 \\ \hline \end{array}$$
$$\begin{array}{r} 4 \\ + 3 \\ \hline \end{array}$$
$$\begin{array}{r} 1 \\ + 0 \\ \hline \end{array}$$
$$\begin{array}{r} 5 \\ + 5 \\ \hline \end{array}$$

10.
$$\begin{array}{r} 2 \\ + 2 \\ \hline \end{array}$$
$$\begin{array}{r} 2 \\ + 1 \\ \hline \end{array}$$
$$\begin{array}{r} 4 \\ + 4 \\ \hline \end{array}$$
$$\begin{array}{r} 0 \\ + 1 \\ \hline \end{array}$$
$$\begin{array}{r} 3 \\ + 2 \\ \hline \end{array}$$
$$\begin{array}{r} 5 \\ + 6 \\ \hline \end{array}$$

11.
$$\begin{array}{r} 3 \\ + 4 \\ \hline \end{array}$$
$$\begin{array}{r} 6 \\ + 6 \\ \hline \end{array}$$
$$\begin{array}{r} 2 \\ + 3 \\ \hline \end{array}$$
$$\begin{array}{r} 6 \\ + 5 \\ \hline \end{array}$$
$$\begin{array}{r} 6 \\ + 7 \\ \hline \end{array}$$
$$\begin{array}{r} 4 \\ + 5 \\ \hline \end{array}$$

 Math Reasoning

Number Sense

12. Ross threw 3 balls.
His total score was 7.
What 3 numbers might
he have scored?

Home Activity Give your child some near-double addition problems (such as 3 + 4) and have him or her tell you the double that helps solve the problem. Homework Workbook 4-5

Name_____

Algebra

There are 3 wagons in the yard.
There are 2 wagons in the path.
How many wagons are there altogether?

Understand

You need to find out how many
wagons there are in all.

Each X is
a wagon on
the path.

Each circle is a
wagon in the yard.

OOO
XX
3+2=5

Plan

You can draw a picture.
Then write the number sentence.

Solve

3 + 2 = 5 wagons

Look Back

How did the picture help you decide
what number sentence to write?

Draw a picture to solve.
Write the addition sentence.

1. 2 boats are in the water.
   7 boats sail in.
   How many boats are there now?

_____ + _____ = _____ boats

California Content Standards *Mathematical Reasoning 1.2
Use tools such as sketches to model problems. Algebra and
Functions 1.1. Also Number Sense 2.5 (⚷), Algebra and
Functions 1.2.*

one hundred fifteen **115**

Draw a picture to solve.
Write the addition sentence.

2. There is 1 big kite.
   There are 3 little kites.
   How many kites are there in all?

   _____ + _____ = _____ kites

3. Mika sees 4 big boats.
   Then she sees 4 little boats.
   How many boats does she see altogether?

   _____ + _____ = _____ boats

4. Rosa has 6 red cars.
   Tom has 3 blue cars.
   How many cars do they have altogether?

   _____ cars

5. Jared has 4 wagons.
   Cora has 2 more wagons than Jared.
   How many wagons does Cora have?

   _____ wagons

Home Activity Have your child make and solve simple addition problems using pennies or buttons.
Homework Workbook 4-6

Count on to find the sum.

1.

4 + 2 = ____

2.

6 + 3 = ____

Find each sum.

3.
$$\begin{array}{r} 1 \\ + 4 \\ \hline \end{array} \quad \begin{array}{r} 7 \\ + 3 \\ \hline \end{array} \quad \begin{array}{r} 2 \\ + 6 \\ \hline \end{array} \quad \begin{array}{r} 8 \\ + 3 \\ \hline \end{array} \quad \begin{array}{r} 3 \\ + 5 \\ \hline \end{array} \quad \begin{array}{r} 9 \\ + 1 \\ \hline \end{array}$$

4.
$$\begin{array}{r} 9 \\ + 3 \\ \hline \end{array} \quad \begin{array}{r} 5 \\ + 1 \\ \hline \end{array} \quad \begin{array}{r} 0 \\ + 7 \\ \hline \end{array} \quad \begin{array}{r} 4 \\ + 3 \\ \hline \end{array} \quad \begin{array}{r} 7 \\ + 1 \\ \hline \end{array} \quad \begin{array}{r} 3 \\ + 6 \\ \hline \end{array}$$

5. 4 + 4 = ____   2 + 2 = ____   6 + 6 = ____

4 + 5 = ____   2 + 3 = ____   6 + 7 = ____

Draw a picture to solve. Write a number sentence.

6. Lisa ate 5 pretzels. Mark ate 4 pretzels.
    How many pretzels did they eat in all?

_____ pretzels

Name_____

1.

10	8	12	11
○	○	○	○

2. $6 + \boxed{} = 9$

4	1	2	NH
○	○	○	○

3. $4 + 4 = 8$
    so $4 + 5 = \boxed{}$

10	9	8	NH
○	○	○	○

4. $7 - \boxed{} = 3$

4	3	5	NH
○	○	○	○

5. $4 + 1 = 5$

      NH

○   ○   ○   ○

6. $10 > 1$ $5 < 6$ $9 > 10$ $11 < 13$

   ○   ○   ○   ○

Oral Directions *Mark the correct answer. NH means "Not here." Mark it whenever the answer is not given.*

#1. Mark the number that shows how many jelly beans are pictured.
#2. Mark the missing number to make the number sentence true.

#3. If four plus four equals eight, then four plus five equals what number?
#4. Mark the missing number to make the number sentence true.
#5. Which picture shows the number sentence four plus one equals five?
#6. Mark the greater than or less than statement that is NOT true.

Name_____ **Counting Back 1 and 2**

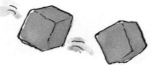

> **Word Bank**
> count back

Start with 5. | Count back 2.

$5 - 2 = 3$

Count back to subtract.

1.

_____

$4 - 1 =$ _____

2.

_____ , _____

$6 - 2 =$ _____

3.

_____

$7 - 1 =$ _____

4.

_____ , _____

$9 - 2 =$ _____

California Content Standards *Number Sense 2.1 (🔑) Know the subtraction facts. Also Number Sense 2.5 (🔑), Mathematical Reasoning 2.1.*

one hundred nineteen **119**

Count back to subtract.

5.  _____ , _____

$$\begin{array}{r} 8 \\ -2 \\ \hline \end{array}$$

6.
$$\begin{array}{r} 5 \\ -2 \\ \hline \end{array}$$
$$\begin{array}{r} 10 \\ -1 \\ \hline \end{array}$$
$$\begin{array}{r} 7 \\ -1 \\ \hline \end{array}$$
$$\begin{array}{r} 4 \\ -2 \\ \hline \end{array}$$
$$\begin{array}{r} 1 \\ -1 \\ \hline \end{array}$$
$$\begin{array}{r} 6 \\ -2 \\ \hline \end{array}$$

7.
$$\begin{array}{r} 6 \\ -1 \\ \hline \end{array}$$
$$\begin{array}{r} 11 \\ -2 \\ \hline \end{array}$$
$$\begin{array}{r} 5 \\ -1 \\ \hline \end{array}$$
$$\begin{array}{r} 9 \\ -2 \\ \hline \end{array}$$
$$\begin{array}{r} 2 \\ -1 \\ \hline \end{array}$$
$$\begin{array}{r} 8 \\ -1 \\ \hline \end{array}$$

8.
$$\begin{array}{r} 9 \\ -1 \\ \hline \end{array}$$
$$\begin{array}{r} 3 \\ -2 \\ \hline \end{array}$$
$$\begin{array}{r} 3 \\ -1 \\ \hline \end{array}$$
$$\begin{array}{r} 4 \\ -1 \\ \hline \end{array}$$
$$\begin{array}{r} 10 \\ -2 \\ \hline \end{array}$$
$$\begin{array}{r} 7 \\ -2 \\ \hline \end{array}$$

Math Reasoning

9. Sam had 4 apples.
He gave 2 apples to Jamie.
Would you *count on* or *count back* to find out
how many apples Sam has left? Why?

Home Activity Have your child use beans, pebbles, or pennies to review the subtraction problems on this page.
Homework Workbook 4-7

Name_____

Counting Back 1, 2, and 3

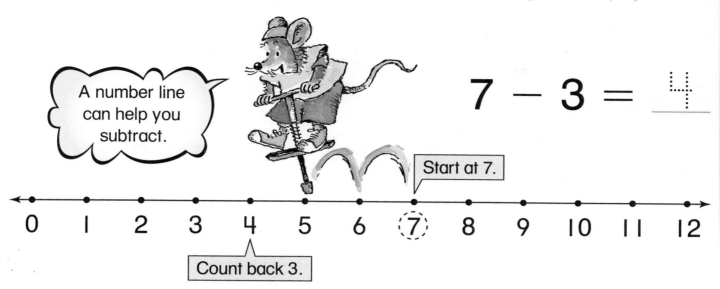

A number line can help you subtract.

Start at 7.

$7 - 3 = 4$

0 1 2 3 4 5 6 (7) 8 9 10 11 12

Count back 3.

Use the number line to count back.
Circle the number where you start.
Write each difference.

1.
$8 - 1 = 7$

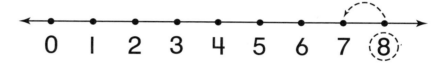

2.
$5 - 2 = \underline{}$

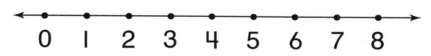

3.
$4 - 3 = \underline{}$

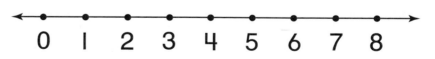

4.
$7 - 1 = \underline{}$

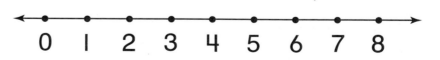

5.
$6 - 3 = \underline{}$

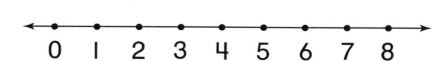

California Content Standards Number Sense 2.1 (🔑) Know the subtraction facts. Also Number Sense 2.5 (🔑), Mathematical Reasoning 1.1.

```
◄──●────●────●────●────●────●────●────●────●────●────●────●────●──►
   0    1    2    3    4    5    6    7    8    9   10   11   12
```

Count back to subtract.
Use the number line to help you.

6. $10 - 3 = \underline{7}$ $6 - 2 = \underline{\hspace{1cm}}$ $9 - 3 = \underline{\hspace{1cm}}$

7. $8 - 2 = \underline{\hspace{1cm}}$ $9 - 2 = \underline{\hspace{1cm}}$ $11 - 2 = \underline{\hspace{1cm}}$

8.
$$\begin{array}{cccccc} 6 & 7 & 8 & 10 & 4 & 8 \\ -1 & -3 & -1 & -2 & -2 & -3 \\ \hline \end{array}$$

9.
$$\begin{array}{cccccc} 2 & 12 & 9 & 7 & 10 & 3 \\ -1 & -3 & -1 & -2 & -1 & -2 \\ \hline \end{array}$$

 Problem Solving

Solve.

10. Earl has 11 big kites and 2 little kites.
   How many more big kites does he have?

   $\underline{\hspace{1.5cm}}$ more big kites

11. Earl has 2 little kites. He buys 2 more little kites.
   How many little kites does he have?

   $\underline{\hspace{1.5cm}}$ little kites

122   one hundred twenty-two

🏠 **Home Activity** Ask your child to show you how he or she used the number line to solve these problems.
Homework Workbook 4-8

Name_____ **Using Doubles to Subtract**

Sometimes doubles can help you subtract.

$2 + 2 = 4$

so $4 - 2 = 2$

$2 + 2 = $ 4

$4 - 2 = $ 2

Find the double. Then subtract.
Use cubes if you like.

1.

$3 + 3 = $ ___

so $6 - 3 = $ ___

2.

$5 + 5 = $ ___

so $10 - 5 = $ ___

3.

$6 + 6 = $ ___

so $12 - 6 = $ ___

4.

$4 + 4 = $ ___

so $8 - 4 = $ ___

California Content Standards *Number Sense 2.2 (⊷) Use the inverse relationship between addition and subtraction. Also Number Sense 2.1 (⊷), Mathematical Reasoning 1.1.*

Add or subtract.

5.
$$\begin{array}{r} 1 \\ -\ 1 \\ \hline 0 \end{array}$$
$$\begin{array}{r} 2 \\ +\ 2 \\ \hline \end{array}$$
$$\begin{array}{r} 6 \\ -\ 3 \\ \hline \end{array}$$
$$\begin{array}{r} 4 \\ +\ 4 \\ \hline \end{array}$$
$$\begin{array}{r} 5 \\ -\ 1 \\ \hline \end{array}$$
$$\begin{array}{r} 3 \\ +\ 3 \\ \hline \end{array}$$

6.
$$\begin{array}{r} 2 \\ -\ 1 \\ \hline \end{array}$$
$$\begin{array}{r} 5 \\ +\ 5 \\ \hline \end{array}$$
$$\begin{array}{r} 4 \\ -\ 2 \\ \hline \end{array}$$
$$\begin{array}{r} 10 \\ -\ 5 \\ \hline \end{array}$$
$$\begin{array}{r} 6 \\ +\ 6 \\ \hline \end{array}$$
$$\begin{array}{r} 8 \\ -\ 4 \\ \hline \end{array}$$

7. $1 + 1 =$ _____ $9 - 2 =$ _____ $4 - 4 =$ _____

8. $8 + 2 =$ _____ $12 - 6 =$ _____ $6 + 3 =$ _____

9. $6 - 0 =$ _____ $8 - 3 =$ _____ $2 - 1 =$ _____

 Problem Solving

Solve.

10. Sam has 6 yellow buttons and 3 blue buttons. How many more yellow buttons does he have?

_____ more yellow buttons

11. Sam has 6 yellow buttons and 3 blue buttons. How many buttons does he have in all?

_____ buttons

Home Activity Have your child add a double, such as $5 + 5 = 10$, and then subtract with five fingers. ($10 - 5 = 5$).
Homework Workbook 4-9

Name_____

Fact Families

Algebra

5 + 4 = 9   9 − 4 = 5

4 + 5 = 9   9 − 5 = 4

Write each fact family.
Use cubes if you like.

1.

___ + ___ = ___   ___ − ___ = ___

___ + ___ = ___   ___ − ___ = ___

2.

___ + ___ = ___   ___ − ___ = ___

___ + ___ = ___   ___ − ___ = ___

3.

___ + ___ = ___   ___ − ___ = ___

___ + ___ = ___   ___ − ___ = ___

California Content Standards *Number Sense 2.1 (🔑) Know the addition facts and the corresponding subtraction facts. Number Sense 2.2 (🔑). Also Algebra and Functions 1.1, 1.2.*

one hundred twenty-five **125**

Use the pictures.
Write each fact family.

4.

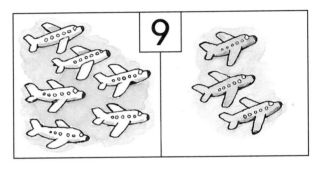

$6 + 3 = 9$

___ + ___ = ___

___ - ___ = ___

___ - ___ = ___

5.

___ + ___ = ___

___ + ___ = ___

___ - ___ = ___

___ - ___ = ___

6.

___ + ___ = ___

___ + ___ = ___

___ - ___ = ___

___ - ___ = ___

7.

___ + ___ = ___

___ + ___ = ___

___ - ___ = ___

___ - ___ = ___

Home Activity Give your child groups of 12 or fewer objects. Have your child divide the group in two and write the fact family. Homework Workbook 4-10

Name_____ **Problem-Solving Application**

Choose the Operation

There are 6 horses.
I more horse joins
them. How many
horses are there in all?

Algebra

6 $\oplus$ 1 = 7 horses

Complete each number sentence.

Think: Do you need to add or subtract?

1. Yoshi has 6 planes.
    He makes 5 more planes.
    How many planes does
    he have now?

    6 $\bigcirc$ 5 = _____ planes

2. There are 6 cars.
    2 cars leave.
    How many cars
    are there now?

    6 $\bigcirc$ 2 = _____ cars

3. Mr. Gomez has 5 bikes.
    Ben has I bike.
    How many more bikes
    does Mr. Gomez have?

    5 $\bigcirc$ 1 = _____ bikes

4. Kim has 4 big trains.
    She has 4 little trains.
    How many trains does
    she have altogether?

    4 $\bigcirc$ 4 = _____ trains

California Content Standards *Algebra and Functions 1.1*
Write and solve number sentences. Algebra and Functions 1.2.
Also Algebra and Functions 1.3, Mathematical Reasoning 1.1.

one hundred twenty-seven **127**

Complete each number sentence.

5. Greg saw 7 balloons.
Then he saw 3 more
balloons. How many
balloons did he see?

$7 \oplus 3 = 10$ balloons

6. The school has 5 buses.
They sell 2 buses.
How many buses
are left?

$5 \bigcirc 2 = \underline{}$ buses

7. There are 9 cars.
2 cars drive away.
How many cars
are there now?

$9 \bigcirc 2 = \underline{}$ cars

8. There are 2 teams.
Each team has 6 bats.
How many bats do
they have altogether?

$6 \bigcirc 6 = \underline{}$ bats

Add or subtract.
Draw a picture or write a story
for each number sentence.

9. $7 + 2 = \underline{}$

10. $9 - 1 = \underline{}$

Home Activity Have your child read these word problems
and explain when to add or subtract, and why.
Homework Workbook 4-11

Name _____   **Diagnostic Checkpoint**

Write the fact family.

1.

_____ + _____ = _____   _____ − _____ = _____

_____ + _____ = _____   _____ − _____ = _____

Count back to subtract.

2.
```
   6        10        5        7        9       11
 − 1       − 2      − 1      − 1      − 2      − 2
```

Find the double. Then subtract.

3.    3 + 3 = _____

6 − 3 = _____

4.   2 + 2 = _____

4 − 2 = _____

Complete the number sentence.

5. There are 2 big kites.
There are 9 little kites.
How many kites are
there in all?

2 ◯ 9 = _____ kites

6. There are 8 boats.
3 boats go away.
How many boats
are left?

8 ◯ 3 = _____ boats

Name_____

1. $4 + 4 = \boxed{}$

   10   8   0   4
   ○   ○   ○   ○

2. $5 - 0 = \boxed{}$

   0   10   1   5
   ○   ○   ○   ○

3.   9
       $+\ 1$

   10   8   12   11
   ○   ○   ○   ○

4.   6
       $-\ 3$

   9   6   1   3
   ○   ○   ○   ○

5. $8 + 3 = \boxed{}$

   5   10   11   NH
   ○   ○   ○   ○

6. $10 - 2 = \boxed{}$

   8   5   12   NH
   ○   ○   ○   ○

7.   ___, 10, 11

   7   12   9   NH
   ○   ○   ○   ○

8.   7, ___, 9

   10   9   6   8
   ○   ○   ○   ○

9.   9   2

   ○ $9 + 2 = 11$
   ○ $9 - 2 = 7$
   ○ $7 + 2 = 9$
   ○ NH

10.   7   3

   ○ 10 notebooks
   ○ 3 notebooks
   ○ 4 notebooks
   ○ NH

Oral Directions *Mark the correct answer. NH means "Not here." Mark it whenever the answer is not given.*

#1–6. Add or subtract.
#7. What number comes just before ten if you are counting by ones?

#8. What number comes between 7 and 9 if you are counting by ones?
#9. Ann has nine pencils. She gives two away. Mark the number sentence that tells how many pencils Ann has left.
#10. Tim has seven notebooks. He buys three more. How many notebooks does he have altogether?

1. Count back to subtract.

_____ , _____

$6 - 2 = $ _____

___

Add. Use the number line if you like.

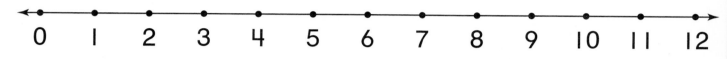

0   1   2   3   4   5   6   7   8   9   10   11   12

2. $6 + 1 = $ _____ $7 + 2 = $ _____ $9 + 3 = $ _____

___

3. Write the fact family.

___ + ___ = ___   ___ = ___   ___ = ___

___ + ___ = ___   ___ = ___   ___ = ___

___

Draw a picture to solve.
Write an addition sentence.

4. There are 6 cars on the table.
   Joe puts 2 more cars on the table.
   How many cars are on the table now?   _____ cars

___

Use the doubles to add.

5. $5 + 5 = $ _____ | 6. $6 + 6 = $ _____

   $5 + 6 = $ _____ | $6 + 7 = $ _____

Add or subtract.

7. $3 + 2 = \underline{\hspace{1cm}}$ $9 - 0 = \underline{\hspace{1cm}}$ $6 + 5 = \underline{\hspace{1cm}}$

8. $10 - 1 = \underline{\hspace{1cm}}$ $2 + 2 = \underline{\hspace{1cm}}$ $5 - 3 = \underline{\hspace{1cm}}$

9.
$$\begin{array}{r} 11 \\ -\ 2 \\ \hline \end{array} \qquad \begin{array}{r} 9 \\ -\ 3 \\ \hline \end{array} \qquad \begin{array}{r} 4 \\ +\ 1 \\ \hline \end{array} \qquad \begin{array}{r} 3 \\ +\ 8 \\ \hline \end{array} \qquad \begin{array}{r} 12 \\ -\ 6 \\ \hline \end{array} \qquad \begin{array}{r} 5 \\ +\ 4 \\ \hline \end{array}$$

Find the double. Then subtract.

10.  $4 + 4 = \underline{\hspace{1cm}}$

$8 - 4 = \underline{\hspace{1cm}}$

11. $3 + 3 = \underline{\hspace{1cm}}$

$6 - 3 = \underline{\hspace{1cm}}$

Complete each number sentence.
Add or subtract.

12. Tom had 9 toy trucks.
He lost 2 of them.
How many trucks
are left?

$9 \bigcirc 2 = \underline{\hspace{1cm}}$ trucks

13. Ann has 4 peanuts.
Jake has 3 more
peanuts than Ann.
How many peanuts
does Jake have?

$4 \bigcirc 3 = \underline{\hspace{1cm}}$ peanuts

Name_____

1.

Count on 1	
4	5
5	6
6	?

   8   5   10   7
   ○   ○   ○   ○

2.

0 1 2 3 4 5 6 7 8 9 10 11 12

$$11 - 2 = \square$$

4   8   9   12
○   ○   ○   ○

3. $7 + 2 = 9$ $2 + 7 = 9$ $9 - 2 = 7$

$7 - 6 = 1$ $7 + 7 = 14$ $9 - 9 = 0$ $9 - 7 = 2$
○   ○   ○   ○

4. $6 + 5 = 11$

$5 + 5 = 10$ $4 + 4 = 8$ $1 + 1 = 2$ $2 + 2 = 4$
○   ○   ○   ○

5. $4 + 4 = 8$

$$\text{so } 8 - 4 = \square$$

8   4   10   0
○   ○   ○   ○

Oral Directions *Mark the correct answer. NH means "Not here." Mark it whenever the answer is not given.*

#1. Follow the rule. Mark the number that is missing.
#2. Subtract. Use the number line to count back if you like.

#3. Which fact belongs to the fact family?
#4. Which doubles fact helps you add six plus five equals eleven?
#5. Use the doubles fact four plus four equals eight to subtract eight minus four equals.

6.

$$2 + 4 = 6$$

○   ○   ○   NH
                                                      ○

---

7. $5 + 3 = \boxed{}$ 7   4   8   10
                                   ○   ○   ○   ○

---

8. $10 - 5 = \boxed{}$ 15   5   0   6
                                   ○   ○   ○   ○

---

9.   8   6   10   12   4
        $- 2$ ○   ○   ○   ○

---

10.   9   10   7   12   11
        $+ 2$ ○   ○   ○   ○

---

11.   7   3

$7 + 7 = 14$ $7 - 3 = 4$ $7 + 3 = 10$ $3 - 3 = 0$
     ○   ○   ○   ○

---

12.   12   6

6 erasers   18 erasers   2 erasers   NH
     ○   ○   ○   ○

Oral Directions *Mark the correct answer. NH means "Not here." Mark it whenever the answer is not given.*

#6. Mark the picture that shows the number sentence two plus four equals six.
#7–10. Add or subtract.

#11. There are seven scissors on the table. Jane put three more scissors on the table. Mark the number sentence you can use to find how many scissors there are now.
#12. Devin had twelve erasers. He lost six erasers. How many erasers does Devin have left?

134   one hundred thirty-four

Diagnosing Readiness
for Chapter 5

1. Color all the white triangles red.
   Color all the white squares blue.

2. Circle the pizza that has
   been cut into equal parts.

3. Draw a line through each item
   to make two equal parts.

To the Family

Looking Back

In Kindergarten children were introduced to two- and three-dimensional shapes. Children also practiced sorting and classifying objects by size, color, and shape.

Chapter 5

Geometry and Fractions

Children learn to identify and compare solid and plane shapes. They also learn to identify fractions (halves, thirds, and fourths).

Looking Ahead

In Grade 2 children will learn to identify more shapes by their attributes and will learn to identify and compare fractions from twelfths to halves.

Page 135 Your child solved problems that review math skills from previous chapters and will help your child with the skills in Chapter 5.

Math at Home Help your child learn two- and three-dimensional shapes by observing objects around the house. Look at packages to compare cylinders, cubes, rectangular prisms, and cones.

Math Literature Read stories and do activities with your child relating to geometry and fractions. Look for the following books in your local library.
Exploring Shapes by Andrew King (Copper Beech Books, 1998)
Fraction Action by Loreen Leedy (Holiday House, 1994)

California Content Standards in Chapter 5 Lessons*

	Teach and Practice	Practice
Number Sense		
4.1 (🔑), Grade 2, Recognize and name unit fractions.	11–13	
4.2 (🔑), Grade 2, Recognize fractions of a whole and parts of a group.	10–14	
Measurement and Geometry		
2.1 Identify, describe, and compare triangles, rectangles, squares, and circles, including the faces of three-dimensional objects.	3, 6, 9	4
2.2 Classify familiar plane and solid objects by common attributes, such as color, position, shape, size, roundness, or number of corners, and explain which attributes are being used for classification.	1, 2, 4	3, 6, 9
2.3 Give and follow directions about location.	7	6, 8
2.4 Arrange and describe objects in space by proximity, position, and direction.	7, 8	

	Teach and Practice	Practice
Statistics, Data Analysis, and Probability		
2.1 (🔑) Describe, extend, and explain ways to get to a next element in simple repeating patterns.	5	1
Mathematical Reasoning		
1.1 Determine the approach, materials, and strategies to be used.		4, 7, 10–14
1.2 Use tools, such as manipulatives or sketches, to model problems.		7, 10–14
2.0 Students solve problems and justify their reasoning.	9	3, 5, 14
2.1 Explain the reasoning used and justify the procedures selected.		1, 4, 10, 11, 13
3.0 Students note connections between one problem and another.		2

* The symbol (🔑) indicates a key standard as designated in the Mathematics Framework for California Public Schools.
  Full statements of the California Content Standards are found at the beginning of this book following the Table of Contents.

Name_____ **Solid Shapes**

rectangular prisms	sphere	cylinder	cone
  cube			

Word Bank

cone
cylinder
sphere
rectangular prism
cube

Circle the objects with the same kind of shape. Write the name of the shape.

1.   _____

_____

2.   _____

_____

3.   _____

_____

4.   _____

California Content Standards *Measurement and Geometry 2.2 Classify familiar solid objects. Also Statistics, Data Analysis, and Probability 2.1 (🔑), Mathematical Reasoning 2.1.*

Put an X on the object that does not belong.
Tell why it is different.

5.

6.

7.

8.

 Problem Solving

Circle the shape that is most likely to
come next in the pattern. Explain why.

9.   _____

Home Activity Point out containers or other objects in your
home that are shaped like cubes, spheres, cones, rectangular
prisms, and cylinders. Homework Workbook 5-1

Name_____ **Attributes of Solid Shapes**

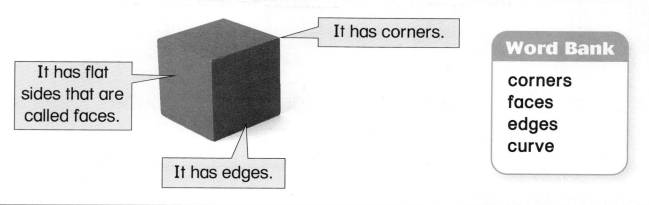

It has corners.

It has flat sides that are called faces.

It has edges.

Word Bank

corners
faces
edges
curve

Use shapes if you like.
Does the shape have corners, faces, and edges?
Write **yes** or **no** in each box.

		Corners	Faces	Edges
1.	rectangular prisms / cube	yes	yes	yes
2.	sphere			
3.	cylinder			
4.	cone			

California Content Standards *Measurement and Geometry 2.2 Classify familiar solid objects by common attributes. Also Mathematical Reasoning 3.0.*

| cone | cylinder | rectangular prism | cube | sphere |

Sort the shapes.
Write the names on the lines.

5. Has a curve

_____

_____

_____

6. Has green color

_____

_____

_____

7. Has only flat faces

_____   _____

 **Problem Solving**

8. Name two shapes that roll.

_____   _____

9. Name two shapes that stack.

_____   _____

Home Activity Give your child household objects such as a cereal box, a funnel, and a paper-towel roll. Ask whether each shape has corners, faces, edges, and/or curves.
Homework Workbook 5–2

Name_____

Relating Solid and Plane Shapes

This object is a cube. The faces of a cube are square.

Look at each shape.
Circle the object with a face that matches the shape.

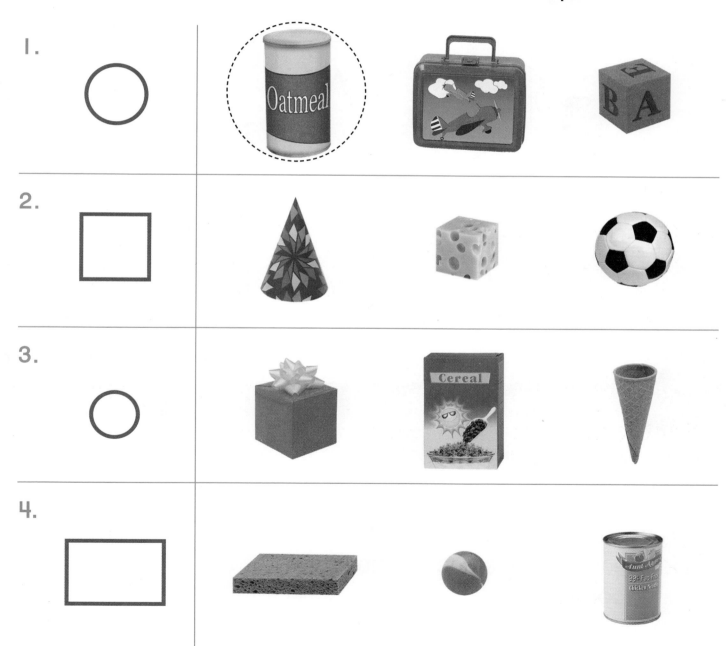

1.

2.

3.

4.

 California Content Standards *Measurement and Geometry 2.1 Identify, describe, and compare triangles, rectangles, squares, and circles, including the faces of three-dimensional objects. Also Measurement and Geometry 2.2, Mathematical Reasoning 2.0.*

one hundred forty-one **141**

Circle the shape that is a face of each object.

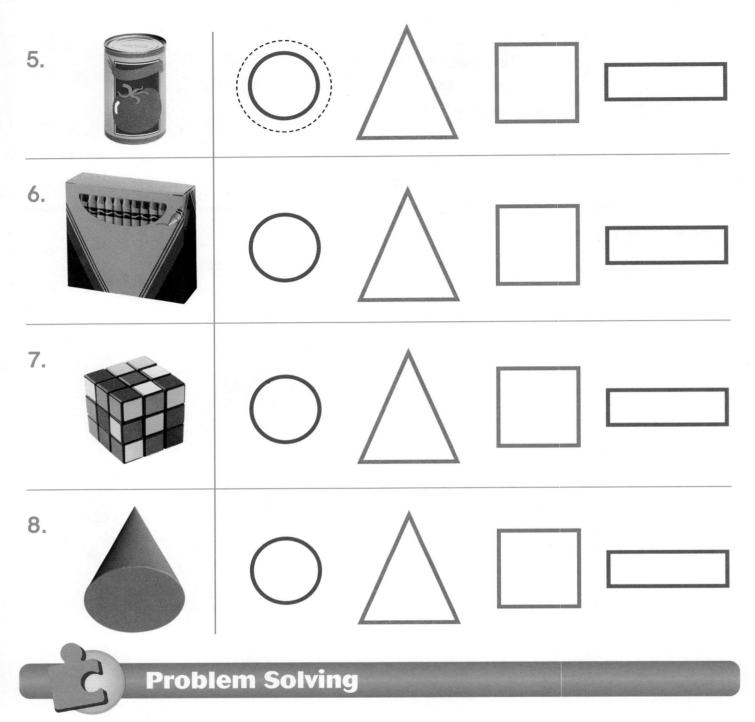

5.

6.

7.

8.

Problem Solving

Solve. Write the number sentence in the rectangle.

9. A cube has 6 faces.
   It has 2 more corners than faces.
   How many corners does a cube have?
   _____ corners

142 one hundred forty-two

Name_____

Which of these shapes do you have?

My shape has 4 corners. All the sides are the same length.

Understand

You need to find the mystery shape.

Plan

You can follow the clues.
Cross out what does not belong.

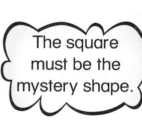

The square must be the mystery shape.

Solve

Clue 1:
My shape has 4 corners.

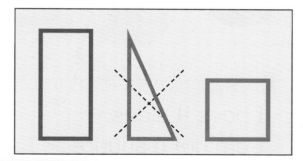

Clue 2:
All the sides are the same length.

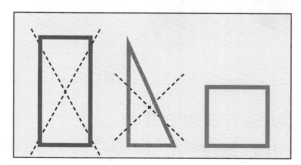

Look Back

How can you check your answer?

___

Circle the correct shape.

1. I am curved.
   I have faces.
   Which shape am I?

 California Content Standards *Measurement and Geometry
2.1 Identify, describe, and compare triangles, rectangles, squares,
and circles by common attributes. Mathematical Reasoning 2.0.
Also Measurement and Geometry 2.2.*

Circle the correct shape.

2. I have sides.
   I do not have 4 corners.
   Which shape am I?

3. I have 0 sides.
   I have 0 corners.
   Which shape am I?

4. I am curved.
   I have 1 face.
   Which shape am I?

5. I am curved.
   I do not have a face.
   Which shape am I?

6. My sides are the same length.
   I have 3 corners.
   Which shape am I?

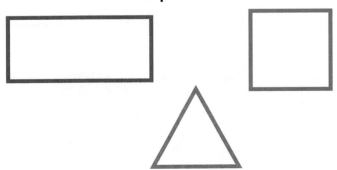

7. I have 4 sides.
   I am not a square.
   Which shape am I?

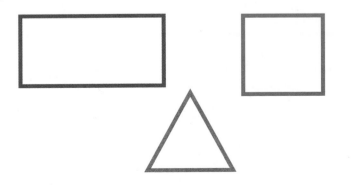

Home Activity Encourage your child to create riddles using two- and three-dimensional shapes. Homework Workbook 5-9

Circle the correct shape.

1. I am curved.
   I have faces.
   Which shape am I?

2. I have sides.
   I do not have 4 corners.
   Which shape am I?

Draw the shape that is most likely to come next.

3. △ ☐ △ ☐ △ ☐ _____

4. _____

Which one is equal in shape and size?
Circle the correct answer.

5. ▭   △   ○   ▭

6. ⬡   ▭   ⬡   △

7. Look at the picture.
   Use the words in the box to fill in the blank.

   | next to |
   | above |
   | below |

   The circle is _____ the triangle.

Name _____

1. (10)   11   0   20   NH
       ○   ○   ○   ○

2. (13)   3   23   10   NH
       ○   ○   ○   ○

3. $5 < 6$ $13 < 11$ $12 > 17$ $1 > 7$
      ○   ○   ○   ○

4.

$4 + 3 = 7$ $6 - 3 = 3$ $5 - 3 = 2$ $10 - 3 = 7$
   ○   ○   ○   ○

5.

$4 + 4 = 8$ $8 - 4 = 4$ $2 + 6 = 8$ $3 + 6 = 9$
   ○   ○   ○   ○

6.

$9 - 3 = 6$ $9 - 6 = 3$ $9 + 3 = 12$ NH
   ○   ○   ○   ○

Oral Directions *Mark the correct answer. NH means "Not here." Mark it whenever the answer is not given.*

#1. What number is ten more than the number in the circle?
#2. What number is ten less than the number in the circle?
#3. Which one is true?
#4. Ten children are jumping rope. Three children stop jumping rope. Mark the number sentence that tells how many children are left jumping rope.

#5. Nick has two red counters and six yellow counters. Mark the number sentence that tells how many counters Nick has altogether.
#6. Sam has nine balloons. Megan has three balloons. How many more balloons does Sam have? Mark the number sentence.

Name_____

Equal Parts

These parts are the same size and shape. The parts are equal.

Circle the shapes that show equal parts.

1.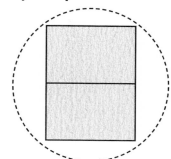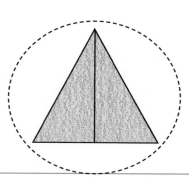

2.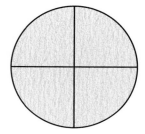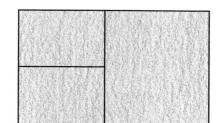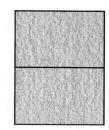

3.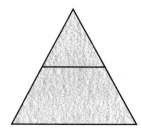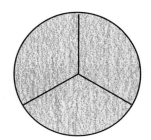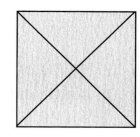

4.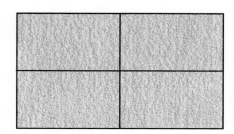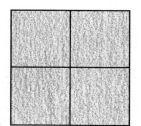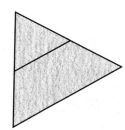

California Content Standards *Number Sense 4.2 (🗝),
Grade 2, Recognize fractions of a whole. Also Mathematical
Reasoning 1.1, 1.2, 2.1.*

one hundred fifty-seven **157**

Write the number of equal parts.

5.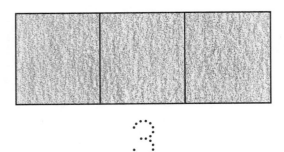

3

6.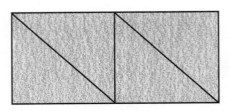

_____

7.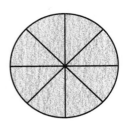

_____

8.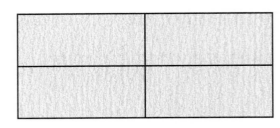

_____

9.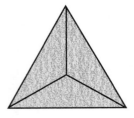

_____

10.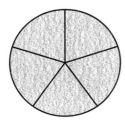

_____

 **Problem Solving**

Solve.

11. Tomás wants to cut this paper into 8 equal parts. Draw lines to show where he could cut. Explain.

Home Activity Cut out some shapes and fold them in different ways. Ask your child to tell how many equal parts are in each shape. Homework Workbook 5-10

Name _____ **Halves**

There are 2 equal parts. Each part is one half of the whole. Each part shows one half.

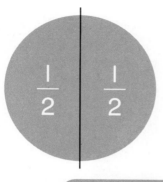

$\frac{1}{2}$ $\frac{1}{2}$

Word Bank

one half

Circle each shape that shows equal halves.

1.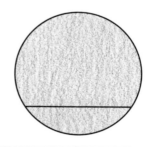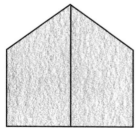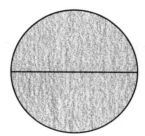

2.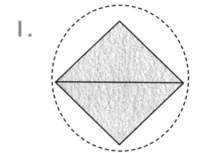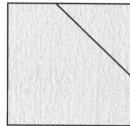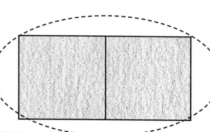

3.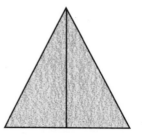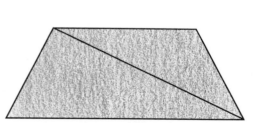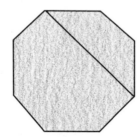

4.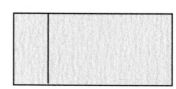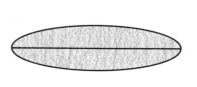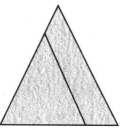

California Content Standards *Number Sense 4.2 (⚷), Grade 2, Recognize fractions of a whole. Number Sense 4.1 (⚷), Grade 2. Also Mathematical Reasoning 1.1, 1.2, 2.1.*

one hundred fifty-nine **159**

Draw a line on each shape to show halves.

Color $\frac{1}{2}$ of each shape.

5.

6.

7.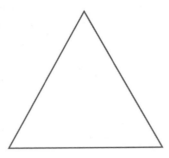

8.

9.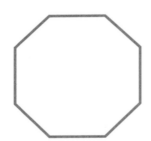

10.

11.

12.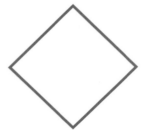

13.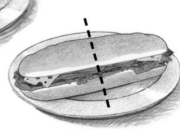

Math Reasoning

Number Sense

14. Andy has $\frac{1}{2}$ of a sandwich.

Eva has $\frac{1}{2}$ of a sandwich.

Eva says she has more than Andy.
Could she be right?
Tell why or why not.

Home Activity Help your child cut paper shapes or objects into two halves (e.g., a slice of bread).
Homework Workbook 5-11

Name_____

Thirds and Fourths

There are 3 equal parts. Each part is one third of the whole.

There are 4 equal parts. Each part is one fourth of the whole.

$\frac{1}{3}$ $\frac{1}{3}$ $\frac{1}{3}$ $\frac{1}{4}$ $\frac{1}{4}$ $\frac{1}{4}$ $\frac{1}{4}$

Word Bank

one third
one fourth

Circle each shape that is cut into thirds.

1.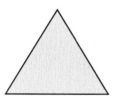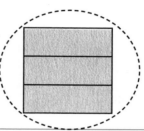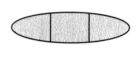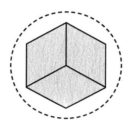

2.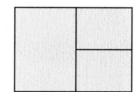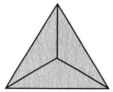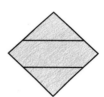

Circle each shape that is cut into fourths.

3.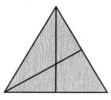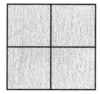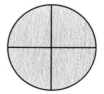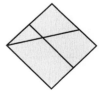

4.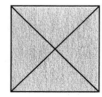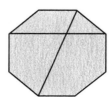

California Content Standards Number Sense 4.2 (🔑), Grade 2, Recognize fractions of a whole. Number Sense 4.1 (🔑), Grade 2. Also Mathematical Reasoning 1.1, 1.2.

Color $\frac{1}{3}$ of each shape.

5.

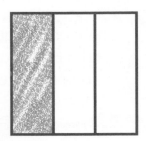

6.

7.

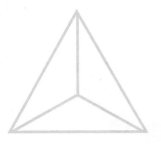

8.

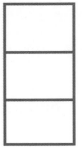

9.

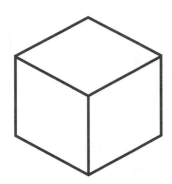

10.

Color $\frac{1}{4}$ of each shape.

11.

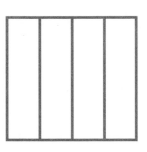

12.

13.

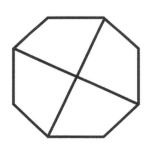

14.

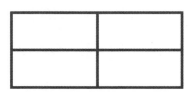

15.

16.

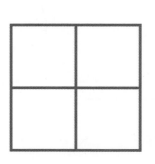

Home Activity Help your child fold and cut out paper shapes into thirds and fourths. Have him or her label the fraction on each piece. Homework Workbook 5-12

Name_____

Fractions of a Group

There are 3 pom pons. One is blue. One third of the group is blue.

$\frac{1}{3}$ is blue.

What part is blue?
Circle the fraction.

1.

$\frac{1}{2}$ $\frac{1}{3}$ $\left(\frac{1}{4}\right)$

2.

$\frac{1}{2}$ $\frac{1}{3}$ $\frac{1}{4}$

3.

$\frac{1}{2}$ $\frac{1}{3}$ $\frac{1}{4}$

4.

$\frac{1}{2}$ $\frac{1}{3}$ $\frac{1}{4}$

5.

$\frac{1}{2}$ $\frac{1}{3}$ $\frac{1}{4}$

6.

$\frac{1}{2}$ $\frac{1}{3}$ $\frac{1}{4}$

California Content Standards *Number Sense 4.2* (🔑), *Grade 2, Recognize fractional parts of a group. Number Sense 4.1* (🔑), *Grade 2. Also Mathematical Reasoning 1.1, 1.2, 2.1.*

one hundred sixty-three **163**

Color to show each fraction.

7. $\frac{1}{3}$

8. $\frac{1}{2}$

9. $\frac{1}{4}$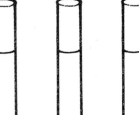

10. $\frac{1}{3}$

11. $\frac{1}{4}$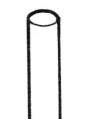

12. $\frac{1}{2}$

Math Reasoning

13. Mike has $\frac{1}{3}$ of a jar of paint.

Lee has $\frac{1}{4}$ of a jar of paint.

The jars are the same size.
Who has more paint? _____
Tell how you know.

$\frac{1}{3}$ $\frac{1}{4}$

🏠 **Home Activity** Show your child 2, 3, or 4 identical objects.
Have your child identify 1/2, 1/3, or 1/4 of each object.
Homework Workbook 5-13

Name_____ **Problem-Solving Application**
Equal Shares

We each have an equal share.

Circle each child's equal share.
Use counters if you like.
Think: An equal share means everyone gets the same amount.

1. **2** children

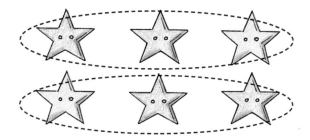

2. **4** children

3. **3** children

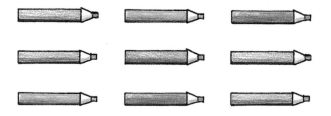

4. **6** children

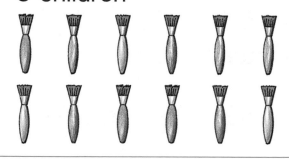

5. **4** children

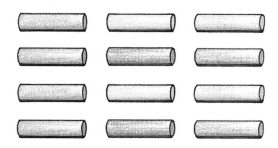

6. **5** children

California Content Standards *Number Sense 4.2 (key), Grade 2, Recognize fractional parts of a group. Also Mathematical Reasoning 1.1, 1.2, 2.0.*

one hundred sixty-five **165**

Solve. Circle **yes** or **no**.

7. Can you make equal shares for 2 children?

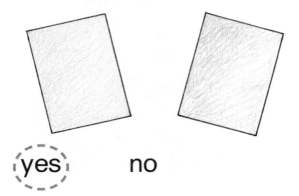

(yes)　　　　no

8. Can you make equal shares for 3 children?

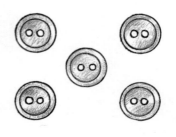

yes　　　　　　　no

9. Can you make equal shares for 4 children?

yes　　　　no

10. Can you make equal shares for 2 children?

yes　　　　　　　no

11. There are 9 marbles. Can you make equal shares for 3 children?

yes　　　　no

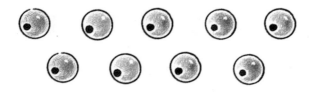

What if one more person comes? Will you be able to make equal shares?

yes　　　　　　　no

12. Tim and Tina have a pie cut into 4 equal pieces. Can they each have an equal share?

yes　　　　　　　no

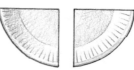

What if 2 more people come? Will they be able to make equal shares?

yes　　　　no

Home Activity Use household items, such as buttons or paper clips, to make equal shares with your child. Homework Workbook 5-14

Name_____

Circle the shapes that show equal parts.

1.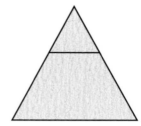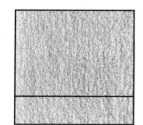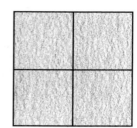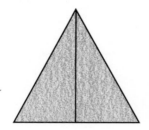

Circle each shape that shows thirds.

2.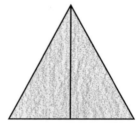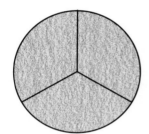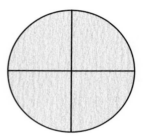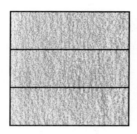

Write the number of equal parts.

3. 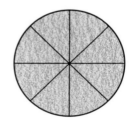 _____ 4.  _____

Color to show each fraction.

5. $\frac{1}{2}$ 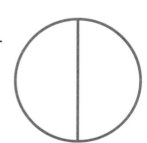 6. $\frac{1}{3}$ 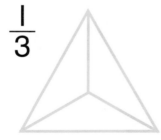 7. $\frac{1}{4}$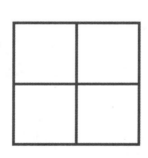

Circle **yes** or **no**.

8. Can you make equal shares for 3 children?

    yes   no

1.

    ○ ◯   △   □   ▭

    ○   ○   ○   ○

2.

    0   1   3   5

    ○   ○   ○   ○

3. $6 + 6 = 12$

so $12 - 6 = \square$

    2   10   4   6

    ○   ○   ○   ○

4. $8 + 3 = 11$

$3 + 8 = 11$

$11 - 3 = 8$

   $7 + 4 = 11$ $9 + 2 = 11$ $11 - 8 = 3$ $12 - 1 = 11$

    ○   ○   ○   ○

5. $\begin{array}{r} 10 \\ -\ 4 \\ \hline \end{array}$

    6   5   4   NH

    ○   ○   ○   ○

6. $4 + 5 = \square$

    12   9   10   NH

    ○   ○   ○   ○

7.  _____

                   NH

    ○   ○   ○   ○

Oral Directions *Mark the correct answer. NH means "Not here." Mark it whenever the answer is not given.*

#1. Mark the shape that is a face of a the cylinder.
#2. How many corners does this triangle have?
#3. Use the doubles fact six plus six equals twelve to solve

twelve minus six equals.
#4. Mark the number sentence that belongs with this fact family.
#5–6. Add or subtract.
#7. Mark the shape that is most likely to come next in the pattern.

Name_____ **Chapter 5 Test**

Circle the objects with the same type of shape.

1.

Draw and color the shape that is most likely to come next in the pattern.

2. _____

Circle the correct shape.

3. I have no edges.
   I do not have a face.
   What shape am I?

Write the number of sides and corners.

4. _____ sides

   _____ corners

5. _____ sides

   _____ corners

Draw a rectangle that is not a square above the circle.

6.

Draw a triangle to the right of the square rectangle.

7.

one hundred sixty-nine **169**

Write the number of equal parts.

8.

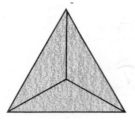

_____

9.

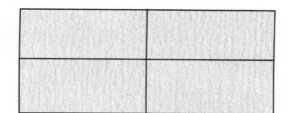

_____

Color $\frac{1}{2}$ of the shape.

10.

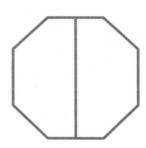

Color $\frac{1}{3}$ of the shape.

11.

Circle what part is red.

12.

$\frac{1}{2}$ $\frac{1}{3}$ $\frac{1}{4}$

13.

$\frac{1}{2}$ $\frac{1}{3}$ $\frac{1}{4}$

Circle each child's equal share.

14. 2 children

15. 3 children

170 one hundred seventy

Name_____

1.

2.

3.   ○   0   2   3   4
         ○   ○   ○   ○

4.   ◁   0   2   3   4
         ○   ○   ○   ○

5. $\frac{1}{2}$ $\frac{1}{3}$ $\frac{1}{4}$ NH
      ○   ○   ○   ○

6. $\frac{1}{2}$ $\frac{1}{3}$ $\frac{1}{4}$ NH
      ○   ○   ○   ○

7. $\frac{1}{2}$ $\frac{1}{3}$ $\frac{1}{4}$ NH
      ○   ○   ○   ○

8.   ○   △   ▢   ▭
      ○   ○   ○   ○

Oral Directions *Mark the correct answer. NH means "Not here." Mark it whenever the answer is not given.*

#1. Look at the drum. Mark the object that has the same type of shape.
#2. Mark the shape that is the same size and shape.

#3. How many corners does a circle have?
#4. How many sides does a triangle have?
#5–6. Look at the drawing. What part is shaded?
#7. Mark the fraction that tells what part is blue.
#8. Mark the shape that is a face of a cone.

9.

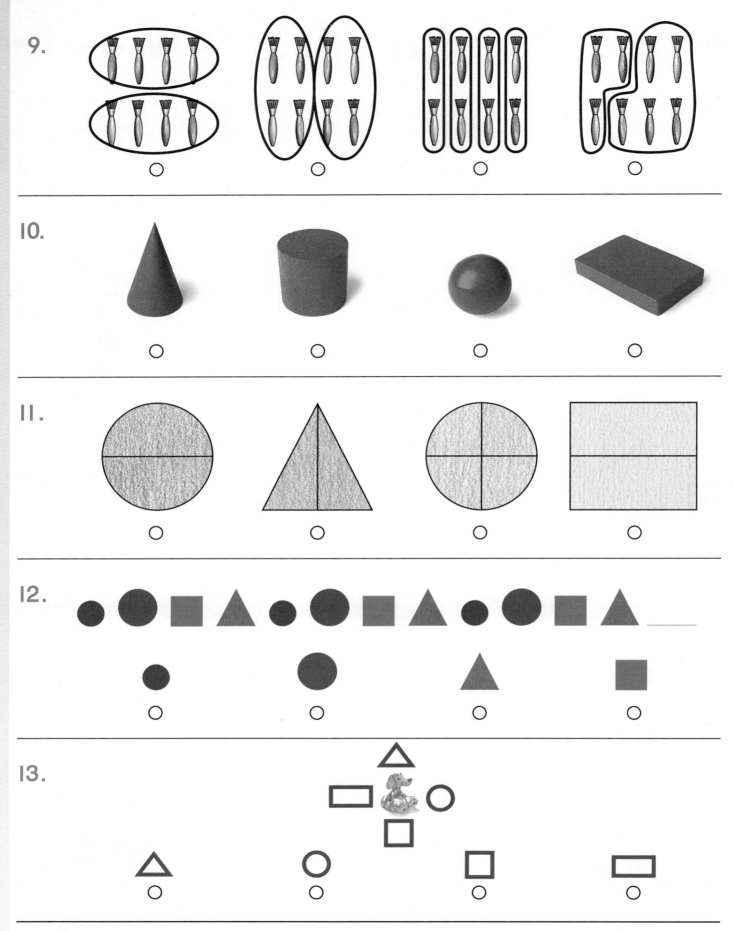

10.

11.

12.

13.

Oral Directions *Mark the correct answer. NH means "Not here." Mark it whenever the answer is not given.*

#9. Mark the drawing that shows equal shares for four children.

#10. I have curves. I have one face. What shape am I?
#11. Mark the shape that is not divided into two equal parts.
#12. What shape is most likely to come next in the pattern?
#13. Mark the shape that is to the right of the dog.

172 one hundred seventy-two

Diagnosing Readiness
For Chapter 6

Write how many.

1. 19

Tens	Ones

2.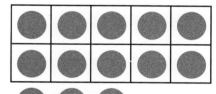

_____ ten and _____ ones is _____

Write >, <, or =.

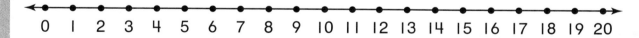

0 1 2 3 4 5 6 7 8 9 10 11 12 13 14 15 16 17 18 19 20

3. 11 ◯ 14

4. 19 ◯ 13

5. Write the missing number. 18, 19, _____

To the Family

Looking Back	Chapter 6	Looking Ahead
Previously in Grade 1 children reviewed counting, reading, and writing numbers to 20. They also compared and ordered numbers using symbols.	**Patterns and Numbers** Children count, read, write, compare, and order numbers to 100. They also work with repeating patterns.	Later in Grade 1 children will use numbers as they learn addition and subtraction facts, work with money and measurement, and tell time.

Page 173 Your child solved problems that review math skills from previous chapters and will help your child with the skills in Chapter 6.

Math at Home Make collections of household items such as buttons, bread tags, twist ties, or rubber bands. Together make groups of tens and ones to find how many of each collection you have. What happens when you add one more item? ten more items?

Math Literature To review counting numbers to 100 with your child, look for the following books in your local library.
Anno's Counting Book by Mitsumasa Anno (HarperTrophy, 1986)
One Watermelon Seed by Celia Barker Lottridge (Oxford University Press, 1990)

California Content Standards in Chapter 6 Lessons*

Number Sense	Teach and Practice	Practice	Statistics, Data Analysis, and Probability	Teach and Practice	Practice
1.1 (🔑) Count, read, and write whole numbers to 100.	1, 3–5, 9, 10	2, 6, 8, 12, 13	1.0 Organize, represent, and compare data by category on simple graphs and charts.	10	
1.2 (🔑) Compare and order whole numbers to 100 by using the symbols for less than, equal to, or greater than (<, =, >).	8, 9		2.0 Create and describe patterns.	10	11
1.3 Represent equivalent forms of the same number through the use of physical models, diagrams, and number expressions (to 20).	2–6		2.1 (🔑) Describe, extend, and explain ways to get to the next element in simple repeating patterns.	7	
1.4 Count and group objects in ones and tens.	1–4, 6	5	**Mathematical Reasoning**		
2.3 (🔑) Identify one more than, one less than, 10 more than, and 10 less than a given number.	13	11	1.0 Make decisions about how to set up a problem.		12
			1.1 Determine the approach, materials, and strategies to be used.		2, 4, 6, 13
2.4 (🔑) Count by 2s, 5s, and 10s to 100.	11, 12		1.2 Use tools, such as manipulatives or sketches, to model problems.		9
3.0 Use estimation strategies in computation and problem solving that involve numbers that use the ones, tens, and hundreds places.		1, 3, 14	2.0 Solve problems and justify reasoning.	7, 14	8–12
			2.1 Explain the reasoning used and justify the procedures selected.		1, 8, 12
3.1 Make reasonable estimates when comparing larger or smaller numbers.	14				

* The symbol (🔑) indicates a key standard as designated in the Mathematics Framework for California Public Schools.
  Full statements of the California Content Standards are found at the beginning of this book following the Table of Contents.

Name_____

Tens

_____ group of ten = _____10

10 ones equal 1 ten.

Word Bank
tens
ones

Circle groups of ten. Write how many.

1.

_____ groups of ten = _____

2.

_____ groups of ten = _____

3.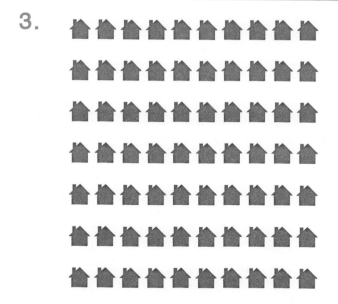

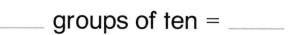
_____ groups of ten = _____

4.

_____ groups of ten = _____

California Content Standards *Number Sense 1.1 ( ) Count and write whole numbers. Number Sense 1.4. Also Number Sense 3.0, Mathematical Reasoning 2.1.*

Estimate how many. Then circle tens and count.

5.

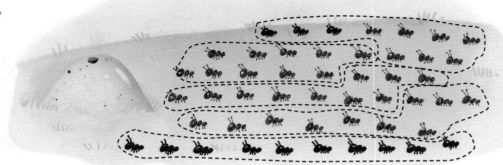

Estimate
40

Count
50

6.

Estimate

Count

7.

Estimate

Count

 Math Reasoning

Visual Thinking

8. Are there more than 10 bees by the hive? Tell why you think as you do.

🏠 **Home Activity** Have your child make groups of ten at home, using toys, coins, or crayons. Help your child count to see how many he or she has in all. Homework Workbook 6-1

Name _____ **Tens and Ones**

Word Bank
regroup

You can show numbers in different ways.

24 ones = **2** tens and **4** ones   or   **20** + **4** = **24**

Use tens, ones, and Workmat 4.
Show the number with ones. Regroup as tens.
Write the number in different ways.

	Ones	Tens and Ones		Addition
1. 15	15	1	5	10 + 5 = 15
2. 22				___ + ___ = ___
3. 11				___ + ___ = ___
4. 18				___ + ___ = ___
5. 20				___ + ___ = ___

California Content Standards *Number Sense 1.4 Count and group objects in ones and tens. Number Sense 1.3. Also Number Sense 1.1 ( ), Mathematical Reasoning 1.1.*

Write the number in different ways.

6.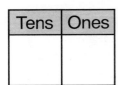

Tens	Ones
1	2

$\underline{10} + \underline{2} = \underline{12}$

_12_

7.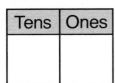

Tens	Ones

_____ + _____ = _____

_____

8.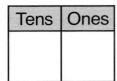

Tens	Ones

_____ + _____ = _____

_____

9.

Tens	Ones

_____ + _____ = _____

_____

10.

Tens	Ones

_____ + _____ = _____

_____

11.

Tens	Ones

_____ + _____ = _____

_____

Problem Solving

Solve.

12. Jake has 2 tens and 4 ones.
     Ann has 2 more tens than Jake.
     How many does Ann have?   _____ tens and _____ ones

     _____ + _____ = _____

Home Activity Ask your child to tell you how he or she
regrouped ones as tens on this page.
Homework Workbook 6-2

Name_____

Representing Numbers to 50

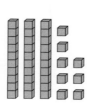

I see 3 tens and 8 ones. 3 tens and 8 ones is 38 or 30 + 8 = 38.

Tens	Ones
3	8

30 + 8 = 38

38

thirty-eight

Write the number in different ways.

1.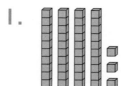

Tens	Ones
4	3

40 + 3 = 43   43

forty-three

2.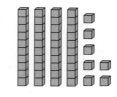

Tens	Ones

____ + ____ = ____   ____

forty-seven

3.

Tens	Ones

____ + ____ = ____   ____

twenty-nine

4.

Tens	Ones

____ + ____ = ____   ____

fifty

California Content Standards *Number Sense 1.1 (⬩—)* *Count, read, and write whole numbers. Number Sense 1.3, 1.4. Also Number Sense 3.0.*

Write the number in different ways.

5.

Tens	Ones
2	6

20 + 6 = 26   26

twenty-six

6.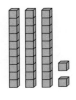

Tens	Ones

_____ + _____ = _____   _____

thirty-two

7.

Tens	Ones

_____ + _____ = _____   _____

thirty-nine

8.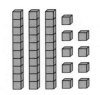

Tens	Ones

_____ + _____ = _____   _____

forty

 **Problem Solving**

Estimation

Estimate how many. Then circle tens and count.

9.

Estimate

Count

Home Activity Ask your child to tell the number of tens and ones in numbers like 42 or 36. Homework Workbook 6-3

Name_____ **Practice with Two-Digit Numbers**

   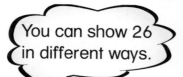

You can show 26 in different ways.

26 ones = 1 ten and 16 ones = 2 tens and 6 ones

Use tens, ones, and Workmat 4. Show each number one way. Then regroup to show each number another way. Record the ways.

1. 32	__3__ tens and __2__ ones	__2__ tens and __12__ ones
2. 25	_____ tens and _____ ones	_____ tens and _____ ones
3. 17	_____ tens and _____ ones	_____ tens and _____ ones
4. 58	_____ tens and _____ ones	_____ tens and _____ ones
5. 44	_____ tens and _____ ones	_____ tens and _____ ones
6. 63	_____ tens and _____ ones	_____ tens and _____ ones

California Content Standards *Number Sense 1.4 Count and group objects in ones and tens. Number Sense 1.3. Also Number Sense 1.1 (🔑), Mathematical Reasoning 1.1.*

one hundred eighty-five **185**

Use tens, ones, and Workmat 4. Show each number.
Regroup to show other ways. Record the ways.

7. 39

Tens	Ones

Tens	Ones

Tens	Ones

8. 86

Tens	Ones

Tens	Ones

Tens	Ones

9. 45

Tens	Ones

Tens	Ones

Tens	Ones

10. 71

Tens	Ones

Tens	Ones

Tens	Ones

Math Reasoning

Fill in the missing numbers.

11.

Tens	Ones

Tens	Ones
1	17

12.

Tens	Ones
3	12

Tens	Ones

186 one hundred eighty-six

Home Activity Ask your child to draw models to show numbers like 36 or 59 in two ways. Homework Workbook 6-6

Name_____

Bill is painting Jake's dog house. The color pattern repeats. What color will the next boards be?

Understand

You need to look for patterns.

Plan

There is a color pattern and a number pattern:
1 green board, 2 red boards, and 3 blue boards.
Then the pattern repeats.

Solve

Color the boards on the house.

Look Back

Tell about the pattern. How do you know what comes next?

California Content Standards *Statistics, Data Analysis, and Probability 2.1 (🔑) Describe, extend, and explain ways to get to the next element in simple repeating patterns. Mathematical Reasoning 2.0.*

These patterns repeat.
What comes next? Tell how you know.

1. 1, 2, 3, 1, 2, 3, 1, 2, _____, _____, _____,

2. ○△□□○△□□○△□□ _____, _____, _____,

3.

These patterns repeat.
Circle what comes next. Tell how you know.

4.

5.

6.

Home Activity Ask your child to tell you about the patterns on this page. Make patterns with household objects and have your child continue the patterns. Homework Workbook 6-7

Name_____

Write how many in different ways.

1.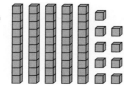

_____ + _____ = _____

2.

_____ groups of 10 = _____

3.

Tens	Ones

_____

4.

_____ tens and _____ ones

Regroup to show other ways to write the number.

5.

29

Tens	Ones

Tens	Ones

Write the number in different ways.

6.

17

Tens	Ones

_____ + _____ = _____

This pattern repeats. Write what comes next.

7.

_____

Name_____

1.   20 〇 19

    >   <   =   NH

    〇   〇   〇   〇

2.   14 〇 14

    >   <   =   NH

    〇   〇   〇   〇

3.   5 〇 8

    >   <   =   NH

    〇   〇   〇   〇

4.   12 〇 18

    >   <   =   NH

    〇   〇   〇   〇

5.

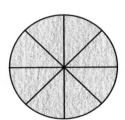

   4   6   8   NH

   〇   〇   〇   〇

6.

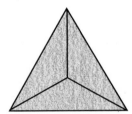

   3   4   5   NH

   〇   〇   〇   〇

7.   4 + ☐ = 8

   2   4   6   8

   〇   〇   〇   〇

8.   6 − ☐ = 1

   6   1   5   NH

   〇   〇   〇   〇

9.   ☐ + 5 = 7

   5   3   1   2

   〇   〇   〇   〇

10.   5 − ☐ = 5

   0   1   10   5

   〇   〇   〇   〇

Oral Directions *Mark the correct answer. NH means "Not here." Mark it whenever the answer is not given.*

#1–4. Mark the symbol that makes the statement true.

#5–6. Mark the number of equal parts.
#7–10. Mark the missing number that makes the number sentence true.

Name_____

Using >, <, and =

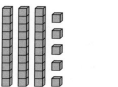

35 > 22	18 = 18	24 < 30
35 is greater than 22.	18 is equal to 18.	24 is less than 30.

Use tens and ones to show each number.
Circle >, <, or =.

1.
$$30 \;\overset{>}{\underset{=}{\textcircled{<}}}\; 32$$

2.
$$87 \;\overset{>}{\underset{=}{<}}\; 78$$

3.
$$23 \;\overset{>}{\underset{=}{<}}\; 23$$

4.
$$54 \;\overset{>}{\underset{=}{<}}\; 45$$

5.
$$36 \;\overset{>}{\underset{=}{<}}\; 26$$

6.
$$74 \;\overset{>}{\underset{=}{<}}\; 74$$

7.
$$91 \;\overset{>}{\underset{=}{<}}\; 99$$

8.
$$67 \;\overset{>}{\underset{=}{<}}\; 76$$

9.
$$48 \;\overset{>}{\underset{=}{<}}\; 81$$

10.
$$52 \;\overset{>}{\underset{=}{<}}\; 52$$

California Content Standards *Number Sense 1.2 (🔑)*
Compare and order whole numbers to 100 by using symbols for
less than, equal to, or greater than (<, =, >). Also Number Sense
1.1 (🔑), Mathematical Reasoning 2.0, 2.1.

one hundred ninety-one **191**

Write >, <, or =.
Use tens and ones if you like.

11.
46 ⬤< 51

12.
82 ◯ 75

13.
98 ◯ 95

14.
65 ◯ 56

15.
10 ◯ 100

16.
39 ◯ 39

17.
35 ◯ 52

18.
15 ◯ 12

19.
98 ◯ 98

20.
54 ◯ 59

Problem Solving

Solve.

21. Timmy has 8  and 7 ✎.
Alicia has 7 🖍 and 8 ✎.
Who has more crayons?
Tell how you know.

Home Activity Ask your child to give examples of numbers that are greater than 51, numbers that are less than 78, and numbers that are equal. Homework Workbook 6-8

Name_____

Write the missing numbers.

You can find patterns in numbers.

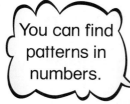

1. Color numbers with 9 ones green.

2. Color numbers with 0 ones blue.

3. Circle numbers with 2 tens.

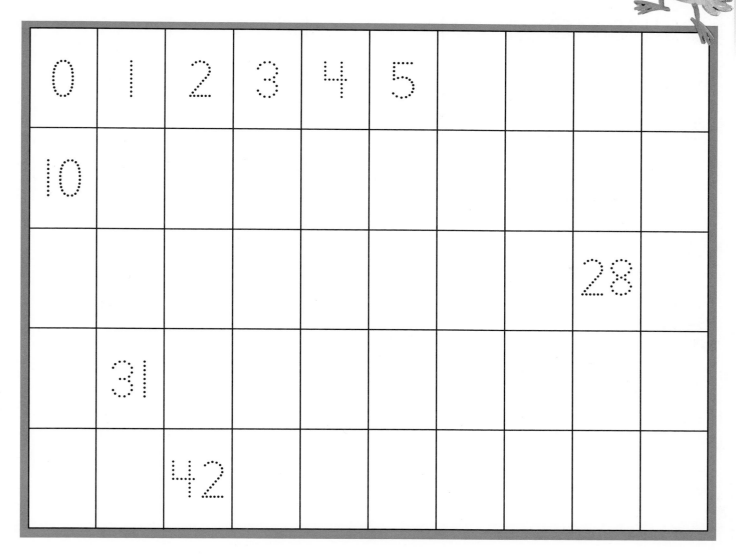

0	1	2	3	4	5				
10									
								28	
	31								
		42							

Find patterns in the chart.

4. Tell about the pattern of numbers colored green.

5. Tell about the pattern of numbers colored blue.

6. Tell about other patterns you find in the chart.

California Content Standards *Number Sense 1.1 (🔑) Count, read, and write whole numbers to 100. Statistics, Data Analysis, and Probability 1.0, 2.0. Also Mathematical Reasoning 2.0.*

one hundred ninety-five **195**

Write the missing numbers.

7. Color numbers with 3 ones red.

8. Circle numbers with 6 tens.

9. Color numbers with 5 ones green.

50	51	52							
60									
					76				
80									

Find patterns in the chart.

10. Tell about the pattern of numbers that are circled.

11. Tell about the pattern of numbers colored green.

12. Tell about other patterns you find in the charts.

196 one hundred ninety-six

Home Activity Look at the chart and have your child tell you how numbers in one row change. Then talk about how numbers in one column change. Homework Workbook 6-10

Name_____

Word Bank

skip count

1. Skip count by twos.

2 ____ 4 ____ ____ ____ ____

2. Skip count by fives.

5 ____ 10 ____ ____ ____ ____

3. Skip count by tens.

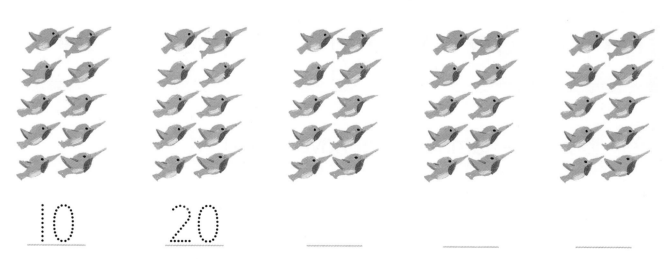

10 ____ 20 ____ ____ ____ ____

California Content Standards *Number Sense 2.4 (🔑) Count by 2s, 5s, and 10s to 100. Also Number Sense 2.3 (🔑), Statistics, Data Analysis, and Probability 2.0, Mathematical Reasoning 2.0.*

4. Start at 2. Skip count by twos. Circle the numbers.

5. Start at 5. Skip count by fives. Put an X on the numbers.

6. Start at 10. Skip count by tens. Color the numbers red.

1	2	3	4	5	6	7	8	9	10
11	12	13	14	15	16	17	18	19	20
21	22	23	24	25	26	27	28	29	30
31	32	33	34	35	36	37	38	39	40
41	42	43	44	45	46	47	48	49	50
51	52	53	54	55	56	57	58	59	60
61	62	63	64	65	66	67	68	69	70
71	72	73	74	75	76	77	78	79	80
81	82	83	84	85	86	87	88	89	90
91	92	93	94	95	96	97	98	99	100

7. Tell about the numbers that have only an X.

8. Tell about the numbers you colored red.

9. Tell about other patterns you see.

Home Activity Invite your child to skip count aloud by twos, fives, and tens to 100. Homework Workbook 6-11

Name_____

Counting from Any Number

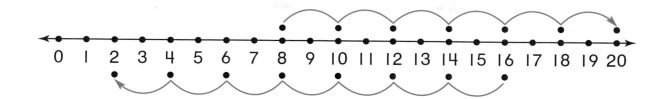

Skip count by twos.
Start with 8.

Skip count backwards
by twos. Start with 16.

Skip count by twos.

1. 8, 10, 12, __14__ , __16__

2. 20, 18, 16, _____, _____

3. 62, 64, _____, _____, _____

4. 46, 44, _____, _____, _____

Skip count by fives.

5. 55, 50, 45, _____, _____

6. 15, 20, 25, _____, _____

7. 80, 85, _____, _____, _____

8. 45, 40, _____, _____, _____

Skip count by tens.

9. 100, 90, 80, _____, _____

10. 22, 32, 42, _____, _____

11. 57, 67, _____, _____, _____

12. 74, 64, _____, _____, _____

California Content Standards *Number Sense 2.4 (🗝) Count by 2s, 5s, and 10s to 100. Also Number Sense 1.1 (🗝), Mathematical Reasoning 1.0, 2.0, 2.1.*

Write the missing numbers.

Skip count by twos.

13. 32, 34, 36, _____, 40, _____, _____, 46, _____, 50

14. 68, 66, _____, 62, _____, _____, 56, 54, 52, _____

Skip count by fives.

15. 15, 20, 25, _____, _____, 40, 45, _____, 55, _____

16. 85, 80, 75, _____, _____, 60, 55, _____, 45, _____

Skip count by tens.

17. 26, 36, _____, _____, 66, _____, _____, 96

18. 87, 77, _____, 57, _____, _____ 27, _____

 Problem Solving

Solve. Tell how you solved the problem.

19. Ally has 5 fish bowls.
    There are 5 fish in each bowl.
    Jack has 3 fish bowls.
    There are 10 fish in each bowl.
    Who has more fish? _____

200 two hundred

Name_____ **Chapter 6 Test**

Write the number in different ways.

1.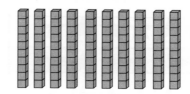

Tens	Ones

_____ + _____ = _____

2.

Hundreds	Tens	Ones

= _____

3. 89 _____ tens and _____ ones | _____ + _____ = _____

Write each number that comes just before or just after.

4.

5.

Circle >, <, or =.

6.
>
76 < 79
=

7.
>
35 < 32
=

8.
>
56 < 56
=

Skip count by fives.

9. 5, 10, _____, _____, _____, _____

Circle the number that makes sense.

10. My bedroom has 2 or 82 windows.

7.   42

    ○   2 tens and 4 ones

    ○   2 tens and 2 ones

    ○   4 tens and 2 ones

    ○   4 tens and 4 ones

8.   100

    ○   10 + 0 = 10

    ○   100 + 0 = 100

    ○   50 + 1 = 51

    ○   NH

---

9.   28, 29, _____

27	30	31	40
○	○	○	○

10.   _____, 71, 72

68	69	70	73
○	○	○	○

---

11.   34 ◯ 43

>	<	=	NH
○	○	○	○

12.   89 ◯ 89

>	<	=	NH
○	○	○	○

---

13.   20, 30, 40, _____, _____

    ○ 50, 60

    ○ 40, 50

    ○ 60, 70

    ○ 30, 40

14.   36, 34, 32, _____, _____

    ○ 31, 32

    ○ 30, 29

    ○ 34, 36

    ○ 30, 28

Oral Directions *Mark the correct answer. NH means "Not here." Mark it whenever the answer is not given.*

#7–8. Mark the one that is a different way to write the number.

#9. Mark the number that comes just after.
#10. Mark the number that comes just before.
#11–12. Mark the symbol that makes the statement true.
#13. If you are counting by tens, what numbers come next?
#14. If you are counting by twos, what numbers come next?

210   two hundred ten

Relating Addition and Subtraction

Diagnosing Readiness
for Chapter 7

1. Solve

   8
   − 6
   ____

2. Write an addition sentence.

   _____ + _____ = _____

3. Write the fact family.

   _____ + _____ = _____

   _____ + _____ = _____

   _____ − _____ = _____

   _____ − _____ = _____

4. Solve.

   Mark ate 7 grapes. There were 12 grapes in the bowl. How many grapes were left?

   _____

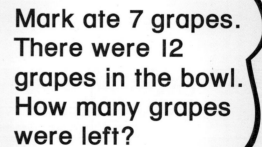

5. Solve. 9 + 0 = _____

To the Family

Looking Back	Chapter 7	Looking Ahead
In Chapters 2, 3, and 4 children learned basic addition facts to 12 and learned addition and subtraction strategies.	**Relating Addition and Subtraction** Children expand their knowledge of basic facts to 16 and build on their understanding of the relationships between addition and subtraction.	Children expand their knowledge of basic facts to 20 in Chapter 8. In Chapter 12 they solve addition and subtraction problems with one- and two-digit numbers.

Page 211 Your child solved problems that review math skills from previous chapters and will help your child with skills in Chapter 7.

Math at Home Help your child memorize basic facts up to 16 by practicing them each day with flash cards or a deck of cards. When using flash cards, turn over two cards and ask your child to add or subtract the numbers on the cards.

Math Literature Read stories and do activities with your child relating to addition and subtraction. Look for the following books in your local library.
Mr. Grumpy's Outing by John Burningham (Holt, 1988)
12 Ways to Get to 11 by Eve Merriam (Simon & Schuster, 1996)

California Content Standards in Chapter 7 Lessons*

	Teach and Practice	Practice		Teach and Practice	Practice
Number Sense			1.3 Create problem situations that might lead to given number sentences involving addition and subtraction.		10
1.3 Represent equivalent forms of the same number through the use of physical models, diagrams, and number expressions.	8		**Statistics, Data Analysis, and Probability**		
2.1 (🔑) Know the addition facts (sums to 20) and the corresponding subtraction facts and commit them to memory.	1–5, 9	7, 8	1.2 Represent and compare data by using pictures and bar graphs.	6	
2.2 (🔑) Use the inverse relationship between addition and subtraction to solve problems.	1–5		2.1 (🔑) Describe, extend, and explain ways to get to the next element in simple repeating patterns.	7	9
Algebra and Functions			**Mathematical Reasoning**		
1.1 Write and solve number sentences from problem situations that express relationships involving addition and subtraction.		1-5, 10	1.1 Determine the approach, materials, and strategies to be used.		2, 4, 5, 10
			1.2 Use tools, such as manipulatives or sketches, to model problems.	6	
1.2 Understand the meaning of the symbols +, −, =.	10	1	2.1 Explain the reasoning used and justify the procedures selected.		3, 7, 8

* The symbol (🔑) indicates a key standard as designated in the Mathematics Framework for California Public Schools.
Full statements of the California Content Standards are found at the beginning of this book following the Table of Contents.

Name_____ **Relating Addition and Subtraction**

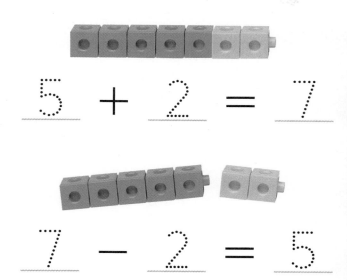

5 + 2 = 7

7 − 2 = 5

Algebra

Use two colors of cubes and
Workmat 3. Show each number.
Write an addition sentence.
Write a subtraction sentence.

1. 6 and 2 | 6 + 2 = 8 | 8 − 2 = 6

2. 4 and 3 | ___ + ___ = ___ | ___ − ___ = ___

3. 5 and 6 | ___ + ___ = ___ | ___ − ___ = ___

4. 8 and 4 | ___ + ___ = ___ | ___ − ___ = ___

5. 5 and 7 | ___ + ___ = ___ | ___ − ___ = ___

California Content Standards *Number Sense 2.1 ( ) Know
the addition facts and the corresponding subtraction facts. Number
Sense 2.2 ( ). Also Algebra and Functions 1.1, 1.2.*

two hundred thirteen 213

Add and subtract.

6.

$3 + 7 = \underline{10}$

$10 - 7 = \underline{}$

7.

$4 + 5 = \underline{}$

$9 - 5 = \underline{}$

8.

$6 + 3 = \underline{}$

$9 - 3 = \underline{}$

9.

$5 + 6 = \underline{}$

$11 - 6 = \underline{}$

Problem Solving

10. Rico has 9 friends.
4 friends move away.
How many friends are left?

$\underline{} \bigcirc \underline{} = \underline{}$

11. Dana finds 4 flowers.
She finds 5 more.
How many flowers does
she find in all?

$\underline{} \bigcirc \underline{} = \underline{}$

Home Activity Ask your child to make up related addition
and subtraction stories about 12 pennies. Homework
Workbook 7-1

Name_____ **Using Addition to Subtract**

What addition fact can
help you find 11 − 7?

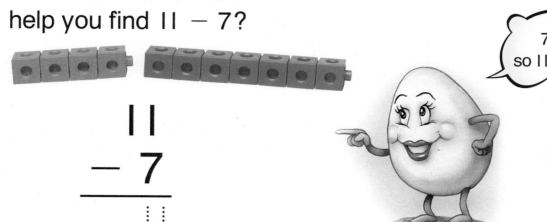

$$7 + 4 = 11$$
so $11 - 7 = 4$.

$$\begin{array}{r} 11 \\ -\ 7 \\ \hline 4 \end{array}$$

Word Bank

related fact

Circle the related addition fact.
Then subtract.

1. $$\begin{array}{r} 12 \\ -\ 7 \\ \hline 5 \end{array}$$
   $7 + 3 = 10$

   $7 + 4 = 11$

   $\boxed{7 + 5 = 12}$

2. $$\begin{array}{r} 10 \\ -\ 6 \\ \hline \end{array}$$
   $6 + 4 = 10$

   $6 + 5 = 11$

   $6 + 6 = 12$

3. $$\begin{array}{r} 11 \\ -\ 5 \\ \hline \end{array}$$
   $5 + 5 = 10$

   $5 + 6 = 11$

   $5 + 7 = 12$

4. $$\begin{array}{r} 9 \\ -\ 4 \\ \hline \end{array}$$
   $4 + 5 = 9$

   $5 + 3 = 8$

   $5 + 5 = 10$

5. $$\begin{array}{r} 12 \\ -\ 8 \\ \hline \end{array}$$
   $8 + 2 = 10$

   $8 + 3 = 11$

   $8 + 4 = 12$

6. $$\begin{array}{r} 10 \\ -\ 3 \\ \hline \end{array}$$
   $3 + 9 = 12$

   $3 + 7 = 10$

   $3 + 8 = 11$

California Content Standards *Number Sense 2.2 ( ) Use the inverse relationship between addition and subtraction to solve problems. Number Sense 2.1 ( ). Also Algebra and Functions 1.1, Mathematical Reasoning 1.1.*

 **Algebra** Write a related addition fact.
Then subtract.

7. 12 − 3 = __9__   __3__ + __9__ = __12__

8. 7 − 3 = ____   ____ + ____ = ____

9. 10 − 8 = ____   ____ + ____ = ____

10. 8 − 6 = ____   ____ + ____ = ____

11. 9 − 1 = ____   ____ + ____ = ____

12. 11 − 3 = ____   ____ + ____ = ____

 Problem Solving

Solve.

13. Carolyn has 10 carrots to feed the horses.
One horse eats 2 carrots.
Another horse eats 3 carrots.
Erin gives Carolyn 5 more carrots.
How many carrots does Carolyn have now? _____ carrots.

216 two hundred sixteen

Home Activity Give your child a subtraction problem. Then challenge your child to think of a related fact. Homework Workbook 7-2

Name_____

This is a fact family.

$3 + 7 = 10$ $10 - 7 = 3$

$7 + 3 = 10$ $10 - 3 = 7$

Complete each fact family.
Use counters if you like.

1.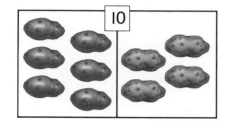

   $6 + 4 = $ _____ $10 - 4 = $ _____

   $4 + 6 = $ _____ $10 - 6 = $ _____

2.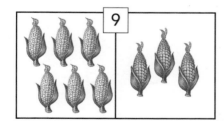

   $6 + 3 = $ _____ $9 - 3 = $ _____

   $3 + 6 = $ _____ $9 - 6 = $ _____

3.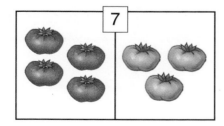

   $4 + 3 = $ _____ $7 - 3 = $ _____

   $3 + 4 = $ _____ $7 - 4 = $ _____

4.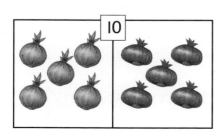

   $5 + 5 = $ _____ $10 - 5 = $ _____

California Content Standards *Number Sense 2.1 (🔑) Know addition facts and corresponding subtraction facts. Number Sense 2.2 (🔑). Also Algebra and Functions 1.1, Mathematical Reasoning 2.1.*

two hundred seventeen **217**

Add or subtract.
Use counters if you like.

5.  $2 + 8 =$ ____ $10 - 8 =$ ____

$8 + 2 =$ ____ $10 - 2 =$ ____

6. 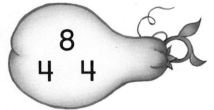 $4 + 4 =$ ____ $8 - 4 =$ ____

7.  $5 + 4 =$ ____ $9 - 4 =$ ____

$4 + 5 =$ ____ $9 - 5 =$ ____

8.  $9 + 1 =$ ____ $10 - 1 =$ ____

$1 + 9 =$ ____ $10 - 9 =$ ____

9. 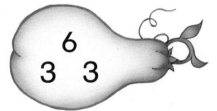 $3 + 3 =$ ____ $6 - 3 =$ ____

 **Problem Solving** **Algebra**

Number Sense

10. Create your own fact family for 9.

_____ _____

11. Share it with a friend. How are your fact families alike?
How are they different?

 Home Activity Ask your child to write the fact family with numbers 4, 5, and 9. Your child may use buttons or other household items to help. Homework Workbook 7-3

Name_____ **Fact Families to 12**

Add or subtract.

1.

| $\begin{array}{r} 7 \\ + 5 \\ \hline 12 \end{array}$ | $\begin{array}{r} 5 \\ + 7 \\ \hline 12 \end{array}$ | $\begin{array}{r} 12 \\ - 7 \\ \hline 5 \end{array}$ | $\begin{array}{r} 12 \\ - 5 \\ \hline 7 \end{array}$ |

2.

| $\begin{array}{r} 3 \\ + 8 \\ \hline \end{array}$ | $\begin{array}{r} 8 \\ + 3 \\ \hline \end{array}$ | $\begin{array}{r} 11 \\ - 3 \\ \hline \end{array}$ | $\begin{array}{r} 11 \\ - 8 \\ \hline \end{array}$ |

3.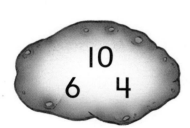

| $\begin{array}{r} 6 \\ + 4 \\ \hline \end{array}$ | $\begin{array}{r} 4 \\ + 6 \\ \hline \end{array}$ | $\begin{array}{r} 10 \\ - 6 \\ \hline \end{array}$ | $\begin{array}{r} 10 \\ - 4 \\ \hline \end{array}$ |

4.

| $\begin{array}{r} 7 \\ + 4 \\ \hline \end{array}$ | $\begin{array}{r} 4 \\ + 7 \\ \hline \end{array}$ | $\begin{array}{r} 11 \\ - 7 \\ \hline \end{array}$ | $\begin{array}{r} 11 \\ - 4 \\ \hline \end{array}$ |

5.

| $\begin{array}{r} 6 \\ + 6 \\ \hline \end{array}$ | $\begin{array}{r} 12 \\ - 6 \\ \hline \end{array}$ |

6 and 6 make one dozen.

California Content Standards Number Sense 2.1 (🔑) Know addition facts and corresponding subtraction facts. Number Sense 2.2 (🔑). Also Algebra and Functions 1.1, Mathematical Reasoning 1.1.

Algebra Write the number sentences for each family.

6.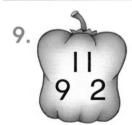

$$5 + 6 = 11 \qquad \underline{\hspace{1cm}} - \underline{\hspace{1cm}} = \underline{\hspace{1cm}}$$

$$\underline{\hspace{1cm}} + \underline{\hspace{1cm}} = \underline{\hspace{1cm}} \qquad \underline{\hspace{1cm}} - \underline{\hspace{1cm}} = \underline{\hspace{1cm}}$$

7. 10 / 2 8

$$\underline{\hspace{1cm}} + \underline{\hspace{1cm}} = \underline{\hspace{1cm}} \qquad \underline{\hspace{1cm}} - \underline{\hspace{1cm}} = \underline{\hspace{1cm}}$$

$$\underline{\hspace{1cm}} + \underline{\hspace{1cm}} = \underline{\hspace{1cm}} \qquad \underline{\hspace{1cm}} - \underline{\hspace{1cm}} = \underline{\hspace{1cm}}$$

8. 12 / 4 8

$$\underline{\hspace{1cm}} + \underline{\hspace{1cm}} = \underline{\hspace{1cm}} \qquad \underline{\hspace{1cm}} - \underline{\hspace{1cm}} = \underline{\hspace{1cm}}$$

$$\underline{\hspace{1cm}} + \underline{\hspace{1cm}} = \underline{\hspace{1cm}} \qquad \underline{\hspace{1cm}} - \underline{\hspace{1cm}} = \underline{\hspace{1cm}}$$

9. 11 / 9 2

$$\underline{\hspace{1cm}} + \underline{\hspace{1cm}} = \underline{\hspace{1cm}} \qquad \underline{\hspace{1cm}} - \underline{\hspace{1cm}} = \underline{\hspace{1cm}}$$

$$\underline{\hspace{1cm}} + \underline{\hspace{1cm}} = \underline{\hspace{1cm}} \qquad \underline{\hspace{1cm}} - \underline{\hspace{1cm}} = \underline{\hspace{1cm}}$$

10. 12 / 3 9

$$\underline{\hspace{1cm}} + \underline{\hspace{1cm}} = \underline{\hspace{1cm}} \qquad \underline{\hspace{1cm}} - \underline{\hspace{1cm}} = \underline{\hspace{1cm}}$$

$$\underline{\hspace{1cm}} + \underline{\hspace{1cm}} = \underline{\hspace{1cm}} \qquad \underline{\hspace{1cm}} - \underline{\hspace{1cm}} = \underline{\hspace{1cm}}$$

 **Problem Solving**

11. Make a fact family with only even numbers.

$$\underline{\hspace{3cm}} \qquad \underline{\hspace{3cm}}$$

$$\underline{\hspace{3cm}} \qquad \underline{\hspace{3cm}}$$

Home Activity Give your child 12 buttons or household items. Ask him or her to use the items to show several different fact families for 12. Homework Workbook 7-4

Name_____**Fact Families to 16**

Add or subtract.

1.
   16
   9 7

   $\begin{array}{r} 9 \\ + 7 \\ \hline 16 \end{array}$
   $\begin{array}{r} 7 \\ + 9 \\ \hline 16 \end{array}$
   $\begin{array}{r} 16 \\ - 9 \\ \hline 7 \end{array}$
   $\begin{array}{r} 16 \\ - 7 \\ \hline 9 \end{array}$

2.
   15
   8 7

   $\begin{array}{r} 8 \\ + 7 \\ \hline \end{array}$
   $\begin{array}{r} 7 \\ + 8 \\ \hline \end{array}$
   $\begin{array}{r} 15 \\ - 8 \\ \hline \end{array}$
   $\begin{array}{r} 15 \\ - 7 \\ \hline \end{array}$

3.
   14
   8 6

   $\begin{array}{r} 8 \\ + 6 \\ \hline \end{array}$
   $\begin{array}{r} 6 \\ + 8 \\ \hline \end{array}$
   $\begin{array}{r} 14 \\ - 8 \\ \hline \end{array}$
   $\begin{array}{r} 14 \\ - 6 \\ \hline \end{array}$

4.
   13
   7 6

   $\begin{array}{r} 7 \\ + 6 \\ \hline \end{array}$
   $\begin{array}{r} 6 \\ + 7 \\ \hline \end{array}$
   $\begin{array}{r} 13 \\ - 7 \\ \hline \end{array}$
   $\begin{array}{r} 13 \\ - 6 \\ \hline \end{array}$

5.
   16
   8 8

   $\begin{array}{r} 8 \\ + 8 \\ \hline \end{array}$
   $\begin{array}{r} 16 \\ - 8 \\ \hline \end{array}$

California Content Standards *Number Sense 2.1 (🔑) Know addition facts and corresponding subtraction facts. Number Sense 2.2 (🔑). Also Algebra and Functions 1.1, Mathematical Reasoning 1.1.*

6.  13   8   5

____ + ____ = ____   ____ − ____ = ____

____ + ____ = ____   ____ − ____ = ____

7. 15   6   9

____ + ____ = ____   ____ − ____ = ____

____ + ____ = ____   ____ − ____ = ____

8. 14   7   7

____ + ____ = ____   ____ − ____ = ____

9. 16   7   9

____ + ____ = ____   ____ − ____ = ____

____ + ____ = ____   ____ − ____ = ____

Problem Solving

Find the number.

10. First double me.
Then subtract 1.
You get 5.
What number am I?

____

11. First double me.
Then subtract 3.
You get 7.
What number am I?

____

 **Home Activity** Have your child demonstrate fact families by using up to 16 paper clips or other objects. Ask your child to state the facts in each family. Homework Workbook 7-5

Name_____ **Diagnostic Checkpoint**

Complete the fact family.

1.

   ____ + ____ = ____   ____ − ____ = ____

   ____ + ____ = ____   ____ − ____ = ____

Circle the related addition fact. Then subtract.

2. 14 $6 + 4 = 10$ 3. 11 $9 + 1 = 10$
    − 6 $7 + 7 = 14$ − 9 $9 + 2 = 11$
    ___ $6 + 8 = 14$ ___ $7 + 4 = 11$

Write a related addition fact. Then subtract.

4. $12 - 9 = $ ____   5. $10 - 1 = $ ____

    ____ + ____ = ____   ____ + ____ = ____

---

6. $13 - 7 = $ ____   7. $16 - 8 = $ ____

    ____ + ____ = ____   ____ + ____ = ____

---

8. Dan had 7 apples.
    He gave 3 to Kathy.
    Then Peter gave Dan 5 more apples.
    How many apples does Dan have now? ____

1.

			◇
○	○	○	○

2. 50, 45, 40, 35, _____

25	20	30	40
○	○	○	○

3.

27	17	10	37
○	○	○	○

4. 7 + 8 = 15

15 − 8 = 7	8 + 8 = 16	8 + 7 = 15	15 − 7 = 8
○	○	○	○

5.

9 tens and 7 ones	8 tens and 17 ones
○	○
6 tens and 27 ones	NH
○	○

6. 5 + 6 = 11

5 + 5 = 10	4 + 4 = 8	7 + 7 = 14	NH
○	○	○	○

7. 16 ◯ 18

<	=	>	NH
○	○	○	○

Oral Directions *Mark the correct answer. NH means "Not here." Mark it whenever the answer is not given.*
#1. Look at the shape on the left. Mark the one that is the same size and shape.
#2. What number comes next?
#3. Mark the number that is ten more than the number in the circle.

#4. Which number sentence does not belong to the same fact family as seven plus eight equals fifteen?
#5. Which is not a way to show ninety-seven in tens and ones?
#6. Which doubles fact helps you solve five plus six equals eleven?
#7. Which symbol makes the statement true?

224 two hundred twenty-four

Name_____

How many of each kind of bread are there?

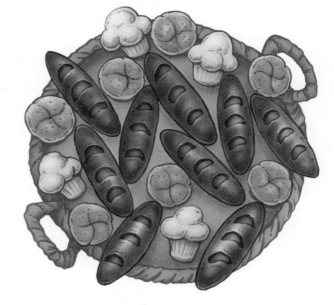

Understand

You need to find how many rolls, muffins, and buns there are.

Plan

You can make a graph.

Solve

Color a box for each kind of bread in the picture.

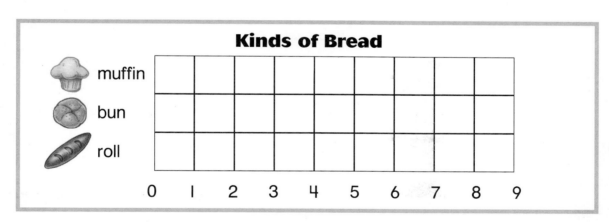

Kinds of Bread

muffin

bun

roll

0   1   2   3   4   5   6   7   8   9

1. How many of each are there?

   muffins _____   buns _____   rolls _____

2. How many more buns than muffins? _____ buns

3. How many fewer buns than rolls? _____ buns

Look Back

4. Do your answers make sense? _____

California Content Standards *Statistics, Data Analysis, and Probability 1.2 Represent and compare data by using pictures and bar graphs. Mathematical Reasoning 1.2.*

two hundred twenty-five **225**

Ask 8 classmates which vegetable they like best.
Color a box for each answer.

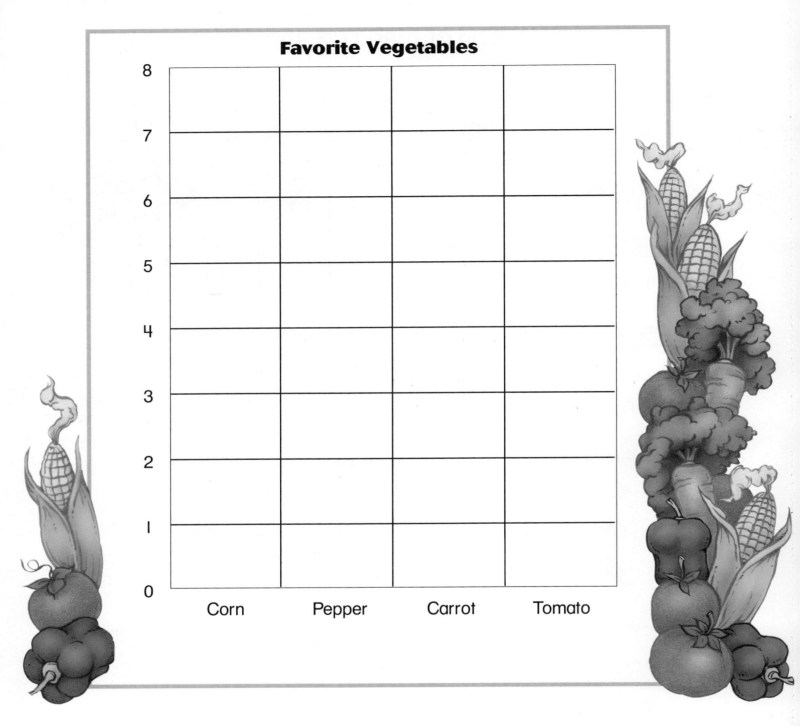

Favorite Vegetables

	Corn	Pepper	Carrot	Tomato

5. How many classmates like each vegetable?

corn _____   pepper _____   carrot _____   tomato _____

6. Which vegetable is the favorite? _____

7. Which vegetable is the least favorite? _____

Home Activity Discuss the graphs with your child. Ask him or her to explain what each colored box means. Homework Workbook 7-6

Name_____

Addition and Subtraction Patterns

  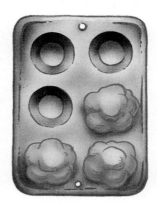 

$$6 - 1 = 5 \qquad 6 - 2 = 4 \qquad 6 - 3 = 3 \qquad 6 - 4 = 2$$

What pattern do you see? What comes next?

Add or subtract.
Look for a pattern in each row.

1.
$$10 + 0 = 10 \qquad 10 + 1 \qquad 10 + 2 \qquad 10 + 3 \qquad 10 + 4 \qquad 10 + 5$$

2.
$$12 - 3 \qquad 12 - 4 \qquad 12 - 5 \qquad 12 - 6 \qquad 12 - 7 \qquad 12 - 8$$

3.
$$11 - 2 \qquad 10 - 2 \qquad 9 - 2 \qquad 8 - 2 \qquad 7 - 2 \qquad 6 - 2$$

California Content Standards *Statistics, Data Analysis, and Probability 2.1 (🔑) Describe, extend, and explain ways to get to the next element in simple repeating patterns. Also Number Sense 2.1 (🔑), Mathematical Reasoning 2.1.*

two hundred twenty-seven **227**

Add or subtract. Look for a pattern.
Write the next fact in the pattern.

4.
$$\begin{array}{r} 5 \\ +1 \\ \hline 6 \end{array}$$
$$\begin{array}{r} 5 \\ +2 \\ \hline \end{array}$$
$$\begin{array}{r} 5 \\ +3 \\ \hline \end{array}$$
$$\begin{array}{r} 5 \\ +4 \\ \hline \end{array}$$
$$\begin{array}{r} 5 \\ +5 \\ \hline \end{array}$$
$$\begin{array}{r} \boxed{5} \\ +\boxed{6} \\ \hline \end{array}$$

5.
$$\begin{array}{r} 7 \\ -6 \\ \hline \end{array}$$
$$\begin{array}{r} 7 \\ -5 \\ \hline \end{array}$$
$$\begin{array}{r} 7 \\ -4 \\ \hline \end{array}$$
$$\begin{array}{r} 7 \\ -3 \\ \hline \end{array}$$
$$\begin{array}{r} 7 \\ -2 \\ \hline \end{array}$$
$$\begin{array}{r} \boxed{} \\ -\boxed{} \\ \hline \end{array}$$

6.
$$\begin{array}{r} 4 \\ +1 \\ \hline \end{array}$$
$$\begin{array}{r} 5 \\ +1 \\ \hline \end{array}$$
$$\begin{array}{r} 6 \\ +1 \\ \hline \end{array}$$
$$\begin{array}{r} 7 \\ +1 \\ \hline \end{array}$$
$$\begin{array}{r} 8 \\ +1 \\ \hline \end{array}$$
$$\begin{array}{r} \boxed{} \\ +\boxed{} \\ \hline \end{array}$$

7.
$$\begin{array}{r} 9 \\ -5 \\ \hline \end{array}$$
$$\begin{array}{r} 10 \\ -5 \\ \hline \end{array}$$
$$\begin{array}{r} 11 \\ -5 \\ \hline \end{array}$$
$$\begin{array}{r} 12 \\ -5 \\ \hline \end{array}$$
$$\begin{array}{r} 13 \\ -5 \\ \hline \end{array}$$
$$\begin{array}{r} \boxed{} \\ -\boxed{} \\ \hline \end{array}$$

Math Reasoning

Look for a pattern. Find the missing numbers.

8.
$$\begin{array}{r} 8 \\ -7 \\ \hline \end{array}$$
$$\begin{array}{r} 8 \\ -6 \\ \hline \end{array}$$
$$\begin{array}{r} 8 \\ -5 \\ \hline \end{array}$$
$$\begin{array}{r} \boxed{} \\ -4 \\ \hline \end{array}$$
$$\begin{array}{r} \boxed{} \\ -\boxed{} \\ \hline \boxed{} \end{array}$$
$$\begin{array}{r} 8 \\ -\boxed{} \\ \hline \boxed{} \end{array}$$

9. Explain the pattern.

Home Activity Make up addition or subtraction problems that follow a pattern and have your child solve them.
Homework Workbook 7-7

Name **Names for Numbers**

$$10 - 2$$

I can name 8 in many ways. Can you think of another way?

$$6 + 2$$ 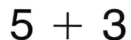 $$5 + 3$$

Circle the names for each number.
Use counters if you like.

1.  3

| $4 - 1$ | $3 + 2$ | $8 + 3$ |
| $2 + 2$ | $9 - 6$ | $1 + 2$ |

2.  7

| $10 - 2$ | $7 + 0$ | $12 - 5$ |
| $3 + 4$ | $5 + 6$ | $11 - 4$ |

3.  6

| $3 + 3$ | $12 - 6$ | $9 - 4$ |
| $7 - 1$ | $6 + 3$ | $4 + 2$ |

4.  9

| $11 - 2$ | $9 - 0$ | $5 + 3$ |
| $12 - 6$ | $5 + 5$ | $4 + 5$ |

California Content Standards *Number Sense 1.3 Represent equivalent forms of the same number. Also Number Sense 2.1 (⚷), Mathematical Reasoning 2.1.*

two hundred twenty-nine **229**

Circle the names for each number.
Then write another name for the number.
Use counters if you like.

5.  9

$\boxed{12-3}$ $\boxed{7+2}$ $9-3$

$4+4$ $\boxed{6+3}$ $\boxed{4 \oplus 5}$

6.  5

$8+4$ $8-3$ $9+3$

$6-1$ $4+1$ ____ ⃝ ____

7.  13

$6+7$ $6+5$ $9+4$

$4+3$ $13-0$ ____ ⃝ ____

8.  11

$11-4$ $12-9$ $7+4$

$9+2$ $3+8$ ____ ⃝ ____

 Math Reasoning

9. Tell why this number sentence makes sense.

$$3 + 1 = 2 + 2$$

Home Activity Ask your child to show different names for 10 and 5. You may wish to use buttons or household items to help. Homework Workbook 7-8

Name_____ **Addition Table**

1. Add.
   Write the numbers in the table.

+	0	1	2	3	4	5	6	7	8	9	10
0	0	1									
1										10	
2											
3											
4					8						
5	5										
6										15	
7											
8											
9											
10											

2. Circle the doubles facts.

3. Put an X on doubles plus 1 facts.

4. How can you use this table to subtract?

California Content Standards *Number Sense 2.1 ( ) Know addition and subtraction facts and commit them to memory. Also Statistics, Data Analysis, and Probability 2.1 ( ).*

Solve.
Use the table if you like.

5.
$$\begin{array}{r} 1 \\ + 2 \\ \hline 3 \end{array}$$
$$\begin{array}{r} 4 \\ + 4 \\ \hline \end{array}$$
$$\begin{array}{r} 10 \\ - 6 \\ \hline \end{array}$$
$$\begin{array}{r} 5 \\ + 4 \\ \hline \end{array}$$
$$\begin{array}{r} 12 \\ - 7 \\ \hline \end{array}$$
$$\begin{array}{r} 0 \\ + 0 \\ \hline \end{array}$$

6.
$$\begin{array}{r} 9 \\ - 3 \\ \hline \end{array}$$
$$\begin{array}{r} 11 \\ - 8 \\ \hline \end{array}$$
$$\begin{array}{r} 6 \\ + 3 \\ \hline \end{array}$$
$$\begin{array}{r} 5 \\ + 5 \\ \hline \end{array}$$
$$\begin{array}{r} 13 \\ - 7 \\ \hline \end{array}$$
$$\begin{array}{r} 6 \\ + 8 \\ \hline \end{array}$$

7.
$$\begin{array}{r} 5 \\ + 6 \\ \hline \end{array}$$
$$\begin{array}{r} 16 \\ - 7 \\ \hline \end{array}$$
$$\begin{array}{r} 8 \\ - 6 \\ \hline \end{array}$$
$$\begin{array}{r} 12 \\ - 4 \\ \hline \end{array}$$
$$\begin{array}{r} 7 \\ + 7 \\ \hline \end{array}$$
$$\begin{array}{r} 4 \\ + 9 \\ \hline \end{array}$$

8. $6 + 7 =$ _____ $14 - 7 =$ _____ $6 + 6 =$ _____

9. $9 + 5 =$ _____ $11 - 6 =$ _____ $15 - 9 =$ _____

10. $8 + 8 =$ _____ $7 - 4 =$ _____ $7 + 8 =$ _____

11. $9 + 6 =$ _____ $16 - 8 =$ _____ $14 - 5 =$ _____

232 two hundred thirty-two

🏠 **Home Activity** Turn over two playing cards and have your child state the sum of the numbers shown. Use the ace for 1 and a face card for zero. Homework Workbook 7-9

Name_____

John has 6 pretzels. He eats 3.
How many pretzels are left?
Think: Do you need to add
or subtract?

$$6 + 3 = \underline{}$$

$$\left(6 - 3 = 3\right)$$

Algebra

Circle the correct number sentence.
Then solve.

1. Chen has 7 oranges.
   He picks 7 more.
   How many oranges does
   he have now?

   $$7 - 7 = \underline{}$$

   $$7 + 7 = \underline{}$$

2. Marco has 12 pears.
   He gives 3 to Kyle.
   How many pears are left?

   $$12 - 3 = \underline{}$$

   $$12 + 3 = \underline{}$$

3. Jess makes 8 sandwiches.
   Steve makes 4 more than Jess.
   How many sandwiches does
   Steve make?

   $$8 - 4 = \underline{}$$

   $$8 + 4 = \underline{}$$

4. Julie has 9 apples.
   She gives 6 to Paul.
   How many apples does
   she have now?

   $$9 + 6 = \underline{}$$

   $$9 - 6 = \underline{}$$

California Content Standards Algebra and Functions 1.2
Understand the meaning of the symbols +, −, =. Also Algebra and
Functions 1.1, 1.3, Mathematical Reasoning 1.1.

Circle the correct number sentence. Then solve.

5. David has 8 drinks.
    He sells 7.
    How many drinks does he have now?

    $8 - 7 =$ _____ $8 + 7 =$ _____

6. Annie makes 6 drinks.
    Betsy makes 8.
    How many drinks are there altogether?

    $8 - 6 =$ _____ $8 + 6 =$ _____

7. Lisa makes 9 drinks.
    She sells 7.
    How many drinks does she have left?

    $9 - 7 =$ _____ $9 + 7 =$ _____

8. Make your own problem.
    Fill in the blanks. Then solve.

    Tanya has _____ drinks.

    She sells _____ .

    How many drinks does she have now?

    _____ $+$ _____ $=$ _____   _____ $-$ _____ $=$ _____

two hundred thirty-four

Home Activity Tell your child a word problem. Ask him or her to decide whether to add or subtract to solve the problem.
Homework Workbook 7-10

© Scott Foresman. All rights reserved.

Name_____

Fruits

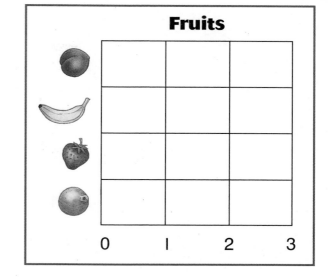

Use the picture.
Complete the graph.
Write how many.

1. Plums and bananas _____

2. How many more bananas than oranges? _____

Add. Look for a pattern.
Write the next fact in the pattern.

3.
$$\begin{array}{ccccc} 8 & 8 & 8 & 8 & 8 \\ +\,1 & +\,2 & +\,3 & +\,4 & +\,5 \end{array}$$

$$\begin{array}{c} \square \\ +\,\square \end{array}$$

Circle the names for each number.

4.
$7+7$	$8+5$	$15-1$
$8+3$	$13-0$	$6+7$

5.
$9-1$	$3+5$	$10-2$
$5+4$	$3+3$	$10-5$

Circle the correct number sentence. Solve.

6. Julie has 11 grapes.
She gives 3 to Brad.
How many grapes does
she have now?

$$11 - 3 = \underline{\quad}$$

$$11 + 3 = \underline{\quad}$$

Name_____

1.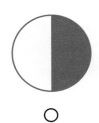

   ○   ○   ○   ○

2.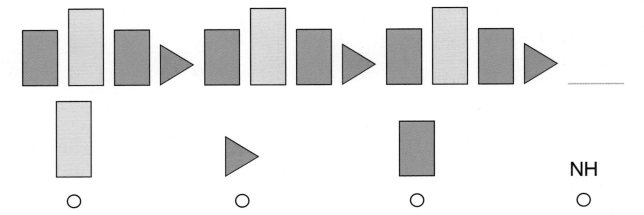

   ○   ○   ○   NH
   ○

3. 14    8

   14 − 8 = 6   8 − 5 = 3   14 − 7 = 7   NH
   ○   ○   ○   ○

4.

   ○   ○   ○   ○

5. 5 + 3 = ☐   10   16   12   NH
   ○   ○   ○   ○

Oral Directions *Mark the correct answer. NH means "Not here." Mark it whenever the answer is not given.*

#1. Mark the shape that shows one-fourth is shaded.
#2. What shape is most likely to come next in the pattern?

#3. Sarah has fourteen rings. Amanda has eight rings. Mark the number sentence that tells how many more rings Sarah has.
#4. Mark the shape that is below the star.
#5. Find the sum.

236   two hundred thirty-six

Name_____ **Chapter 7 Test**

Write the related addition or subtraction fact. Solve.

1. 10 − 2 = _____

    _____ + _____ = _____

2. 6 + 7 = _____

    _____ − _____ = _____

Add or subtract.

3.
    14
    6   8

    $$6 + 8$$ $$8 + 6$$ $$14 - 6$$ $$14 - 8$$

4. Complete the graph.

Flowers

	🌼	🌷	🌸	🌼
5				
4				
3				
2				
1				
0				

5. How many more tulips than daisies are there? _____

Add or subtract. Look for a pattern.
Write the next fact in the pattern.

6. $\begin{array}{r} 12 \\ -\ 6 \\ \hline \end{array}$ $\begin{array}{r} 12 \\ -\ 5 \\ \hline \end{array}$ $\begin{array}{r} 12 \\ -\ 4 \\ \hline \end{array}$ $\begin{array}{r} \square \\ -\ \square \\ \hline \end{array}$

Circle the names for the number.
Then write another name for the number.

7.  $1 + 8$ $7 + 3$ $3 + 6$

       $8 + 7$ $12 - 3$ ___ ◯ ___

---

8. Write the number sentences for the fact family.

   ___ + ___ = ___   ___ − ___ = ___

       ___ + ___ = ___   ___ − ___ = ___

Circle the correct number sentence. Solve.

9. Mike had 9 eggs.
   He gave 2 eggs to Tom.
   How many are left?

   $9 + 2 =$ ___

   $9 - 2 =$ ___

10. Mary made 6 pies.
    Mark made 6 pies.
    How many pies did they
    make altogether?

    $6 + 6 =$ ___

    $6 - 6 =$ ___

I.   12
     − 5 | 5 + 7 = 12   4 + 7 = 11   5 + 5 = 10   NH
              ○   ○   ○   ○

2. 7 + 7 = 14 | 13 − 7 = 6   10 − 7 = 3   14 − 7 = 7   NH
                  ○   ○   ○   ○

3.   13 | 8 + 7   6 + 7   12 − 3   NH
              ○   ○   ○   ○

4.   9 | 11 − 2   5 + 4   6 + 3   NH
              ○   ○   ○   ○

5.

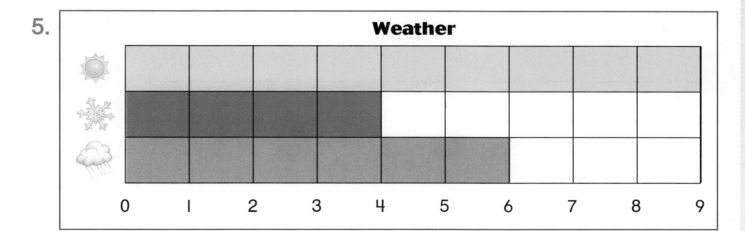

Weather

0   1   2   3   4   5   6   7   8   9

6 − 4 = 2   9 − 6 = 3   4 + 6 = 10   9 + 4 = 13
    ○   ○   ○   ○

Oral Directions *Mark the correct answer. NH means "Not here." Mark it whenever the answer is not given.*

#1. Mark the related addition fact.
#2. Mark the related subtraction fact.

#3. Which is another name for thirteen?
#4. Which is not another name for nine?
#5. Which number sentence tells how many more sunny days there are than rainy days?

6.

$8 + 4 = 12$

$4 + 8 = 12$

$12 - 8 = 4$

| $4 + 4 = 8$ ○ | $12 - 4 = 8$ ○ | $6 + 6 = 12$ ○ | NH ○ |

---

7. $8 + 8 = \boxed{}$

| 16 ○ | 13 ○ | 12 ○ | NH ○ |

8.

| $9 + 5 = 14$ ○ | $14 - 5 = 9$ ○ | $14 - 9 = 5$ ○ | $5 + 6 = 11$ ○ |

9.

$$\begin{array}{r} 13 \\ -\ 4 \\ \hline 9 \end{array} \qquad \begin{array}{r} 13 \\ -\ 5 \\ \hline 8 \end{array} \qquad \begin{array}{r} 13 \\ -\ 6 \\ \hline 7 \end{array} \qquad \underline{}$$

$$\begin{array}{r} 13 \\ -\ 7 \\ \hline 6 \end{array} \qquad \begin{array}{r} 13 \\ -\ 8 \\ \hline 5 \end{array} \qquad \begin{array}{r} 13 \\ +\ 4 \\ \hline 17 \end{array} \qquad \begin{array}{r} 13 \\ -\ 9 \\ \hline 4 \end{array}$$

○ ○ ○ ○

10.

8 7

| 14 ○ | 13 ○ | 15 ○ | NH ○ |

---

11. 12

3

| $12 + 3 = 15$ ○ | $12 - 3 = 9$ ○ | $6 + 6 = 12$ ○ | NH ○ |

Oral Directions *Mark the correct answer. NH means "Not here." Mark it whenever the answer is not given.*

#6. Mark the number sentence that belongs in this fact family.
#7. Add.
#8. Mark the number sentence that does not belong in the fact family.

#9. What comes next in the pattern?
#10. Mia picked eight cherries. Max picked seven cherries. How many cherries did they pick altogether?
#11. Twelve flowers were blooming in the garden. Martin picked three of the flowers. Which number sentence tells how many flowers are left in the garden?

240 two hundred forty

Diagnosing Readiness
for Chapter 8

Write the missing numbers.

1. 5 + 5 = _____

    5 + 6 = _____

2. 5 + 7 = _____

    12 − 7 = _____

3. 6 + 7 = _____   13 − _____ = 6

    7 + _____ = 13   13 − 7 = _____

4. 16 − 8 = _____

    14 − 7 = _____

To the Family

Looking Back	Chapter 8	Looking Ahead
In Chapters 2, 3, 4, and 7 children learned addition and subtraction facts to 16 and learned addition and subtraction strategies.	**Addition and Subtraction to 20** — Children practice addition and subtraction facts to 20, add three numbers, and build on their understanding of the relationships between addition and subtraction.	In Chapter 12 children will solve addition and subtraction problems with one- and two- digits and will apply addition and subtraction skills when solving number stories.

Page 241 Your child solved problems that review math skills from previous chapters and will help your child with the skills in Chapter 8.

Math at Home Help your child memorize basic facts up to 20 by practicing them each day with flash cards. Encourage your child to use basic facts when solving everyday problems such as, "There are 15 oranges in the bag. We ate 6 of them. How many are left?"

Math Literature Read stories and do activities with your child relating to addition and subtraction. Look for the following books in your local library.
Caps for Sale by Esphyr Slobodikina (HarperTrophy, 1987)
Eat Up, Gemma by Sarah Hayes (Mulberry Books, 1994)

California Content Standards in Chapter 8 Lessons*

Number Sense	Teach and Practice	Practice
1.3 Represent equivalent forms of the same number.	4, 5	8
2.1 (🔑) Know the addition facts (sums to 20) and the corresponding subtraction facts and commit them to memory.	1–5, 7, 11–13	6, 8–10, 14
2.2 (🔑) Use the inverse relationship between addition and subtraction to solve problems.	8, 10	
2.3 Identify 10 more than a given number.		3
2.5 (🔑) Show the meaning of addition and subtraction.		1, 2, 11
2.6 Solve addition problems with one- and two-digit numbers.		3
2.7 Find the sum of three one-digit numbers.	6	
Algebra and Functions		
1.1 Write and solve number sentences from problem situations.	9, 14	10, 12
1.2 Understand the meaning of the symbols +, −, =.	9	14

	Teach and Practice	Practice
Statistics, Data Analysis, and Probablity		
2.0 Students describe patterns by numbers.	3, 13	
Mathematical Reasoning		
1.1 Determine the approach, materials, and strategies to be used.		6, 7, 10–14
1.2 Use tools, such as manipulatives or sketches, to model problems.		1, 2, 5, 11
2.0 Students solve problems and justify their reasoning.	14	3, 5, 12
2.1 Explain the reasoning used and justify the procedures selected.		9
2.2 Make precise calculations and check the validity of the results from the context of the problem.		13
3.0 Students note connections between one problem and another.	2	4, 6–8, 13

* The symbol (🔑) indicates a key standard as designated in the Mathematics Framework for California Public Schools.
  Full statements of the California Content Standards are found at the beginning of this book following the Table of Contents.

Name_____ **Doubles to 20**

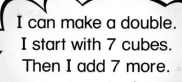
I can make a double.
I start with 7 cubes.
Then I add 7 more.

$$7 + 7 = 14$$

Use two colors of cubes and Workmat 3.
Show each number. Then show the double.
Complete the addition sentence.

1. Show 3. $3 + \underline{\quad} = \underline{\quad}$	2. Show 5. $5 + \underline{\quad} = \underline{\quad}$
3. Show 4. $4 + \underline{\quad} = \underline{\quad}$	4. Show 7. $7 + \underline{\quad} = \underline{\quad}$
5. Show 6. $6 + \underline{\quad} = \underline{\quad}$	6. Show 9. $9 + \underline{\quad} = \underline{\quad}$
7. Show 8. $8 + \underline{\quad} = \underline{\quad}$	8. Show 10. $10 + \underline{\quad} = \underline{\quad}$

California Content Standards *Number Sense 2.1 (✪) Know the addition facts and commit them to memory. Also Number Sense 2.5 (✪), Mathematical Reasoning 1.2.*

two hundred forty-three **243**

Add. Circle the doubles.
Use cubes if you like.

9. $\left(\,2 + 2 = \underline{4}\,\right)$ $7 + 3 = \underline{\quad}$ $6 + 6 = \underline{\quad}$

10. $7 + 7 = \underline{\quad}$ $3 + 9 = \underline{\quad}$ $8 + 8 = \underline{\quad}$

11.
$$\begin{array}{r} 8 \\ + 2 \\ \hline \end{array} \qquad \begin{array}{r} 5 \\ + 4 \\ \hline \end{array} \qquad \begin{array}{r} 0 \\ + 0 \\ \hline \end{array} \qquad \begin{array}{r} 9 \\ + 9 \\ \hline \end{array} \qquad \begin{array}{r} 2 \\ + 6 \\ \hline \end{array} \qquad \begin{array}{r} 5 \\ + 5 \\ \hline \end{array}$$

12.
$$\begin{array}{r} 10 \\ + 10 \\ \hline \end{array} \qquad \begin{array}{r} 4 \\ + 8 \\ \hline \end{array} \qquad \begin{array}{r} 7 \\ + 8 \\ \hline \end{array} \qquad \begin{array}{r} 4 \\ + 4 \\ \hline \end{array} \qquad \begin{array}{r} 5 \\ + 6 \\ \hline \end{array} \qquad \begin{array}{r} 6 \\ + 4 \\ \hline \end{array}$$

 **Problem Solving**

Solve.

13. Clara has the same number of red and blue blocks. She has 16 blocks altogether. How many blocks of each color does she have?

   _____ red   _____ blue

14. Rico has 14 blocks altogether. He has 2 more red blocks than blue blocks. How many blocks of each color does he have?

   _____ red   _____ blue

Home Activity Use buttons or other household items to practice doubles with your child. Homework Workbook 8-1

Name_____ **Using Doubles to Add**

How can you use doubles to add 7 + 8?

Think 7 + 7 and
1 more is 15.

$7 + 7 = 14$ $\qquad$ $7 + 8 = 15$

Use cubes. Write each sum.

1. $3 + 3 = \underline{\quad}$

   $3 + 4 = \underline{\quad}$

2. $4 + 4 = \underline{\quad}$

   $4 + 5 = \underline{\quad}$

3. $6 + 6 = \underline{\quad}$

   $6 + 7 = \underline{\quad}$

4. $1 + 1 = \underline{\quad}$

   $2 + 1 = \underline{\quad}$

5. $5 + 5 = \underline{\quad}$

   $5 + 6 = \underline{\quad}$

6. $8 + 8 = \underline{\quad}$

   $9 + 8 = \underline{\quad}$

7. $2 + 2 = \underline{\quad}$

   $2 + 3 = \underline{\quad}$

8. $9 + 9 = \underline{\quad}$

   $9 + 10 = \underline{\quad}$

California Content Standards *Number Sense 2.1 (⟶) Know addition facts and commit them to memory. Mathematical Reasoning 3.0. Also Number Sense 2.5 (⟶), Mathematical Reasoning 1.2.*

Write each sum.
Use cubes if you like.

9.
$$3 + 3 = 6$$
$$3 + 4 = 7$$

10.
$$0 + 0 =$$
$$0 + 1 =$$

11.
$$6 + 6 =$$
$$7 + 6 =$$

12.
$$7 + 7 =$$
$$7 + 8 =$$

13.
$$5 + 5 =$$
$$5 + 6 =$$

14.
$$8 + 8 =$$
$$9 + 8 =$$

15.
$$4 + 4 =$$
$$5 + 4 =$$

16.
$$9 + 9 =$$
$$10 + 9 =$$

 Problem Solving

Solve.

17. There are 7 owls on a cactus.
There are double that many
and one more flying away.
How many owls are flying away? _____ owls

Home Activity Ask your child to use items such as paper clips or buttons to show doubles. Then add one item to the number and ask what the new sum is. Homework Workbook 8-2

Name_____ **Patterns with Tens**

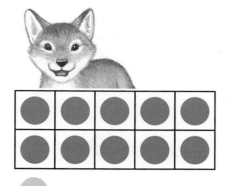

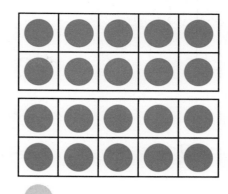

1 ten + 1 one

$10 + 1 =$ _11_

2 tens + 1 one

$20 + 1 =$ _21_

Write each sum. Look for a pattern.

1. $10 + 1 =$ _11_

   $10 + 2 =$ ____

   $10 + 3 =$ ____

   $10 + 4 =$ ____

   $10 + 5 =$ ____

   $10 + 6 =$ ____

   $10 + 7 =$ ____

   $10 + 8 =$ ____

   $10 + 9 =$ ____

   $10 + 10 =$ ____

2. $20 + 1 =$ ____

   $20 + 2 =$ ____

   $20 + 3 =$ ____

   $20 + 4 =$ ____

   $20 + 5 =$ ____

   $20 + 6 =$ ____

   $20 + 7 =$ ____

   $20 + 8 =$ ____

   $20 + 9 =$ ____

   $20 + 10 =$ ____

3. $30 + 1 =$ ____

   $30 + 2 =$ ____

   $30 + 3 =$ ____

   $30 + 4 =$ ____

   $30 + 5 =$ ____

   $30 + 6 =$ ____

   $30 + 7 =$ ____

   $30 + 8 =$ ____

   $30 + 9 =$ ____

   $30 + 10 =$ ____

California Content Standards *Number Sense 2.1 (🔑) Know the addition facts. Statistics, Data Analysis, and Probability 2.0. Also Number Sense 2.3 (🔑), 2.6, Mathematical Reasoning 2.0.*

Write each sum.

4. $10 + 5 =$ 15 $20 + 7 =$ ____ $1 + 30 =$ ____

5. $50 + 2 =$ ____ $6 + 70 =$ ____ $60 + 9 =$ ____

6.
$$\begin{array}{r} 20 \\ + 3 \\ \hline \end{array} \quad \begin{array}{r} 10 \\ + 6 \\ \hline \end{array} \quad \begin{array}{r} 7 \\ + 50 \\ \hline \end{array} \quad \begin{array}{r} 90 \\ + 5 \\ \hline \end{array} \quad \begin{array}{r} 2 \\ + 40 \\ \hline \end{array} \quad \begin{array}{r} 70 \\ + 10 \\ \hline \end{array}$$

7.
$$\begin{array}{r} 90 \\ + 9 \\ \hline \end{array} \quad \begin{array}{r} 4 \\ + 80 \\ \hline \end{array} \quad \begin{array}{r} 7 \\ + 30 \\ \hline \end{array} \quad \begin{array}{r} 60 \\ + 4 \\ \hline \end{array} \quad \begin{array}{r} 6 \\ +20 \\ \hline \end{array} \quad \begin{array}{r} 5 \\ + 70 \\ \hline \end{array}$$

 Math Reasoning

Number Sense

Complete the pattern. Tell about the pattern.

8. $10 + 10 =$ 20 $60 + 10 =$ ____

   $20 + 10 =$ ____ $70 + 10 =$ ____

   $30 + 10 =$ ____ $80 + 10 =$ ____

   $40 + 10 =$ ____ $90 + 10 =$ ____

   $50 + 10 =$ ____ $100 + 10 =$ ____

Home Activity Encourage your child to talk about patterns when adding ones to tens. Homework Workbook 8-3

Name_____

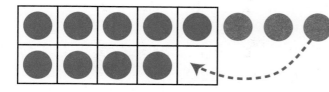

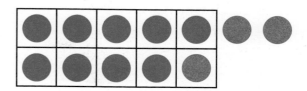

9 + 3

10 + 2 = 12

so 9 + 3 = 12

Make 10.
Then add 2.

Use counters and Workmat 2.
Show 9 in the ten-frame.
Make 10. Add.

1.
9 + 6

10 + 5 = ____

so 9 + 6 = ____

2.
9 + 4

10 + 3 = ____

so 9 + 4 = ____

3.
9 + 8

10 + 7 = ____

so 9 + 8 = ____

4.
9 + 2

10 + 1 = ____

so 9 + 2 = ____

5.
9 + 7

10 + 6 = ____

so 9 + 7 = ____

6.
9 + 5

10 + 4 = ____

so 9 + 5 = ____

California Content Standards *Number Sense 2.1 (🔑) Know addition facts and commit them to memory. Number Sense 1.3. Also Mathematical Reasoning 3.0.*

two hundred forty-nine **249**

Make 10.
Draw squares to add.

7.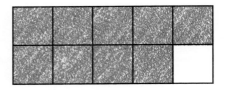

$$\begin{array}{r} 9 \\ + 7 \\ \hline 16 \end{array}$$

8.

$$\begin{array}{r} 9 \\ + 3 \\ \hline \end{array}$$

9.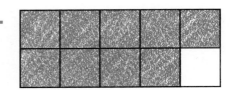

$$\begin{array}{r} 9 \\ + 5 \\ \hline \end{array}$$

10.

$$\begin{array}{r} 9 \\ + 8 \\ \hline \end{array}$$

11.

$$\begin{array}{r} 9 \\ + 6 \\ \hline \end{array}$$

12.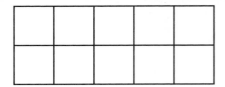

$$\begin{array}{r} 9 \\ + 9 \\ \hline \end{array}$$

Problem Solving

Solve.
The sum of two numbers fits
in a ten-frame with 3 left over.

13. What two numbers could they be? _____ and _____

14. Tell other numbers that could also solve the problem.

Home Activity Making 10 can help children find sums where one number is 9. Ask your child to explain how making 10 can help find sums on this page. Homework Workbook 8-4

Name_____

Making 10 to Add 7, 8, and 9

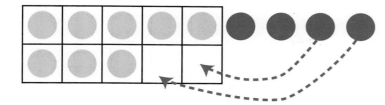

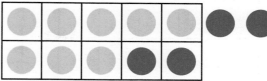

$$8 + 4$$

$$10 + 2 = \underline{12}$$

so $8 + 4 = \underline{12}$

Make 10. Then add the others.

Draw more dots to add.

1.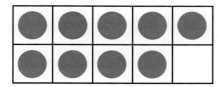

$$\begin{array}{r} 8 \\ + 6 \\ \hline 14 \end{array}$$

2.

$$\begin{array}{r} 7 \\ + 4 \\ \hline \end{array}$$

3.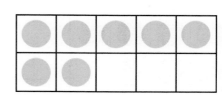

$$\begin{array}{r} 9 \\ + 7 \\ \hline \end{array}$$

4.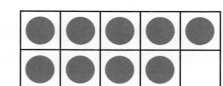

$$\begin{array}{r} 9 \\ + 4 \\ \hline \end{array}$$

5.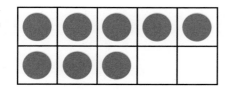

$$\begin{array}{r} 8 \\ + 7 \\ \hline \end{array}$$

6.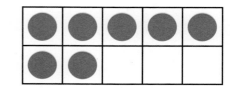

$$\begin{array}{r} 7 \\ + 5 \\ \hline \end{array}$$

California Content Standards *Number Sense 2.1 (🔑) Know the addition facts and commit them to memory. Number Sense 1.3. Also Mathematical Reasoning 1.2, 2.0.*

Draw more dots to add.

7. 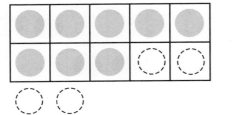 $\begin{array}{r} 8 \\ + 4 \\ \hline 12 \end{array}$

8. 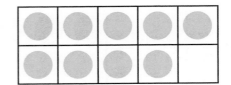 $\begin{array}{r} 9 \\ + 5 \\ \hline \end{array}$

9. 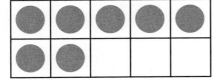 $\begin{array}{r} 7 \\ + 6 \\ \hline \end{array}$

10. 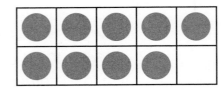 $\begin{array}{r} 9 \\ + 6 \\ \hline \end{array}$

11. 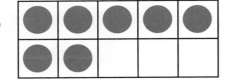 $\begin{array}{r} 7 \\ + 9 \\ \hline \end{array}$

12. 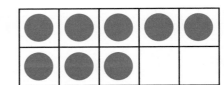 $\begin{array}{r} 8 \\ + 5 \\ \hline \end{array}$

13. 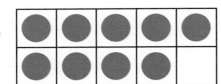 $\begin{array}{r} 9 \\ + 8 \\ \hline \end{array}$

14. 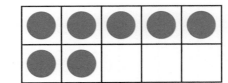 $\begin{array}{r} 7 \\ + 8 \\ \hline \end{array}$

 **Problem Solving**

15. Tom is fixing lunch for 14 friends.
How many more plates, glasses, and spoons
does Tom need so that he will have 14 of each?

_____ more plates | _____ more glasses | _____ more spoons

Home Activity Have your child use paper clips or buttons to show a fact like 8 + 5. Then have him or her make 10 and find the sum. Homework Workbook 8-5

Name_____ **Adding Three Numbers**

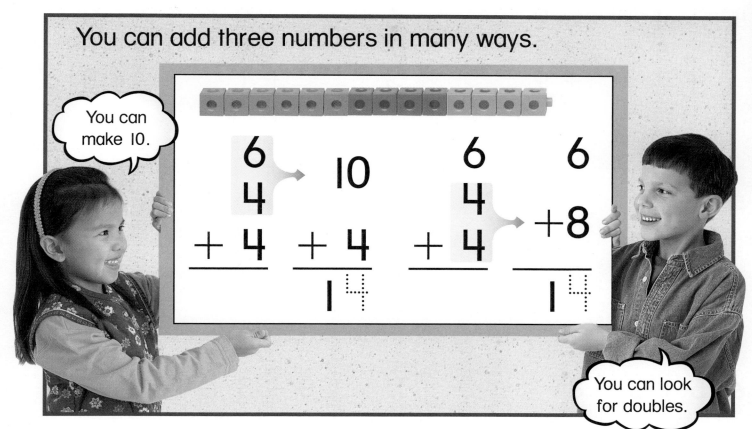

You can add three numbers in many ways.

You can make 10.

$$\begin{array}{r} 6 \\ 4 \\ +\ 4 \\ \hline \end{array} \rightarrow \begin{array}{r} 10 \\ +\ 4 \\ \hline 14 \end{array}$$

$$\begin{array}{r} 6 \\ 4 \\ +\ 4 \\ \hline \end{array} \rightarrow \begin{array}{r} 6 \\ +\ 8 \\ \hline 14 \end{array}$$

You can look for doubles.

Find each sum.

1.
$$\begin{array}{r} 6 \\ 5 \\ +\ 5 \\ \hline \end{array} \rightarrow \boxed{10}$$
$$\begin{array}{r} 7 \\ 3 \\ +\ 1 \\ \hline \end{array} \rightarrow \boxed{}$$
$$\begin{array}{r} 2 \\ 2 \\ +\ 8 \\ \hline \end{array} \rightarrow \boxed{}$$
$$\begin{array}{r} 6 \\ 3 \\ +\ 3 \\ \hline \end{array} \rightarrow \boxed{}$$

2.
$$\begin{array}{r} 4 \\ 4 \\ +\ 5 \\ \hline \end{array}$$
$$\begin{array}{r} 6 \\ 3 \\ +\ 7 \\ \hline \end{array}$$
$$\begin{array}{r} 9 \\ 1 \\ +\ 5 \\ \hline \end{array}$$
$$\begin{array}{r} 7 \\ 7 \\ +\ 1 \\ \hline \end{array}$$
$$\begin{array}{r} 7 \\ 4 \\ +\ 6 \\ \hline \end{array}$$
$$\begin{array}{r} 6 \\ 6 \\ +\ 8 \\ \hline \end{array}$$

3.
$$\begin{array}{r} 8 \\ 1 \\ +\ 1 \\ \hline \end{array}$$
$$\begin{array}{r} 4 \\ 3 \\ +\ 7 \\ \hline \end{array}$$
$$\begin{array}{r} 2 \\ 2 \\ +\ 5 \\ \hline \end{array}$$
$$\begin{array}{r} 8 \\ 8 \\ +\ 4 \\ \hline \end{array}$$
$$\begin{array}{r} 6 \\ 1 \\ +\ 9 \\ \hline \end{array}$$
$$\begin{array}{r} 5 \\ 5 \\ +\ 7 \\ \hline \end{array}$$

California Content Standards *Number Sense 2.7 Find the sum of three one-digit numbers. Also Number Sense 2.1 (🔑), Mathematical Reasoning 1.1, 3.0.*

Find each sum.

4.

4	2	6	2	3
6	2	7	9	8
+ 7	+ 9	+ 3	+ 1	+ 8
17				

5.

7	5	2	0	9
3	6	8	9	8
+ 6	+ 4	+ 4	+ 9	+ 2

6. $5 + 3 + 3 =$ _____ $8 + 8 + 4 =$ _____

7. $8 + 2 + 7 =$ _____ $1 + 9 + 9 =$ _____

 Problem Solving

Add across. Add down.
The sum is the same. Complete each number square.

8.

4	9	
	5	7
8		

Each sum is 15.

9.

7		3
	4	
5	6	

Each sum is 12.

Home Activity Ask your child how he or she found the sums on these pages. Ask which number he or she added first and why. Homework Workbook 8-6

Name_____ **Using Addition Strategies**

You can add in many ways.

Add. Tell how you found each sum.

1.
$$\begin{array}{r} 5 \\ + 6 \\ \hline \end{array}$$
$$\begin{array}{r} 9 \\ + 4 \\ \hline \end{array}$$
$$\begin{array}{r} 7 \\ + 3 \\ \hline \end{array}$$
$$\begin{array}{r} 8 \\ + 8 \\ \hline \end{array}$$
$$\begin{array}{r} 10 \\ + 6 \\ \hline \end{array}$$
$$\begin{array}{r} 4 \\ + 8 \\ \hline \end{array}$$

2.
$$\begin{array}{r} 6 \\ + 7 \\ \hline \end{array}$$
$$\begin{array}{r} 20 \\ + 3 \\ \hline \end{array}$$
$$\begin{array}{r} 8 \\ + 2 \\ \hline \end{array}$$
$$\begin{array}{r} 4 \\ + 7 \\ \hline \end{array}$$
$$\begin{array}{r} 9 \\ + 8 \\ \hline \end{array}$$
$$\begin{array}{r} 8 \\ + 5 \\ \hline \end{array}$$

3.
$$\begin{array}{r} 9 \\ + 3 \\ \hline \end{array}$$
$$\begin{array}{r} 10 \\ + 9 \\ \hline \end{array}$$
$$\begin{array}{r} 7 \\ + 8 \\ \hline \end{array}$$
$$\begin{array}{r} 4 \\ + 9 \\ \hline \end{array}$$
$$\begin{array}{r} 9 \\ + 9 \\ \hline \end{array}$$
$$\begin{array}{r} 30 \\ + 5 \\ \hline \end{array}$$

California Content Standards *Number Sense 2.1 (🔑) Know the addition facts and commit them to memory. Also Mathematical Reasoning 1.1, 3.0.*

two hundred fifty-five 255

Follow each rule.

4.

Double it.	
4	8
5	
6	
7	
8	
9	

5.

Add 3.	
4	
5	
6	
7	
8	
9	

6.

Add 7.	
10	
9	
8	
7	
6	
5	

7.

Add 8.	
3	
6	
9	
4	
8	
7	

8.

Add 9.	
4	
6	
5	
8	
7	
10	

Home Activity Have your child tell you how he or she found the sums on this page. Homework Workbook 8-7

Add.

1. 8 + 8 = _____   2. 7 + 7 = _____   3. 9 + 9 = _____

    8 + 9 = _____   8 + 7 = _____   9 + 10 = _____

Find each sum.

4.
```
    7        9        4        7        5        8
    3        9        8        7        5        8
  + 2      + 2      + 2      + 5      + 6      + 0
```

Draw more dots to add.

5.
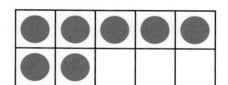
```
    9
  + 5
```

6.
```
    7
  + 6
```

Follow each rule.

7.

Double it.	
6	
7	
8	
9	
10	

8.

Add 8.	
5	
6	
7	
8	
9	

1.   ⑨ $5 + 4$ $15 - 6$ $6 + 3$ $16 - 8$
    ○   ○   ○   ○

2.

Tens	Ones
5	6

Tens	Ones
3	6

Tens	Ones
2	6

NH

    ○   ○   ○   ○

3.   ○   △   ☐   ▭
    ○   ○   ○   ○

4.   0   2   3   4
    ○   ○   ○   ○

5.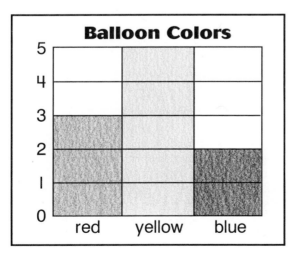

$3 - 2 = 1$ $2 + 3 = 5$
   ○   ○

$5 - 2 = 3$ $5 - 3 = 2$
   ○   ○

Oral Directions *Mark the correct answer. NH means "Not here." Mark it whenever the answer is not given.*

#1. Mark the statement that is not another name for nine.
#2. Count the tennis balls. Mark the one that shows a way to regroup the number in tens and ones.

#3. Mark the shape that is the face of the cube.
#4. Look at the plane shape. How many corners does it have?
#5. Look at the graph. Mark the number sentence that tells how many more yellow balloons than blue balloons there are.

Name_____ **Relating Addition and Subtraction**

Subtracting a number is the opposite of adding that number.

$$6 + 4 = 10$$
$$10 - 4 = 6$$

Use two colors of counters and Workmat 3.
Show each number.
Add. Then subtract.

1. Start with 8. Add 7.

   Now subtract 7.

   $$8 + 7 = 15$$
   $$15 - 7 = 8$$

2. Start with 7. Add 6.

   ___ + ___ = ___

   Now subtract 6.

   ___ − ___ = ___

3. Start with 8. Add 8.

   ___ + ___ = ___

   Now subtract 8.

   ___ − ___ = ___

4. Start with 8. Add 9.

   ___ + ___ = ___

   Now subtract 9.

   ___ − ___ = ___

California Content Standards Number Sense 2.2 (🔑) Use the inverse relationship between addition and subtraction to solve problems. Also Number Sense 1.3, 2.1(🔑), Mathematical Reasoning 3.0.

Use two colors of counters and Workmat 3.
Show each number. Add. Then subtract.

	Add	Subtract
5. **4** **9**	$4 + 9 = 13$	$13 - 9 = 4$
6. **6** **8**	___ + ___ = ___	___ − ___ = ___
7. **9** **9**	___ + ___ = ___	___ − ___ = ___
8. **7** **8**	___ + ___ = ___	___ − ___ = ___
9. **7** **10**	___ + ___ = ___	___ − ___ = ___

Problem Solving

Solve.

10. The sum of two numbers is 8.
The difference of the numbers is 4.
What are the numbers? _____ and _____

Home Activity Ask your child to use buttons or other household items to show an addition fact and the related subtraction fact. Then write both number sentences. Homework Workbook 8-8

Name_____

Problem-Solving Strategy
Write a Number Sentence

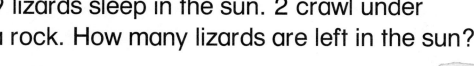

9 lizards sleep in the sun. 2 crawl under
a rock. How many lizards are left in the sun?

Understand

You need to find how many
lizards are left.

Plan

You can write a number sentence.
Decide whether to add or subtract.

Solve

$$9 - 2 = 7 \text{ lizards}$$

Look Back

Did you answer the question?

Write a number sentence. Solve.

1. 14 bats are in a cave. 7 fly away.
   How many bats are there now?

   ____ ◯ ____ = ____ bats

2. 8 owls are on a cactus.
   7 more join them.
   How many owls are there?

   ____ ◯ ____ = ____ owls

California Content Standards *Algebra and Functions 1.1
Write and solve number sentences from problem situations.
Algebra and Functions 1.2. Also Number Sense 2.1 (🔑),
Mathematical Reasoning 2.1.*

two hundred sixty-one **261**

Write a number sentence. Solve.

3. 14 big bears and 8 little bears play.
How many more big bears are playing?

14 − 8 = 6 big bears

4. A rabbit eats 7 plants.
It eats that many plants again.
How many plants does it eat in all?

_____ ◯ _____ = _____ plants

5. 12 owls sleep.
4 of them wake up.
How many owls are left sleeping?

_____ ◯ _____ = _____ owls

6. 9 deer drink at the creek.
6 more join them.
Now how many are drinking?

_____ ◯ _____ = _____ deer

Math Reasoning

7. Tell why this makes sense.
5 + 2 = 15 − 8

8. Write the numbers to make
the number sentence true.

5 + 4 = _____ − _____

Home Activity Make up addition and subtraction stories.
Ask your child to write a number sentence for each story.
Homework Workbook 8-9

Name_____ **Fact Families**

$7+5=\underline{12}$ $12-5=\underline{7}$

$5+7=\underline{12}$ $12-7=\underline{5}$

Every fact has the same numbers. This must be a fact family.

Add or subtract.
Use the numbers to write the fact family.

1.
   14
   9   5

   $9+5=\underline{\quad}$ $14-5=\underline{\quad}$

   $5+9=\underline{\quad}$ $14-9=\underline{\quad}$

2.
   15
   8   7

   $8+7=\underline{\quad}$ $15-7=\underline{\quad}$

   $7+8=\underline{\quad}$ $15-8=\underline{\quad}$

3.
   16
   9   7

   $9+7=\underline{\quad}$ $16-7=\underline{\quad}$

   $7+9=\underline{\quad}$ $16-9=\underline{\quad}$

4.
   13
   8   5

   $8+5=\underline{\quad}$ $13-5=\underline{\quad}$

   $5+8=\underline{\quad}$ $13-8=\underline{\quad}$

California Content Standards Number Sense 2.2 (🔑) Use the inverse relationship between addition and subtraction to solve problems. Also Number Sense 2.1 (🔑), Algebra and Functions 1.1, Mathematical Reasoning 1.1.

Add and subtract.
Use the numbers to write the fact family.

5.  $3 + 9 =$ 12 $12 - 9 =$ 3

$9 + 3 =$ 12 $12 - 3 =$ 9

6.  $6 + 7 =$ ___ $13 - 7 =$ ___

$7 + 6 =$ ___ $13 - 6 =$ ___

7.  $6 + 9 =$ ___ $15 - 9 =$ ___

$9 + 6 =$ ___ $15 - 6 =$ ___

8.  $9 + 8 =$ ___ $17 - 8 =$ ___

$8 + 9 =$ ___ $17 - 9 =$ ___

9.  $6 + 8 =$ ___ $14 - 8 =$ ___

$8 + 6 =$ ___ $14 - 6 =$ ___

Math Reasoning

10. Make your own fact family.
Write the number sentences.

___ $+$ ___ $=$ ___   ___ $-$ ___ $=$ ___

___ $+$ ___ $=$ ___   ___ $-$ ___ $=$ ___

264 two hundred sixty-four

Home Activity Ask your child to write number sentences for a fact family like 7, 8, and 15. Homework Workbook 8-10

Using 10 to Subtract

Name_____

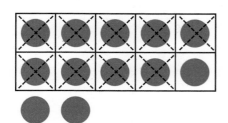

$$12 - 9$$

There are 10 counters in the ten-frame and 2 extra. So 12 − 9 = 3.

Cross out to subtract.
Use counters and Workmat 2 if you like.

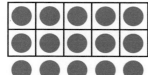 1. $$15 - 8$$

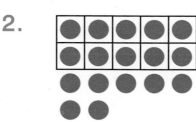 2. $$17 - 9$$

3. 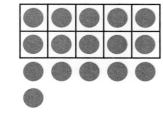 $$16 - 9$$

4. 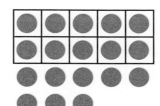 $$18 - 9$$

5. 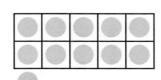 $$11 - 8$$

6. 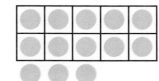 $$13 - 8$$

7. 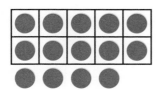 $$14 - 8$$

8. 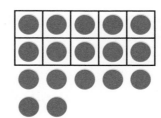 $$17 - 8$$

California Content Standards Number Sense 2.1 (🔑) Know the subtraction facts and commit them to memory. Also Number Sense 2.5 (🔑), Mathematical Reasoning 1.1, 1.2.

Cross out to subtract.

9. 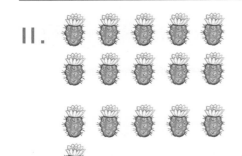 $\begin{array}{r} 13 \\ -9 \\ \hline 4 \end{array}$

10. 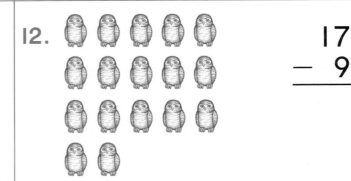 $\begin{array}{r} 15 \\ -9 \\ \hline \end{array}$

11.  $\begin{array}{r} 16 \\ -8 \\ \hline \end{array}$

12.  $\begin{array}{r} 17 \\ -9 \\ \hline \end{array}$

13. 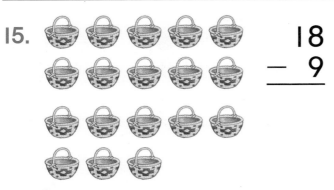 $\begin{array}{r} 14 \\ -9 \\ \hline \end{array}$

14.  $\begin{array}{r} 17 \\ -8 \\ \hline \end{array}$

15. $\begin{array}{r} 18 \\ -9 \\ \hline \end{array}$

16. $\begin{array}{r} 16 \\ -9 \\ \hline \end{array}$

Problem Solving

17. Circle 2 toys you can buy with these coins.

     8¢   5¢   9¢

18. How much money will you have left? _____

Home Activity Have your child use buttons or pennies and a hand-drawn ten-frame to practice using ten to subtract 8 or 9.
Homework Workbook 8-11

Name_____ **Using Subtraction Strategies**

You can subtract in many ways.

Subtract. Tell how you found each difference.

1.
12	15	17	14	16	13
− 4	− 7	− 9	− 6	− 6	− 4

2.
18	14	13	19	16	12
− 9	− 7	− 5	−10	− 7	− 7

3.
16	15	12	17	20	9
− 9	− 6	− 6	− 8	−10	− 0

California Content Standards *Number Sense 2.1 (🔑) Know addition and subtraction facts and commit them to memory. Also Algebra and Functions 1.1, Mathematical Reasoning 1.1, 2.0.*

Follow the path to add and subtract.

4. Write the missing numbers.

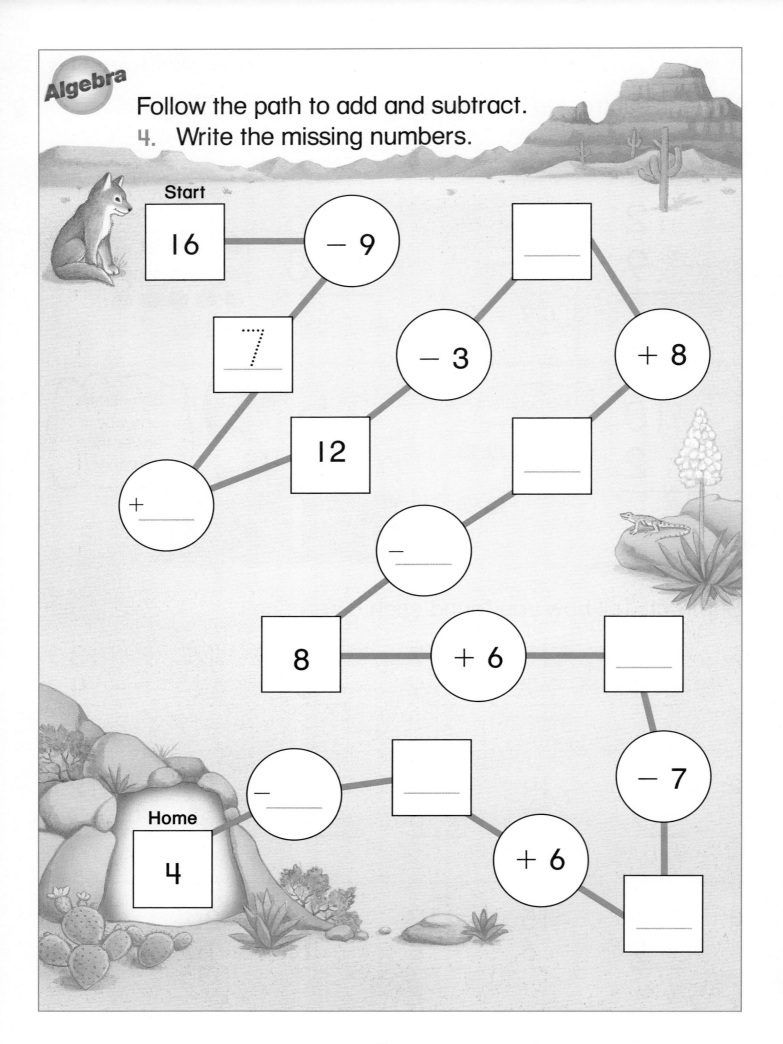

Start
16 — −9 — [ ]
7 — −3 — +8
+ — 12 — [ ]
8 — − — [ ]
8 — +6 — [ ]
− — [ ] — −7
Home
4 — [ ] — +6 — [ ]

Home Activity Write two problems similar to those on page 267. Ask your child to solve the problems and describe the strategy he or she used to find the answer. Homework Workbook 8-12

Name_____

Look for a pattern in the table. It will help you find the missing numbers.

coyotes	1	2	3	4
eyes	2	4	6	8

Look for a pattern.
Complete each table.

1.

foxes	1	2	3	4	5	6
legs	4	8	12			

2.

cactuses	1	2	3	4	5	6
flowers	3	6				

3.

owls	6	5	4	3	2	1
wings	12	10				

California Content Standards *Number Sense 2.1 (🔑) Know addition and subtraction facts and commit them to memory. Statistics, Data Analysis, and Probability 2.0. Also Mathematical Reasoning 1.1, 2.2, 3.0.*

Look for the pattern.
Complete each table.

4.

rabbits	1	2	3	4	5	6
ears	2	4				

5.

bats	8	7	6	5	4	3
wings	16	14				

6.

lizard's feet	1	2	3	4	5	6
toes	5	10				

Problem Solving

7. Make your own table.

8. How can you check your answers?

Home Activity Make function tables at home using addition facts to 20. Ask your child to complete each table and describe the pattern. Homework Workbook 8-13

Name_____

Problem-Solving Application

Too Much Information

Read carefully.
Think: What do I need to find out?
Cross out the information you do not need.
Write the number sentence.

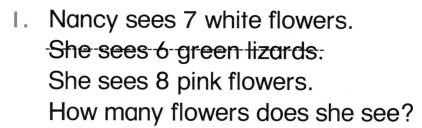

1. Nancy sees 7 white flowers.
~~She sees 6 green lizards.~~
She sees 8 pink flowers.
How many flowers does she see?

$7 + 8 = 15$ flowers

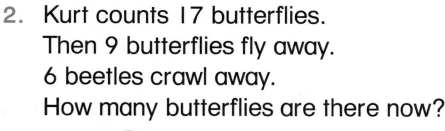

2. Kurt counts 17 butterflies.
Then 9 butterflies fly away.
6 beetles crawl away.
How many butterflies are there now?

____ ◯ ____ = ____ butterflies

3. Jenny sees 8 big deer and 6 little deer.
The deer are behind 6 cactuses.
How many deer does she see altogether?

____ ◯ ____ = ____ deer

4. Alex sees 18 lizards.
The lizards are on 2 rocks.
9 of the lizards hide.
How many lizards are left?

____ ◯ ____ = ____ lizards

 California Content Standards Algebra and Functions 1.1
Write and solve number sentences from problem situations.
Mathematical Reasoning 2.0. Also Number Sense 2.1 (⚸),
Algebra and Functions 1.2, Mathematical Reasoning 1.1.

Cross out the information you do not need.
Write the number sentence.

5. Rachel has 13 pieces of fruit.
   She has 2 baskets.
   She gives 8 pieces of fruit to friends.
   How many pieces of fruit does she have now?

   _____ ◯ _____ = _____ pieces of fruit

6. Cody's family sees 16 deer.
   8 deer run away.
   Cody sees 2 bobcats.
   How many deer are left?

   _____ ◯ _____ = _____ deer

7. José sees 8 owls.
   He sees 7 bats.
   He sees 4 deer.
   How many bats and owls does José see?

   _____ ◯ _____ = _____ bats and owls

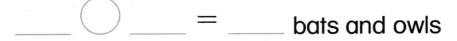

8. Sara sees 10 birds.
   Then she sees 7 more.
   Sara sees 8 squirrels.
   How many birds does she see in all?

   _____ ◯ _____ = _____ birds

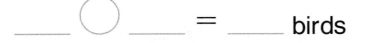

Home Activity Make up word problems with extra information for your child to solve. Ask what information is extra.
Homework Workbook 8-14

Name_____

Write the fact family.

1.

   17
   8   9

   8 + 9 = ____   17 − 9 = ____

   9 + 8 = ____   17 − 8 = ____

Look at the pattern.
Complete the table.

2.

lizards	1	2	3	4	5
stripes	5	10			

Subtract.

3.
   15   14   18   13   20   16
   − 7   − 5   − 9   − 8   − 10   − 9

---

4. 17 − 8 = ____   16 − 8 = ____   15 − 9 = ____

Cross out the information you do not need.
Write the number sentence.

5. Joy sees 15 bats.
    7 bats fly away.
    4 deer run by.
    How many bats are there now?

    ____ ◯ ____ = ____

Name_____

1. $9 + \boxed{} = 11$

4	3	2	1
○	○	○	○

2.

NH

○   ○   ○   ○

3.

$7 + 2 = 9$	$9 - 7 = 2$	$9 - 2 = 7$	$9 + 2 = 11$
○	○	○	○

4.

$8 + 9 = 17$	$10 + 9 = 20$	$6 + 8 = 15$	$7 + 7 = 13$
○	○	○	○

5.

$16 - 8 = 7$	$7 - 3 = 5$	$15 - 7 = 7$	$5 - 3 = 2$
○	○	○	○

6.

6   13

7	6	19	4
○	○	○	○

Oral Directions *Mark the correct answer. NH means "Not here." Mark it whenever the answer is not given.*

#1. Mark the missing number that makes the number sentence true.
#2. There are eight butterflies. Three fly away. Mark the picture that shows this.

#3. Look at the four number sentences. Three of them belong to the same family of facts. Mark the number sentence that does not belong.
#4–5. Mark the number sentence that is true.
#6. Jack's class has six footballs and thirteen baseballs. How many more baseballs than footballs are there?

Name_____

Draw dots to add.

1.

$$\begin{array}{r} 9 \\ + \ 6 \\ \hline \end{array}$$

Cross out to subtract.

2.

$$\begin{array}{r} 14 \\ - \ 8 \\ \hline \end{array}$$

Add.

3. $8 + 8 =$ _____

$8 + 9 =$ _____

4. $9 + 9 =$ _____

$10 + 9 =$ _____

Add and subtract.

5. $7 + 6 =$ _____

$13 - 6 =$ _____

6. $5 + 10 =$ _____

$15 - 10 =$ _____

Look at the pattern.
Complete the table.

7.

birds	9	8	7	6	5
wings	18	16			

Use the numbers to write the fact family.

8.

14
9   5

_____ + _____ = _____   _____ − _____ = _____

_____ + _____ = _____   _____ − _____ = _____

Add or subtract.

9.
$$\begin{array}{r} 7 \\ + 7 \\ \hline \end{array}$$
$$\begin{array}{r} 15 \\ - 9 \\ \hline \end{array}$$
$$\begin{array}{r} 9 \\ + 7 \\ \hline \end{array}$$
$$\begin{array}{r} 17 \\ - 8 \\ \hline \end{array}$$
$$\begin{array}{r} 10 \\ + 10 \\ \hline \end{array}$$
$$\begin{array}{r} 13 \\ - 8 \\ \hline \end{array}$$

10.
$$\begin{array}{r} 16 \\ - 9 \\ \hline \end{array}$$
$$\begin{array}{r} 9 \\ + 9 \\ \hline \end{array}$$
$$\begin{array}{r} 19 \\ - 9 \\ \hline \end{array}$$
$$\begin{array}{r} 10 \\ + 8 \\ \hline \end{array}$$
$$\begin{array}{r} 15 \\ - 6 \\ \hline \end{array}$$
$$\begin{array}{r} 20 \\ + 10 \\ \hline \end{array}$$

11. $7 + 7 + 5 =$ _____ $9 + 8 + 1 =$ _____

Follow the rule.

12.

Add 10.	
7	
6	
5	

13.

Add 9.	
3	
4	
5	

Cross out the information you do not need.
Write the number sentence.

14. Tina had 6 rings.
Sara had 9 rings.
Jan had 2 hats.
How many rings in all?

_____ ◯ _____ = _____

15. There were 15 lions playing.
8 lions walked away.
6 monkeys played in the tree.
How many lions were left?

_____ ◯ _____ = _____

1. $5 + 5 = 10$ $8 + 8 = 16$ $7 + 7 = 15$ $10 + 10 = 20$
○   ○   ○   ○

2. $9 + 6 = 15$ $6 + 9 = 15$ $16 - 9 = 7$ $15 - 9 = 6$
○   ○   ○   ○

3. $7 + 6 = 13$
so $13 - 6 = \boxed{}$

7	6	5	13
○	○	○	○

4. $8 + 8 = 16$
so $8 + 9 = \boxed{}$

16	18	20	17
○	○	○	○

5.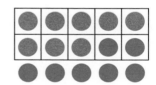

$8 + 6 = 14$	$8 + 7 = 15$	$10 + 3 = 13$	NH
○	○	○	○

6. $9 + 9 + 0 = \boxed{}$

16	18	9	NH
○	○	○	○

7. $17 - 10 = \boxed{}$

10	27	7	NH
○	○	○	○

Oral Directions *Mark the correct answer. NH means "Not here." Mark it whenever the answer is not given.*

#1. Mark the doubles fact that is not true.
#2. Look at the four number sentences. Three of them belong to the same family of facts. Mark the number sentence that does not belong.

#3. Seven plus six equals thirteen so thirteen minus six equals which number?
#4. Use the doubles fact eight plus eight equals sixteen to help you solve eight plus nine.
#5. Look at the picture. What basic fact does it show?
#6–7. Solve

8.

9 − 5 = 4	9 + 5 = 14	14 − 5 = 9	NH
○	○	○	○

9. 6 + 4 + 9 = ☐

10	13	15	19
○	○	○	○

10.

dogs	1	2	3
paws	4	8	

12	10	18	NH
○	○	○	○

11.   8   5

8 − 5 = 3	13 − 5 = 8	8 + 5 = 13	NH
○	○	○	○

12.   10 🦋   4 🦋

10 + 4 = 14	10 − 4 = 6	14 − 2 = 1	NH
○	○	○	○

Oral Directions *Mark the correct answer. NH means "Not here." Mark it whenever the answer is not given.*

#8. Look at the picture. What basic fact does it show?
#9. Add.
#10. Look for the pattern. Mark the number that is missing.

#11. There are eight rabbits hopping in the park. Five more rabbits join them. How many rabbits are there in all?
#12. Ten butterflies are in the garden. Four more butterflies join them. Two birds fly by. How many butterflies are in the garden?

Money

Diagnosing Readiness
for Chapter 9

1. Circle >, <, or =.

$$25 \quad \begin{matrix} > \\ < \\ = \end{matrix} \quad 17$$

2. Solve.

$$\begin{array}{r} 6 \\ +\ 1 \\ \hline \end{array}$$

3. Count the coins.

 ¢

4. Count by 5s.

5, 10, _____, _____

20, 25, _____, _____

To the Family

| Looking Back | Chapter 9 | Looking Ahead |

Chapter 9

Money

Children learn the values of individual coins and groups of mixed coins are used to solve problems.

Looking Back

In Kindergarten children were introduced to pennies, nickels, and dimes. The value of each coin was presented and children counted and sorted coins.

Looking Ahead

By the end of Grade 1 problems are solved that involve addition and subtraction of money.

Page 279 Your child solved problems that review math skills from previous chapters and will help your child with skills in Chapter 9.

Math at Home If your child has a coin bank at home, empty the contents and count the coins together. Encourage your child to group like coins together and begin counting with the coins of greatest value.

Math Literature Read stories about money with your child. Look for the following books in your local library.
Yard Sale by James Stevenson (Greenwillow Books, 1996)
Dollars and Cents for Harriet by Betsy and Giulio Maestro (Crown, 1988)

California Content Standards in Chapter 9 Lessons*

Number Sense	Teach and Practice	Practice
1.2 (🔑) Compare and order whole numbers to 100 by using the symbols for less than, equal to, or greater than ($<, =, >$).	9	
1.5 Identify and know the value of coins.	1–10	
2.1 (🔑) Know addition and subtraction facts and commit them to memory.	11	
Statistics, Data Analysis, and Probability		
1.1 Sort objects and data by common attributes and describe the categories.		1

	Teach and Practice	Practice
1.2 Represent and compare data.	8	
Mathematical Reasoning		
1.1 Determine the approach, materials, and strategies to be used.	10	1, 6, 11
1.2 Use tools, such as manipulatives or sketches, to model problems.		1, 3, 5, 8, 9
2.0 Students solve problems and justify their reasoning.		2, 4, 6, 8
2.1 Explain the reasoning used and justify the procedures selected.		1, 7

* The symbol (🔑) indicates a key standard as designated in the Mathematics Framework for California Public Schools.
 Full statements of the California Content Standards are found at the beginning of this book following the Table of Contents.

Name_____

Sorting Coins

What You Need

2 pennies

2 nickels

2 dimes

2 quarters

1. Use the boxes to sort the coins.
   Make as many groups as you like.

2. Then sort another way.
   Tell about ways to group the coins.
   Can you sort another way?

California Content Standards *Number Sense 1.5 Identify and know the value of coins. Also Statistics, Data Analysis, and Probability 1.1, Mathematical Reasoning 1.1, 1.2, 2.1.*

two hundred eighty-one **281**

Circle the coins that are the same kind.

3.

4.

5.

6.

Home Activity Give your child a handful of coins. Ask him or her to sort them in different ways. Homework Workbook 9-1

Name_____

Pennies and Nickels

 I penny
I ¢
I cent

 I nickel
5¢
5 cents

I can show 5¢ with 5 pennies or with I nickel.

 or

Count on. Write how much in all.

Word Bank
penny
nickel

1.

   1¢   2¢   3¢   4¢   5¢   in all 5¢

2.

   ___¢   ___¢   ___¢   ___¢   ___¢   in all ___¢

3.

   ___¢   ___¢   ___¢   ___¢   ___¢   in all ___¢

4.

   ___¢   ___¢   ___¢   ___¢   ___¢   in all ___¢

California Content Standards *Number Sense 1.5 Identify and know the value of coins. Also Mathematical Reasoning 2.0.*

Circle the coins to match each price.

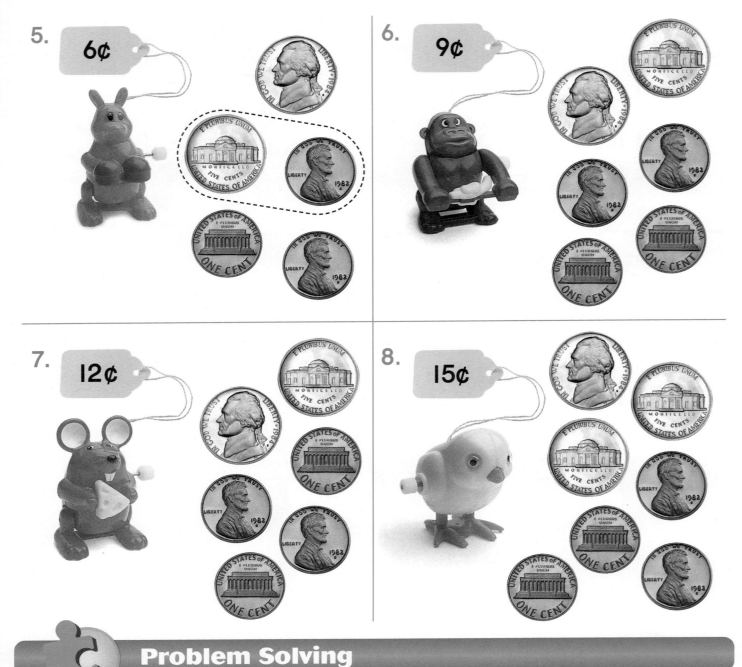

5. 6¢

6. 9¢

7. 12¢

8. 15¢

Problem Solving

Solve.

9. Carol has 3 nickels and 3 pennies. How much money does she have? _____ ¢

10. Can Carol buy the toy frog with 3 nickels and 3 pennies? Explain.

20¢

Home Activity Give your child a set of coins containing nickels and pennies. Have him or her determine the total value of each set. Homework Workbook 9-2

Name_____ **Pennies and Dimes**

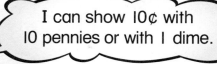
I can show 10¢ with 10 pennies or with 1 dime.

1 dime
10¢
10 cents

 or

Count on. Write how much in all.

1.

   $\underset{¢}{10}$ $\underset{¢}{20}$ $\underset{¢}{30}$ $\underset{¢}{40}$ $\underset{¢}{50}$ in all $\underset{¢}{50}$

2.

   ____¢ ____¢ ____¢ ____¢ ____¢ ____¢ in all ____¢

3.

   ____¢ ____¢ ____¢ ____¢ ____¢ ____¢ in all ____¢

4.

   ____¢ ____¢ ____¢ ____¢ ____¢ ____¢ in all ____¢

California Content Standards *Number Sense 1.5 Identify and know the value of coins. Also Mathematical Reasoning 1.2.*

two hundred eighty-five **285**

Circle the coins to match each price.

5. 14¢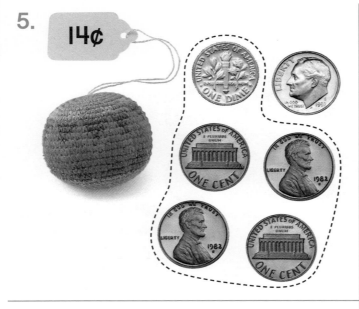

6. 23¢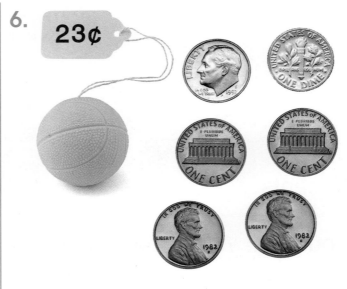

7. 44¢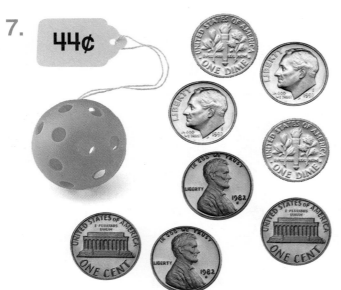

8. 32¢

 **Problem Solving**

Solve.

You have pennies and dimes.
You pick up 3 coins.

9. What is the greatest amount you could have? _____ ¢

10. What is the least amount you could have? _____ ¢

286 two hundred eighty-six

Home Activity Give your child sets of coins containing pennies and dimes. Have your child count the coins.
Homework Workbook 9-3

Name_____ **Pennies, Nickels, and Dimes**

To count coins, start with the coins of greatest value.

22¢

Count on.
Write how much you have in all.

1.

5 ¢   10 ¢   15 ¢   20 ¢   21 ¢   22 ¢   in all 22 ¢

2.

___ ¢   ___ ¢   ___ ¢   ___ ¢   ___ ¢   in all ___ ¢

3.

___ ¢   ___ ¢   ___ ¢   ___ ¢   ___ ¢   ___ ¢ in all ___ ¢

4.

___ ¢   ___ ¢   ___ ¢   ___ ¢   ___ ¢   ___ ¢ in all ___ ¢

California Content Standards Number Sense 1.5 Identify and know the value of coins. Also Mathematical Reasoning 2.0.

two hundred eighty-seven **287**

Remember to start with the coins of greatest value.

Write each amount.

5.  | 17 ¢

6.  | ¢

7.  | ¢

8.  | ¢

9.  | ¢

10.  | ¢

Problem Solving

11. You have

19¢

Do you have enough money to buy the bear?

Circle **yes** or **no**. Explain.

yes   **no**

🏠 **Home Activity** Have your child count sets of coins containing pennies, nickels, and dimes. Homework Workbook 9-4

Name_____

Name_____ **Quarters**

or

quarter

25¢

Word Bank

quarter

25¢

Circle the coins you could trade for a quarter.

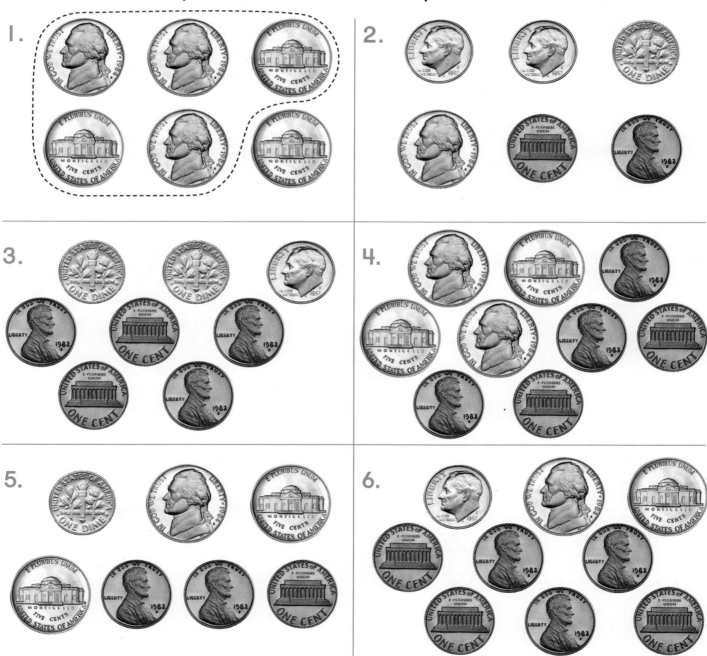

1.

2.

3.

4.

5.

6.

California Content Standards *Number Sense 1.5 Identify and know the value of coins. Also Mathematical Reasoning 1.2.*

two hundred eighty-nine **289**

Circle the coins to match each price.

7. 25¢

8. 35¢

9. 26¢

10. 25¢

Math Reasoning

11. You have 3 coins.
They equal one quarter.
Circle the coins you have.

🏠 **Home Activity** Have your child take and count a handful of coins. Encourage your child to explain the order in which he or she counted the coins and why. Homework Workbook 9-5

Name_____

Counting with Quarters
Coin Purses Around the World

Count the coins.
Write how much in all.

1.

25¢ 30¢ 31¢ 32¢   32¢
                                      in all

2.

___¢ ___¢ ___¢ ___¢ ___¢   ___¢
                                        in all

3.

___¢ ___¢ ___¢ ___¢   ___¢
                                        in all

4.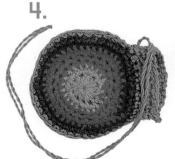

___¢ ___¢ ___¢ ___¢ ___¢   ___¢
                                        in all

 **California Content Standards** *Number Sense 1.5 Identify and know the value of coins. Also Mathematical Reasoning 1.1, 2.0.*

Circle the coins to show how much.

5.

6.

7.

8.

Math Reasoning

9. Ryan has 1 coin.
June has 3 coins.
Each has 25¢.
Use words to tell what coins they have.

Home Activity Have your child empty a coin purse. Ask him or her to count five of the coins and tell you how much money there is. Homework Workbook 9-6

Name_____ **Diagnostic Checkpoint**

Count on.
Write how much in all.

1.

____¢   ____¢   ____¢   ____¢   ____¢   ____¢   ____¢

in all

2.

____¢   ____¢   ____¢   ____¢   ____¢   ____¢   ____¢

in all

Circle the coins to match the price.

3.  **41¢**

4. **27¢**

5. **36¢**

Name_____

1.   20 > 18   9 < 6   33 > 31   40 < 50
        ○   ○   ○   ○

2.

 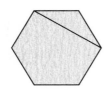 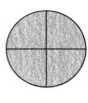

        ○   ○   ○   ○

3.

 |

                       ○   ○   ○   ○

4.

 | $\frac{1}{2}$ $\frac{1}{3}$ $\frac{1}{4}$ NH

                      ○   ○   ○   ○

5.

 |  pencil

                        25¢   60¢   50¢   55¢

                        ○   ○   ○   ○

Oral Directions *Mark the correct answer. NH means "Not here." Mark it whenever the answer is not given.*

#1. Mark under the statement that is not true.
#2. Which shape shows fourths?

#3. Which shape matches the first shape?
#4. Which part is blue?
#5. Which item has the same price as the coins shown?

294   two hundred ninety-four

Name_____ **Choosing Coins**

What coins could you use to buy the book?

Do You See?

_3_ pennies

____ nickels

_2_ dimes

____ quarters

or

_3_ pennies

_4_ nickels

____ dimes

____ quarters

23¢

Show two ways you could buy each item.

1.

32¢

____ pennies

____ nickels

____ dimes

____ quarters

or

____ pennies

____ nickels

____ dimes

____ quarters

2.

48¢

____ pennies

____ nickels

____ dimes

____ quarters

or

____ pennies

____ nickels

____ dimes

____ quarters

---

3. 29¢

____ pennies

____ nickels

____ dimes

____ quarters

or

____ pennies

____ nickels

____ dimes

____ quarters

California Content Standards *Number Sense 1.5 Identify and know the value of coins. Also Mathematical Reasoning 2.1.*

Use coins to solve.
How much more money
do you need to buy each item?
Tell which coins you need.

	You Have	You Need
4. 43¢	quarter	_____ pennies _____ nickels _____ dimes _____ quarters
5. 36¢	dime dime, nickel	_____ pennies _____ nickels _____ dimes _____ quarters
6. 50¢	dime, dime, nickel	_____ pennies _____ nickels _____ dimes _____ quarters

Math Reasoning

Number Sense

7. Can every amount of money from 1¢ to 50¢ be shown in more than one way? Tell why or why not.

Home Activity Place many different coins in a pile. Ask your child to choose coins to make a given amount. Homework Workbook 9-7

Name_____

Make a table.
Use coins to find
ways to show 10¢.

I have 10¢.
What coins
could I have?

Understand

You need to find all
possible groups of coins.

Plan

You can make a table.
Use pennies, nickels,
and dimes to make 10¢.

Solve

Finish the table.

		1
	2	
5	1	
10		

Look Back

Does each row total 10¢?

California Content Standards *Statistics, Data Analysis, and
Probability 1.2 Represent and compare data. Number Sense 1.5.
Also Mathematical Reasoning 1.2, 2.0.*

Use coins to find ways to show 25¢.

1.

 Home Activity Look for tables in newspapers or magazines. Discuss with your child how tables organize information.
Homework Workbook 9-8

Name_____ **Comparing Amounts**

35¢ is greater than 24¢.

35¢   24¢

Count the coins.
Write each amount.
Circle >, <, or =.

1.

6¢
> / < / =

7¢

2.

___¢
> / < / =
___¢

3.

___¢
> / < / =
___¢

 California Content Standards *Number Sense 1.2 (⚷)*
*Compare and order whole numbers to 100 by using the symbols
for less than, equal to, or greater than. Number Sense 1.5. Also
Mathematical Reasoning 1.2.*

two hundred ninety-nine **299**

Count the coins.
Write each amount.
Circle >, <, or =.

4.

>

_____ ¢   <   _____ ¢

=

5.

>

_____ ¢   <   _____ ¢

=

6.

>

_____ ¢   <   _____ ¢

=

Math Reasoning

7. You have 25¢. What three items can you buy for exactly 25¢?

ring	yo yo	horn	ball	charm
10¢	15¢	20¢	5¢	5¢

_____ , _____ , and _____

Home Activity Give your child groups of coins to compare values. Homework Workbook 9-9

Name_____ **Problem-Solving Application**

Making Purchases

Write how much money you have.
Circle the item you would buy.
Think: Use the picture to find the prices.

1.  10¢

2.   ____¢

3.  ____¢

4.   ____¢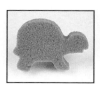

California Content Standards *Number Sense 1.5 Identify and know the value of coins. Mathematical Reasoning 1.1.*

40¢   25¢   27¢

6¢   19¢   31¢

Write how much money you have.
Circle the item you would buy.

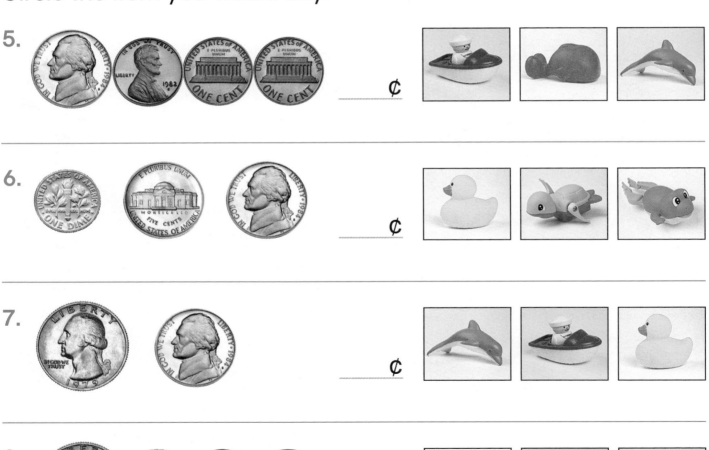

5. _____ ¢

6. _____ ¢

7. _____ ¢

8. _____ ¢

Home Activity Give your child a handful of coins. Set up a home store and have your child purchase different items.
Homework Workbook 9-10

Name_____ **Adding and Subtracting Money**

$$10¢$$
$$+ 3¢$$
$$13¢$$

$$10¢$$
$$- 3¢$$
$$7¢$$

Add or subtract. Use coins if you like.

1.
$$3¢$$
$$+ 2¢$$
$$\rule{1cm}{0.4pt}¢$$

$$4¢$$
$$- 1¢$$
$$\rule{1cm}{0.4pt}¢$$

2.
$7¢$	$13¢$	$6¢$	$16¢$	$9¢$
$+ 8¢$	$- 5¢$	$+ 6¢$	$- 8¢$	$+ 4¢$
___¢	___¢	___¢	___¢	___¢

3.
$20¢$	$6¢$	$17¢$	$14¢$	$10¢$
$- 10¢$	$+ 7¢$	$- 9¢$	$- 7¢$	$+ 6¢$
___¢	___¢	___¢	___¢	___¢

4.
$5¢$	$9¢$	$12¢$	$15¢$	$4¢$
$+ 9¢$	$+ 9¢$	$- 7¢$	$- 8¢$	$+ 7¢$
___¢	___¢	___¢	___¢	___¢

California Content Standards *Number Sense 2.1 (🔑) Know addition and subtraction facts and commit them to memory. Also Mathematical Reasoning 1.1.*

Add or subtract.

5.
$$18¢ - 8¢ = \underset{10}{}¢$$
$$3¢ + 10¢ = \underline{}¢$$
$$11¢ - 3¢ = \underline{}¢$$
$$9¢ + 8¢ = \underline{}¢$$
$$16¢ - 7¢ = \underline{}¢$$

6.
$$6¢ + 8¢ = \underline{}¢$$
$$15¢ - 5¢ = \underline{}¢$$
$$4¢ + 9¢ = \underline{}¢$$
$$10¢ + 7¢ = \underline{}¢$$
$$12¢ - 8¢ = \underline{}¢$$

7.
$$19¢ - 9¢ = \underline{}¢$$
$$7¢ + 7¢ = \underline{}¢$$
$$8¢ + 5¢ = \underline{}¢$$
$$11¢ - 8¢ = \underline{}¢$$
$$10¢ + 10¢ = \underline{}¢$$

8.
$$12¢ - 4¢ = \underline{}¢$$
$$8¢ + 7¢ = \underline{}¢$$
$$13¢ - 9¢ = \underline{}¢$$
$$7¢ + 5¢ = \underline{}¢$$
$$14¢ - 9¢ = \underline{}¢$$

9.
$$8¢ + 6¢ = \underline{}¢$$
$$13¢ - 6¢ = \underline{}¢$$
$$6¢ + 9¢ = \underline{}¢$$
$$18¢ - 9¢ = \underline{}¢$$
$$14¢ - 6¢ = \underline{}¢$$

Problem Solving

Each pocket has one nickel and some pennies.
Solve.

10. You have 8¢.
How many pennies
are in the pocket?

8¢

_____ pennies

11. You have 11¢.
How many pennies
are in the pocket?

11¢

_____ pennies

304 three hundred four

Home Activity Give your child various numbers of pennies, and have him or her add or subtract. Ask your child to write the fact. Homework Workbook 9-11

Name_____

1. Circle the coins to match the price.

 47¢

Write each amount.
Circle >, <, or =.

2.

          >

_____ ¢   <   _____ ¢

          =

3.

          >

_____ ¢   <   _____ ¢

          =

4. Add or subtract.

7¢	8¢	13¢	4¢	10¢	7¢
+ 5¢	− 6¢	− 4¢	+ 0¢	+ 5¢	− 4¢
___¢	___¢	___¢	___¢	___¢	___¢

5. Write the amount. Circle what you can buy.

 _____ ¢  40¢    30¢

1. $9 + 2 = \square$

    10   11   12   NH
    ○   ○   ○   ○

2. $10 - 6 = \square$

    5   3   4   NH
    ○   ○   ○   ○

3.   12
      $- \ 4$

    8   11   9   5
    ○   ○   ○   ○

4.   5¢
      $+ 2$¢

    9¢   3¢   7¢   4¢
    ○   ○   ○   ○

5. $9 - 9 = \square$

    9   0   2   3
    ○   ○   ○   ○

6. $3 + 3 = \square$

    9   6   0   3
    ○   ○   ○   ○

7. 5, 10, 15, 20, ____

    30   35   25   21
    ○   ○   ○   ○

8. 90, 89, 88, ____

    89   91   87   86
    ○   ○   ○   ○

9.

    ○ 46¢
    ○ 36¢
    ○ 31¢
    ○ NH

10.

    ○ 1¢
    ○ 10¢
    ○ 5¢
    ○ 25¢

Oral Directions *Mark the correct answer. NH means "Not here." Mark it whenever the answer is not given.*

#1–6. Add or subtract.
#7. What number comes after twenty if you are counting by fives?

#8. What number comes just after eighty-eight if you are counting backwards by ones?
#9. How much money is there?
#10. How much more money do you need to make thirty cents?

Name_____

1. Circle the coins to match the price.

2. Count the coins. Write how much in all.

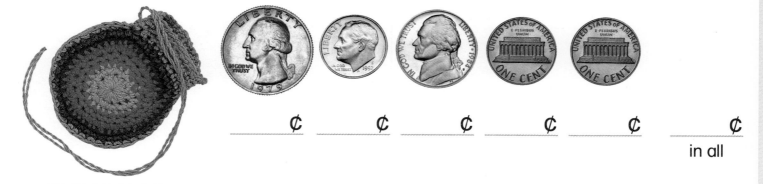

_____ ¢   _____ ¢   _____ ¢   _____ ¢   _____ ¢   _____ ¢

in all

Write each amount.
Circle >, <, or =.

3.

>
_____ ¢ < _____ ¢
=

4.

>
_____ ¢ < _____ ¢
=

5. Use coins to find ways to show 15¢.

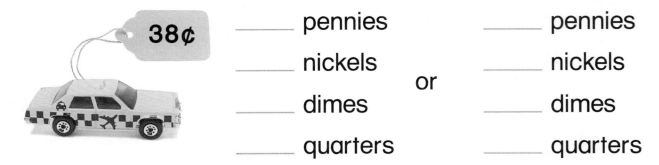

6. Show two ways you could buy the toy car.

38¢

_____ pennies   _____ pennies

_____ nickels   _____ nickels

        or

_____ dimes   _____ dimes

_____ quarters   _____ quarters

Add or subtract.

7.
$$\begin{array}{r} 7¢ \\ + 3¢ \\ \hline ¢ \end{array}$$
$$\begin{array}{r} 18¢ \\ - 9¢ \\ \hline ¢ \end{array}$$
$$\begin{array}{r} 10¢ \\ - 5¢ \\ \hline ¢ \end{array}$$
$$\begin{array}{r} 4¢ \\ + 4¢ \\ \hline ¢ \end{array}$$
$$\begin{array}{r} 9¢ \\ - 3¢ \\ \hline ¢ \end{array}$$
$$\begin{array}{r} 10¢ \\ + 4¢ \\ \hline ¢ \end{array}$$

8.
$$\begin{array}{r} 6¢ \\ + 6¢ \\ \hline ¢ \end{array}$$
$$\begin{array}{r} 2¢ \\ + 5¢ \\ \hline ¢ \end{array}$$
$$\begin{array}{r} 7¢ \\ - 3¢ \\ \hline ¢ \end{array}$$
$$\begin{array}{r} 10¢ \\ + 8¢ \\ \hline ¢ \end{array}$$
$$\begin{array}{r} 6¢ \\ - 4¢ \\ \hline ¢ \end{array}$$
$$\begin{array}{r} 7¢ \\ + 8¢ \\ \hline ¢ \end{array}$$

1.

32¢	42¢	27¢	35¢
○	○	○	○

2.

○	○	○	○

3.
$$\begin{array}{r} 8¢ \\ + 7¢ \\ \hline \end{array}$$

1¢	15¢	16¢	NH
○	○	○	○

4.
$$\begin{array}{r} 12¢ \\ - 6¢ \\ \hline \end{array}$$

6¢	18¢	20¢	NH
○	○	○	○

5.
$$\begin{array}{r} 17¢ \\ - 9¢ \\ \hline \end{array}$$

8¢	9¢	10¢	NH
○	○	○	○

Oral Directions *Mark the correct answer. NH means "Not here." Mark it whenever the answer is not given.*

#1. How much money is there?

#2. Which coin shows the same amount?
#3–5. Add or subtract.

6.

7¢	17¢	27¢	22¢
○	○	○	○

7.

45¢	35¢	25¢	55¢
○	○	○	○

8.

36¢	30¢	26¢	20¢
○	○	○	○

9.

1¢	10¢	5¢	NH
○	○	○	○

Oral Directions *Mark the correct answer. NH means "Not here." Mark it whenever the answer is not given.*

#6. The price of the toy car is the total value of the coins shown. Mark the space under the amount that shows the price.

#7. Count the coins in each set. Which amount is more?
#8. Count the coins in each set. Which amount is less?
#9. You have two nickels. How much more money do you need to make twenty cents?

CHAPTER 10 Time and Probability

Diagnosing Readiness
for Chapter 10

1. What time is it? _____

Help the pigs count the wood.
Fill in the missing numbers.

2. I, _____, _____, 4, _____, 6, 7, _____, _____

3. Circle the third pig.

first

What happened first? What happened last?

4. Write I, 2, and 3 to show the order.

_____ _____ _____

To the Family

Looking Back	Chapter 10	Looking Ahead

Looking Back

In Kindergarten children learned the concept of time, order of events, and telling time to the hour.

Chapter 10

Time and Probability

In Chapter 10 children learn to tell time to the hour and half hour and use a calendar. Children also explore the concept of probability.

Looking Ahead

In Grade 2 children will learn to tell time to the quarter hour and to five-minute intervals.

Page 311 Your child solved problems that review math skills from previous chapters and will help your child with skills in Chapter 10.

Math at Home Help your child learn about the concept of time by making a schedule of your child's day and posting it on the refrigerator. Call your child's attention to the schedule and help him or her relate the time of scheduled activities to time on a clock.

Math Literature Read stories about time with your child. Look for the following books in your local library.

Tick-tock by James Dunbar (Lerner Publishing Group, 1998)

What's the Time? Benjamin Learns to Tell Time by Anne Leblanc, Inc. Staff Sterling Publishing Company (Sterling Publishing Company, 1997)

California Content Standards in Chapter 10 Lessons*

	Teach and Practice	Practice		Teach and Practice	Practice
Measurement and Geometry			**1.1**, Grade 3, Identify whether common events are certain, likely, unlikely, or improbable.	10	
1.2, Kindergarten, Demonstrate an understanding of concepts of time and tools that measure time.	8		**1.2** Represent and compare data by using pictures, bar graphs, tally charts, and picture graphs.	11	
1.2 Tell time to the nearest half hour and relate time to events.	1–7, 9		**Mathematical Reasoning**		
1.3, Kindergarten, Name the days of the week.		8	**1.0** Students make a decision about how to set up a problem.	7	
Statistics, Data Analysis, and Probability			**1.2** Use tools, such as manipulatives or sketches, to model problems.	11	10
1.0 Students organize, represent, and compare data by category on simple graphs and charts.	9		**2.0** Students solve problems and justify their reasoning.	7, 9	2, 4–6
1.1 Sort objects and data by common attributes and describe the categories.	11		**2.1** Explain the reasoning used and justify the procedures selected.		2, 11

* The symbol (🔑) indicates a key standard as designated in the Mathematics Framework for California Public Schools. Full statements of the California Content Standards are found at the beginning of this book following the Table of Contents.

Name_____ **Ordering Events**

What happened first? What happened last?

3   1   2

Write 1, 2, and 3 to show the order.

1.

_____   _____   _____

2.

_____   _____   _____

3.

_____   _____   _____

California Content Standards *Measurement and Geometry*
1.2 Tell time to the nearest half hour and relate time to events.

Look at the picture in the middle.
What comes before? What comes after?
Write the words.

4.

before   after

5.

_____   _____

6.

_____   _____

7.

_____   _____

Home Activity Discuss the events of the day with your child.
Help your child describe what happened first, next, and last.
Homework Workbook 10-1

Name_____ **Minutes**

What can you do in a minute?

I can count to 60.

I can tie my shoes.

Try each activity.
Can you do it in a minute?
Circle **yes** or **no**.

Word Bank

minute

1. Write your name 10 times.

yes   (no)

2. Say the alphabet.

yes   no

3. Write 1 to 100.

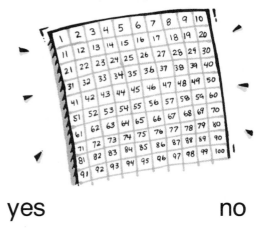

yes   no

4. Put on your coat.

yes   no

California Content Standards *Measurement and Geometry 1.2 Tell time to the nearest half hour and relate time to events. Also Mathemathical Reasoning 2.0, 2.1.*

three hundred fifteen **315**

Does each activity take more or less than a minute?
Circle more or less.

5. Eat lunch.

(more)   less

6. Brush your teeth.

more   less

7. Sharpen a pencil.

more   less

8. Read a book.

more   less

 Math Reasoning

9. Look at the activities on this page.
   Think about how long each one takes.
   Order them from shortest to longest.

10. What if the book were very short?
    Would your answer change? Explain.

Home Activity Ask your child to estimate how long a minute is. Use a clock with a second hand to show your child how accurate his or her estimate is. Homework Workbook 10-2

Name_____ **Minutes and Hours**

minutes

hours

About how long does each take?
Circle **minutes** or **hours**.

1. Get dressed.

(minutes)   hours

2. Watch a movie.

minutes   hours

3. Be at school.

minutes   hours

4. Set the table.

minutes   hours

California Content Standards *Measurement and Geometry*
1.2 Tell time to the nearest half hour and relate time to events.

5. Circle activities that take about an hour.

Eat a snack.

Play soccer.

Have a picnic.

Mow the lawn.

Paint a house.

Wash a car.

Walk the dog.

Mail a letter.

Home Activity Discuss with your child activities that take hours and activities that take minutes to complete. Homework Workbook 10-3

Name_____ **Hour and Minute Hands**

The hour hand points to the 5. The minute hand points to the 12.

hour ➤ 5

minute ➤ 12

___ o'clock

Word Bank

hour hand
minute hand
o'clock

Where do the hands point?
Write each time.

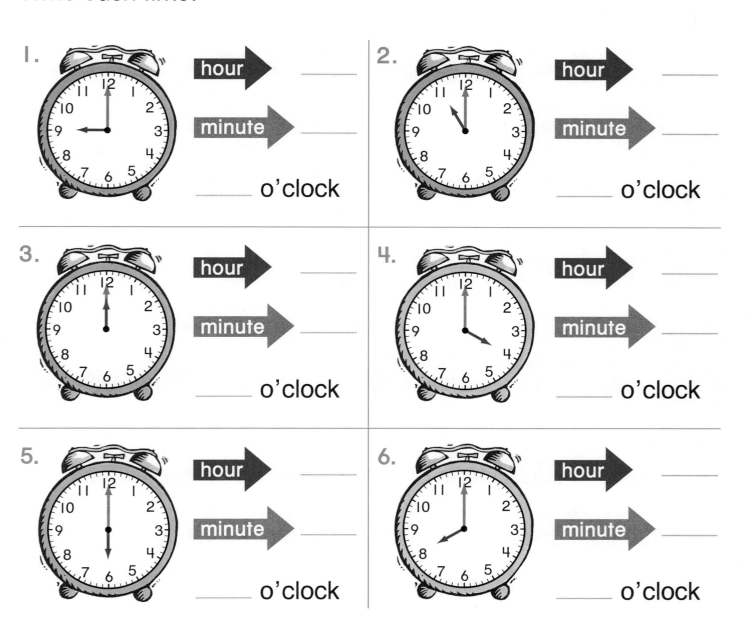

1.
hour ➤ ___
minute ➤ ___
___ o'clock

2.
hour ➤ ___
minute ➤ ___
___ o'clock

3.
hour ➤ ___
minute ➤ ___
___ o'clock

4.
hour ➤ ___
minute ➤ ___
___ o'clock

5.
hour ➤ ___
minute ➤ ___
___ o'clock

6.
hour ➤ ___
minute ➤ ___
___ o'clock

California Content Standards *Measurement and Geometry*
1.2 Tell time to the nearest half hour and relate time to events. Also
Mathematical Reasoning 2.0.

Write each time.

7.

_7_ o'clock

8.

_____ o'clock

9.

_____ o'clock

10.

_____ o'clock

11.

_____ o'clock

12.

_____ o'clock

 **Problem Solving**

Solve.

13. At school, lunch starts at 12 o'clock. It lasts 1 hour. What time does lunch end?

_____ o'clock

14. The soccer game began at 2 o'clock. It ended at 4 o'clock. How long was the game?

_____

Home Activity Ask your child to tell you the time at the next hour. What time will it be at the following hour? Homework Workbook 10-4

Name_____ **Time to the Hour**

5 o'clock

5:00

Draw the hour hand.
Write each time.

1.   3 o'clock

2.   6 o'clock

3.   8 o'clock

4.   1 o'clock

5.   11 o'clock

6.   12 o'clock

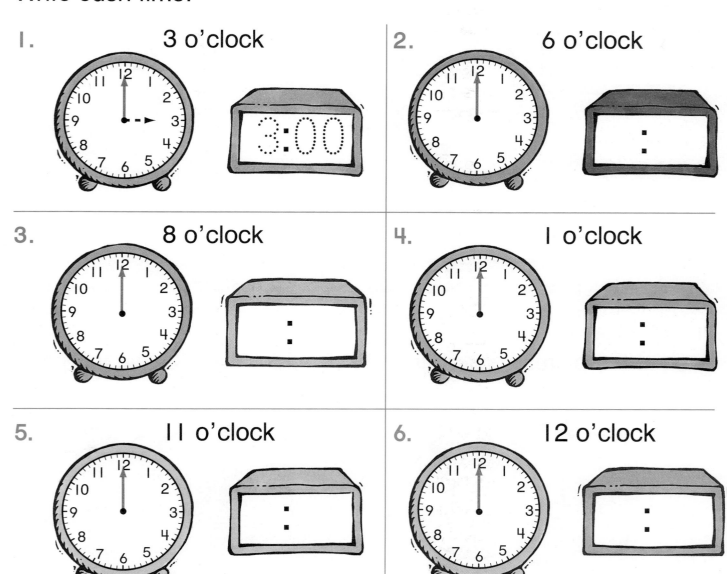

California Content Standards *Measurement and Geometry
1.2 Tell time to the nearest half hour and relate time to events.
Also Mathematical Reasoning 2.0.*

three hundred twenty-one   **321**

Write the time.
Draw the clock hands.

7.

5 o'clock

8.

_____ o'clock

9.

_____ o'clock

10.

_____ o'clock

 **Problem Solving**

Visual Thinking

Look at the picture. What time do you think it is? Circle the time.

11.

8:00   4:00

12.

7:00   12:00

322 three hundred twenty-two

Home Activity Help your child tell time on an analog clock and on a digital clock. Homework Workbook 10-5

Name_____

Diagnostic Checkpoint

1. Write **1**, **2**, and **3** to show the order.

_____ _____ _____

2. Does it take **more** or **less** than a minute? Circle.

more   less

3. Write the time.

┌─────┐
│ : │
└─────┘

Draw the clock hands. Write the time.

4. 2 o'clock

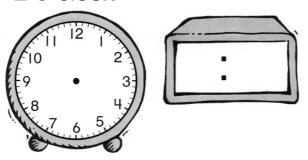

5. 11 o'clock

Write the time. Draw the clock hands.

6.

3:00

_____ o'clock

7.

8:00

_____ o'clock

three hundred twenty-three **323**

1. 15
    − 9
    ○ 14
    ○ 10
    ○ 6
    ○ 4

2. 10
    + 7
    ○ 17
    ○ 18
    ○ 3
    ○ 16

3. 16
    − 8
    ○ 7
    ○ 8
    ○ 12
    ○ 2

4. 8
    + 6
    ○ 14
    ○ 2
    ○ 15
    ○ 16

5. ○ 32, 34, 36, 38, 40
    ○ 32, 35, 38, 30, 45
    ○ 32, 38, 42, 46, 50
    ○ 32, 34, 40, 44, 48

6. ○ 4, 8, 12, 16, 20
    ○ 4, 6, 8, 10, 12
    ○ 4, 8, 16, 32, 64
    ○ 4, 5, 6, 7, 8

7. ○ 15, 20, 25, 35, 45
    ○ 15, 20, 25, 30, 35
    ○ 15, 25, 35, 45, 50
    ○ 15, 17, 19, 21, 23

8. ○ 43, 53, 63, 73, 83
    ○ 10, 20, 40, 80, 100
    ○ 10, 15, 20, 25, 30
    ○ 20, 30, 60, 70, 100

9. 15 − ☐ = 7

    2   9   12   8
    ○   ○   ○   ○

10. 7 + 6 = ☐

    13   1   14   12
    ○   ○   ○   ○

Oral Directions *Mark the correct answer. NH means "Not here." Mark it whenever the answer is not given.*

#1–4. Add or subtract. Mark the correct answer.

#5–6. Mark the pattern that shows counting by twos.
#7. Mark the pattern that shows counting by fives.
#8. Mark the pattern that shows counting by tens.
#9–10. Mark the missing number that makes the number sentence true.

324 three hundred twenty-four

Name_____ **Time to the Half-Hour**

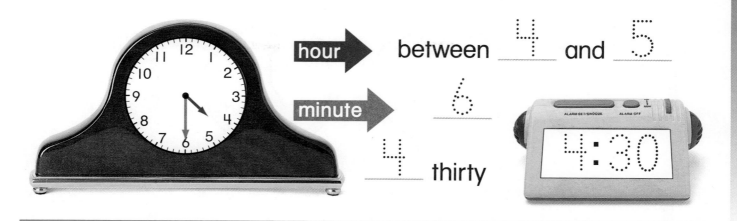

between __4__ and __5__

minute → __6__

__4__ thirty

4:30

Where do the hands point?
Tell and write each time.

1.

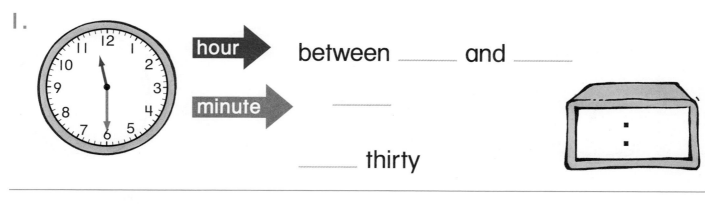

hour → between _____ and _____

minute → _____

_____ thirty

2.

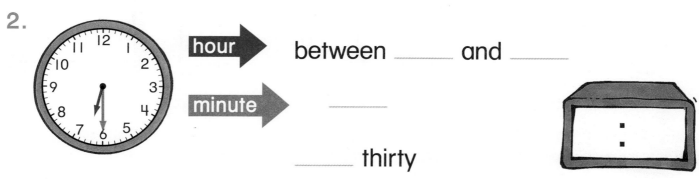

hour → between _____ and _____

minute → _____

_____ thirty

3.

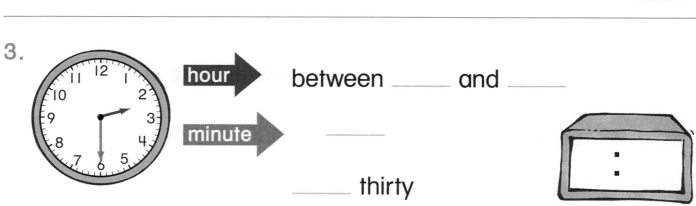

hour → between _____ and _____

minute → _____

_____ thirty

California Content Standards *Measurement and Geometry*
1.2 Tell time to the nearest half hour and relate time to events. Also
Mathematical Reasoning 2.0.

three hundred twenty-five **325**

Write the time.

4.

5.

6.

7.

6:30

8.

9.

10.

11.

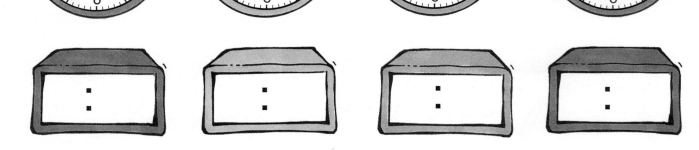

Problem Solving

Solve.

12. I am meeting Steve at 10:30. I get there at 10:00. Steve is not there. Am I late or early? Explain.

13. I wake up at 7:00. I go to sleep at 7:00. Could this be true? Explain.

326 three hundred twenty-six

Home Activity Ask your child where the hour hand and minute hand point at 2:30, 5:30, 7:30, and 10:30. Homework Workbook 10-6

Name_____

Soo Lin starts dance class at 3:00.
She has class for 1 hour.
What time will dance class be over?

> When an hour goes by, the hour hand moves to the next number.

Understand

You need to find what time it will be
1 hour after 3:00.

Plan

You can draw a clock to find the time.

Solve

Draw a clock with the starting time.
Then draw the hour hand 1 hour later.

1 hour later

Look Back

How does drawing a clock with the
time help you?

What time will it be?
Draw the clock hands for the starting and ending times.
Write the ending time.

Start	How long?	What time will it be?
I. 11:00	The men paint for 2 hours.	1:00

California Content Standards *Measurement and Geometry*
1.2 Tell time to the nearest half hour and relate time to events.
Mathematical Reasoning, 1.0, 2.0.

three hundred twenty-seven **327**

What time will it be?
Draw the clock hands for the starting and ending times.
Write the ending time.

Start	How long?	What time will it be?
2. 1:00	Benito bakes for 3 hours.	
3. 3:30	Tom works for 2 hours.	
4. 10:00	Vicki rides for 1 hour.	
5. 4:00	They eat for 30 minutes.	

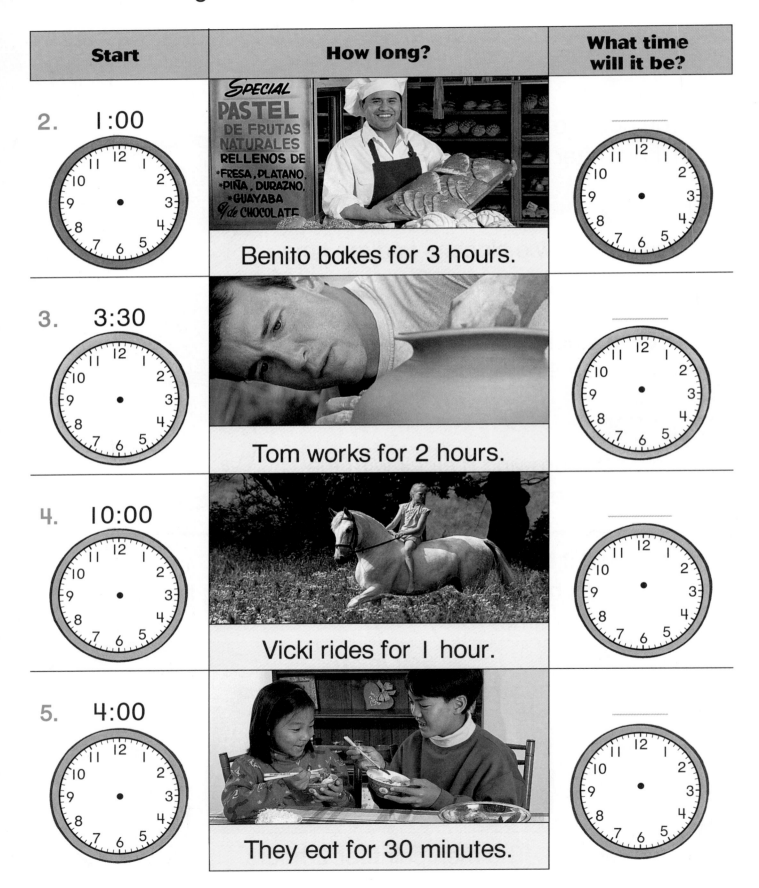

Home Activity Have your child write down the start and stop time for an activity he or she has done. Ask how long the activity took. Homework Workbook 10-7

Name_____ **Using a Calendar**

July

Sunday	Monday	Tuesday	Wednesday	Thursday	Friday	Saturday
	1	2	3	4	5	6
7	8	9	10	11	12	13
14	15	16	17	18	19	20
21	22	23	24	25	26	27
28	29	30	31			

Word Bank

calendar

Use the calendar above.

1. How many days are in a week? _____

2. How many days are in this month? _____

3. How many Thursdays are in this month? _____

4. How many Mondays are in this month? _____

5. What is the date of the third Saturday? _____

6. On what day is July 19? _____

7. On what day does this month end? _____

California Content Standards *Measurement and Geometry 1.2, Kindergarten, Demonstrate an understanding of concepts of time and tools that measure time. Also Measurement and Geometry 1.3, Kindergarten.*

three hundred twenty-nine **329**

Sunday	Monday	Tuesday	Wednesday	Thursday	Friday	Saturday

Create a calendar for this month.
Use your calendar to answer each question.

8. On what day of the week does this month start? _____

9. What is the date of the first Tuesday? _____

10. What is today's date? _____

11. What date is tomorrow? _____

12. What date was yesterday? _____

330 three hundred thirty

Home Activity Show your child a calendar for the present month. Discuss the days that various dates fall on. Have your child mark family birthdays, holidays, or events. Homework Workbook 10-8

Name_____

Morning Schedule

Time	Subject
9:00	Reading
10:00	Math
11:00	Lunch
11:30	Recess

Use the schedule.
Circle the correct activity for each time.
Think: The schedule tells when each activity starts.

1.

 Reading   Math    Lunch

2.

 Lunch   Reading   Recess

3.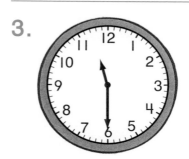

 Recess   Lunch    Math

California Content Standards *Measurement and Geometry*
1.2 Tell time to the nearest half hour and relate time to events.
Mathematical Reasoning 2.0. Statistics, Data Analysis, and
Probability 1.0.

three hundred thirty-one **331**

Billy's After-School Schedule

Time	Event
3:00	Leave school.
3:30	Have a snack.
4:00	Play.
5:30	Eat dinner.

Use the schedule. Solve.

4. What does Billy do at 4:00?

_____

5. What time does Billy eat dinner?

_____

6. Does Billy have a snack before or after he plays?

_____

7. What does Billy do before having a snack?

_____

8. What do you think Billy does after dinner?

_____

Home Activity Have your child make a schedule of his or her day. Read the schedule together and discuss the day's events. Homework Workbook 10-9

Name_____ **Probability**

Use a counter like the one above.
Toss it a few times.
Will the counter land as shown?
Circle **certain**, **impossible**, or **maybe**.

1.	●	certain	impossible	⟨maybe⟩
2.	●	certain	impossible	maybe
3.	●	certain	impossible	maybe
4.	● or ●	certain	impossible	maybe
5.	● or ●	certain	impossible	maybe

California Content Standards *Statistics, Data Analysis, and Probability 1.1, Grade 3, Identify whether common events are certain, likely, unlikely, or improbable. Also Mathematical Reasoning 1.2.*

Will it happen?
Mark **certain**, **impossible**, or **maybe**.

6. 
It will rain tomorrow.

☐ certain
☐ impossible
☐ maybe

7. 
A dog will talk.

☐ certain
☐ impossible
☐ maybe

8. 
I will get mail today.

☐ certain
☐ impossible
☐ maybe

9. 
A cat will fly.

☐ certain
☐ impossible
☐ maybe

10. 
A kangaroo will hop.

☐ certain
☐ impossible
☐ maybe

334 three hundred thirty-four

Home Activity Ask your child to think about some events that definitely happen (certain), some events that cannot happen (impossible), and some events that might happen (maybe).
Homework Workbook 10-10

Name_____

Where do the hands point?
Tell and write each time.

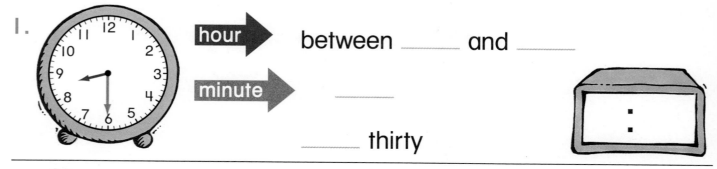

1.   hour ➡ between _____ and _____

minute ➡ _____

_____ thirty

June

Sunday	Monday	Tuesday
1	2	3
8	9	10

2. What is the date of the second Sunday? _____

3. On what day is June 2?

_____

What time will it be?
Draw the clock hands for the starting and ending times.
Write the ending time.

Start	How long?	What time will it be?
4. 10:00	Zach naps for 2 hours.	_____

Will it happen? Circle **certain**, **impossible**, or **maybe**.

5.    A fish will play ball.

certain   maybe

impossible

1.   81 > 53   27 = 19   39 < 41   77 > 71
     ○   ○   ○   ○

2.

     ○   ○   ○   ○

3.

first

     ○   ○   ○   ○

4.
     ○   ○   ○   ○

5.

     ○   ○   ○   ○

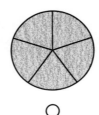 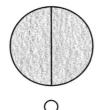 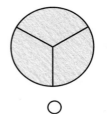 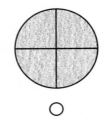

Oral Directions *Mark the correct answer. NH means "Not here." Mark it whenever the answer is not given.*

#1. Mark the statement that is not true.
#2. Count the money. Mark the item you can buy using the money shown.

#3. Mark the train car that is fourth in line.
#4. Mark the circle that shows four equal parts.
#5. Ben has three balloons. Joy has four more balloons than Ben. Mark the picture that shows how many balloons Joy has.

338 three hundred thirty-eight

1. Write **1**, **2**, and **3** to show the order.

_____ _____ _____

About how long does each take?
Circle minutes or hours.

2. Brush your teeth.

minutes   hours

3. Play baseball.

minutes   hours

Where do the hands point?
Write each time.

4.  hour ▶ _____
   minute ▶ _____

   _____ o'clock

5.  hour ▶ _____
   minute ▶ _____

   _____ o'clock

Where do the hands point?
Write the time.

6.  hour ▶ between _____ and _____
   minute ▶ _____

   _____ thirty

Use the calendar.

7. On what day is May 10?

_____

8. What is the date of the first
   Wednesday of May?

   _____

	May	
Sunday	Monday	Tuesday
1	2	3
8	9	10

Use the schedule.
Circle the correct activity for the time.

9.  Games   Swimming   Lunch

Camp Schedule

Time	Activity
10:00	Swimming
11:00	Crafts
12:00	Lunch
1:00	Games

Will it happen? Circle **certain**, **impossible**, or **maybe**.

10. A lion will read a book.

   certain   maybe   impossible

11. Lea will catch the ball.

   certain   maybe   impossible

What time will it be?
Draw the clock hands for the starting and ending times.
Write the ending time.

Start	How long?	What time will it be?
12. 2:00	Sam rides for 2 hours.	

1.   get on the bus   put on your coat   wake up   eat lunch
     ○   ○   ○   ○

2.   read a book   paint a fence   brush your teeth   make a kite
     ○   ○   ○   ○

3.   go to the zoo   eat an apple   wash your hands   make the bed
     ○   ○   ○   ○

4.

     ○   ○   ○   ○

5.

     ○   ○   ○   ○

6.
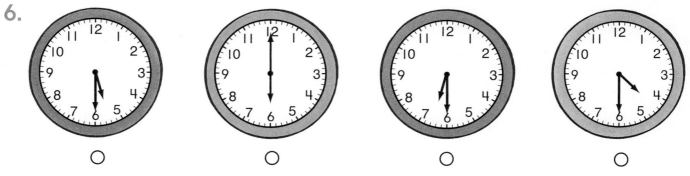
     ○   ○   ○   ○

Oral Directions *Mark the correct answer. NH means "Not here." Mark it whenever the answer is not given.*

#1. Mark the activity that happens first on a school day.
#2. Mark the activity that takes minutes.

#3. Mark the activity that takes hours.
#4. Mark the clock that shows seven o'clock.
#5. Mark the clock that shows eleven thirty.
#6. Mark the clock that shows five thirty.

7.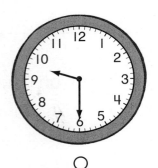

○   ○   ○   ○

April

Sunday	Monday	Tuesday	Wednesday	Thursday	Friday	Saturday
	1	2	3	4	5	6
7	8	9	10	11	12	13

8. Monday   Tuesday   Friday   NH
         ○   ○   ○   ○

9. Monday   Sunday   Friday   NH
         ○   ○   ○   ○

10.

Time	Activity
1:00	Basketball
2:00	Soccer
3:00	Baseball
4:30	Tennis

1:00   2:00   4:30   NH
 ○   ○   ○   ○

11. ○ A tiger will sing.

○ It will be warm today.

○ A fish will drive a car.

○ You will find a gold egg.

Oral Directions *Mark the correct answer. NH means "Not here." Mark it whenever the answer is not given.*

#7. Kim begins to read at nine o'clock. She reads for thirty minutes. What time does she finish?

#8. On what day is April 13?
#9. On what day of the week does this month start?
#10. Mark the time for tennis.
#11. Mark the activity that may happen.

Diagnosing Readiness
for Chapter 11

Circle each answer.

1. Which is the longer object?

2. Which holds more?

3. Who is heavier?

4. Which is the taller plant?

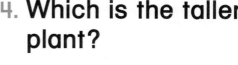

To the Family

Looking Back	Chapter 11	Looking Ahead
Children compared and ordered the length, weight, and capacity of objects in Kindergarten.	**Measurement** Children compare the length, weight, and capacity of objects and measure with nonstandard units. They also become familiar with measurement terms and concepts.	In Grade 2 children will estimate and measure length, weight, and capacity using standard units.

Page 343 Your child solved problems that review math skills from previous chapters and will help your child with the skills in Chapter 11.

Math at Home Provide several empty containers and have your child estimate how many 8-oz cups of water each container will hold. Then use a measuring cup to see how much water is needed to fill each container. Compare the containers with the actual amounts.

Math Literature To read more about measurement with your child, look for these books in your local library.
The Carrot Seed by Ruth Krauss (Harper Trophy, 2000)
How Big Is a Foot? By Rolf Myller (Young Yearling, 1991)

California Content Standards in Chapter 11 Lessons*

	Teach and Practice	Practice		Teach and Practice	Practice
Number Sense			1.3 (🔑) (Gr. 2) Measure the length of an object to the nearest inch and/or centimeter.	3,4	
6.1 (Gr. 2) Recognize when an estimate is reasonable in measurements (e.g. closest inch).	4	3, 10	**Mathematical Reasoning**		
Measurement and Geometry			1.2 Use tools such as manipulatives or sketches, to model problems.		2–6, 10
1.0 Use direct comparison and nonstandard units to describe the measurements of objects.	7, 12		2.0 Solve problems and justify their reasoning.	11	1, 2, 5, 7–9
1.1 Compare the length, weight, and volume of two or more objects by using direct comparison or a nonstandard unit.	1, 2, 5, 6, 8–10		2.1 Explain the reasoning used and justify the procedures selected.		1, 2, 5, 7–9, 11
1.1 (Gr. 2) Measure the length of objects by iterating (repeating) a nonstandard or standard unit.	3		3.0 Note connections between one problem and another.	2	
1.1 (Gr. 3) Choose the appropriate tools and units (metric and U.S.) and estimate the length, liquid volume, and weight/mass of given objects.	11				

* The symbol (🔑) indicates a key standard as designated in the Mathematics Framework for California Public Schools.
Full statements of the California Content Standards are found at the beginning of this book following the Table of Contents.

Name_____

Understanding Length and Height

Are you shorter or taller than the real object? Compare to find out. Circle **shorter** or **taller**.

Word Bank
shorter
taller
longer

1.  shorter (taller)
trash can

2.  shorter taller
door

3.  shorter taller
closet

4.  shorter taller
desk

5.  shorter taller
watering can

6.  shorter taller
bookshelf

California Content Standards Measurement and Geometry 1.1 Compare the length of two or more objects. Also Mathematical Reasoning 2.0, 2.1.

Circle the longer object.
Put an X on the shorter object.

7.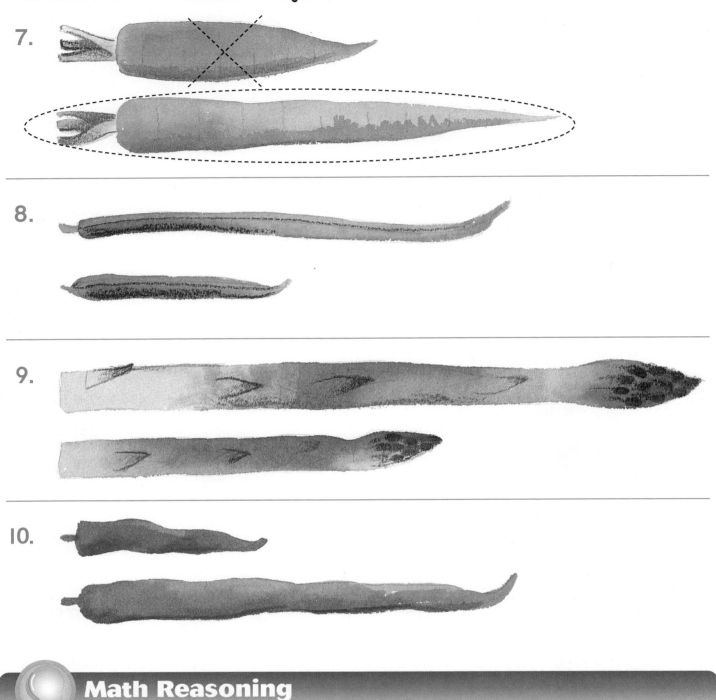

8.

9.

10.

Math Reasoning

11. Look at all the objects on this page.
Which one is the longest?
Tell how you know.

 Home Activity Have your child compare the lengths and heights of objects at home, using the words "shorter," "longer," and "taller." Homework Workbook 11-1

Name_____

Problem-Solving Strategy

Make a List

Do you use more cubes or more paper clips to measure the worm?

Understand

You need to find out how many cubes and how many paper clips fit along the length of the worm.

Plan

Measure by lining up the cubes under the worm. Then measure using paper clips. Make a list to record the results.

Solve

I used more cubes than paper clips to measure the worm.

Worm:
about 4 cubes
about 3 clips

Look Back

Why did I use more cubes than paper clips?

1. About how long is the bug? Measure with cubes and paper clips.

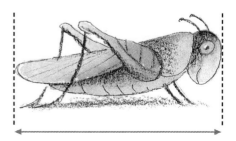

Bug:

about _____ cubes

about _____ clips

California Content Standards *Measurement and Geometry 1.1 Compare the length of two or more objects by using direct comparison or a nonstandard unit. Mathematical Reasoning 3.0. Also Mathematical Reasoning 1.2, 2.0, 2.1.*

How wide is your chair?
Use straws, paper clips, and cubes
to measure. Make a list to record
the results.

2. How wide?

How wide?	
about _____	straws
about _____	clips
about _____	cubes

3. How tall?

How tall?	
about _____	straws
about _____	clips
about _____	cubes

4. Choose an object from your
classroom. Measure using straws,
paper clips, and cubes.
Make a list to record your results.

about _____	straws
about _____	clips
about _____	cubes

5. Did you use more straws, clips, or cubes to measure?
Why do you think that happened?

_____

_____

Home Activity Ask your child to measure the lengths of
objects at home using pennies, paper clips, or spoons placed
end to end. Record the measurements in a list. Discuss the
results. Homework Workbook 11-2

Name_____Inches

The crayon is about 3 paper clips long.
It is about 4 cubes long.
It is about 3 inches long.

Word Bank
inch

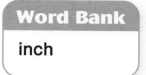

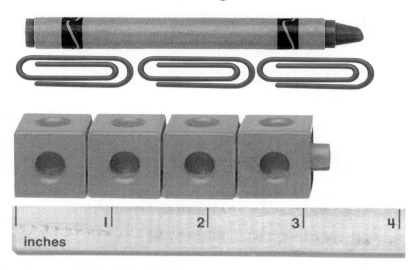

About how long is the real object?
Use cubes and paper clips to measure.
Then use an inch ruler.

1. book

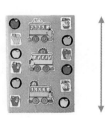

about _____ cubes

about _____ clips

about _____ inches

---

2. eraser

about _____ cubes

about _____ clips

about _____ inches

---

3. marker

about _____ cubes

about _____ clips

about _____ inches

California Content Standards *Measurement and Geometry 1.1, Grade 2, Measure the length of objects by iterating a nonstandard unit. Measurement and Geometry 1.3 (🔑), Grade 2, Also, Number Sense 6.1, Grade 2, Mathematical Reasoning 1.2.*

Use cubes and an inch ruler to measure.
Write how long or tall.

4.

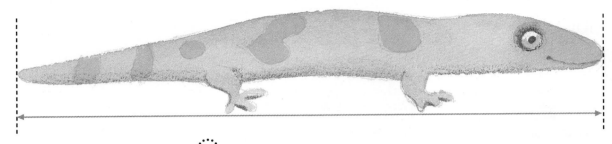

about ⬚8⬚ cubes long

about ⬚6⬚ inches long

5.

about _____ cubes tall

about _____ inches tall

6.

about _____ cubes tall

about _____ inches tall

7.

about _____ cubes long

about _____ inches long

Home Activity Have your child use pennies or paper clips to measure the length of items at home, such as spoons, toys, pencils, or books. Then measure using a ruler. Homework Workbook 11-3

Name_____ **Centimeters**

About how long is the mouse's tail?

I centimeter

Work with a partner.
Use a centimeter ruler to measure.

1. **Your ear**

   about _____

   centimeters

2. **Your thumb**

   about _____

   centimeters

3. **Your hand**

   about _____

   centimeters

4. **Your forearm**

   about _____

   centimeters

5. **Your foot**

   about _____

   centimeters

 California Content Standards *Measurement and Geometry
1.3 (🔑), Grade 2, Measure the length of an object to the nearest
centimeter. Number Sense 6.1, Grade 2. Also Mathematical
Reasoning 1.2.*

Use a centimeter ruler to measure.

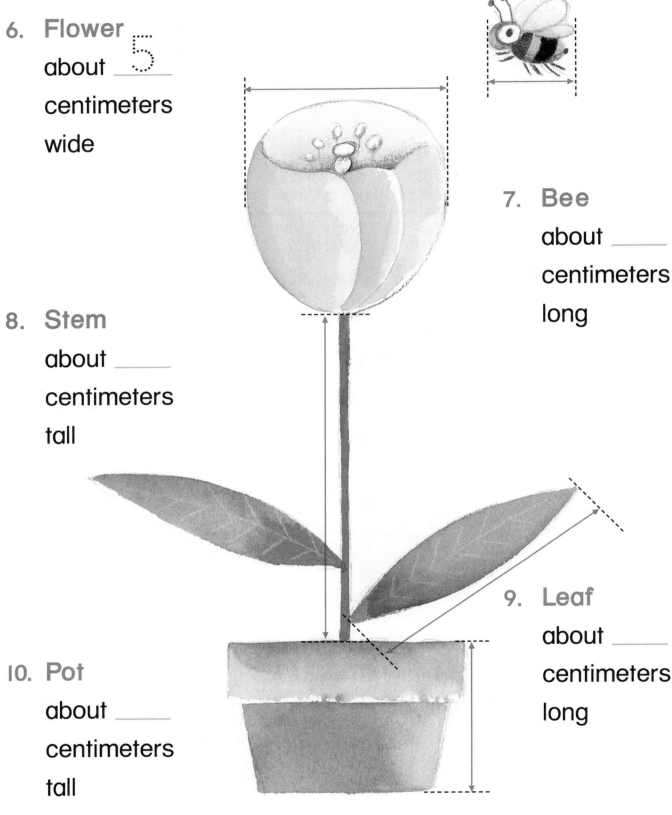

6. **Flower**

about ⁙5⁙

centimeters

wide

7. **Bee**

about _____

centimeters

long

8. **Stem**

about _____

centimeters

tall

9. **Leaf**

about _____

centimeters

long

10. **Pot**

about _____

centimeters

tall

Home Activity Have your child find things at home that are about 10 centimeters long. Help your child check the measurements with a centimeter ruler. Homework Workbook 11-4

Name_____ **Weight**

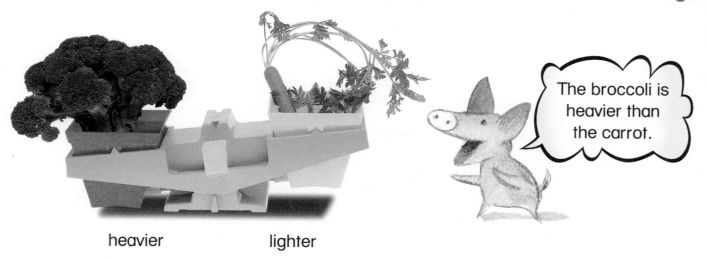

heavier   lighter

The broccoli is heavier than the carrot.

Which object is heavier?
Use a scale and real objects.
Circle the heavier object.

1.

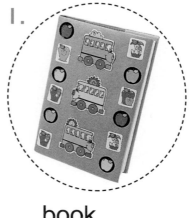   

book   tape

2.

ruler   crayons

3.

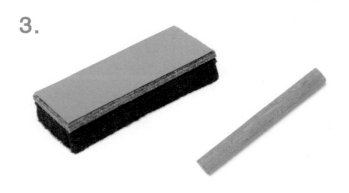

eraser   chalk

4.

calculator   paint

California Content Standards *Measurement and Geometry 1.1 Compare the weight of two or more objects by using direct comparison or a nonstandard unit. Also Mathematical Reasoning 1.2, 2.0, 2.1.*

three hundred fifty-three **353**

Circle the one that is lighter.

5.

6.

7.

8.

Math Reasoning

9. Is something big always heavier than something small? Explain.

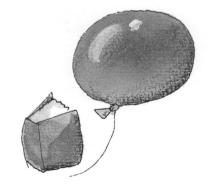

_____

_____

Home Activity Encourage your child to pick up different objects in each hand and tell which is heavier and which is lighter. Homework Workbook 11-5

Name_____ **Pounds**

less than 1 pound

about 1 pound

more than 1 pound

Does each weigh **more** or **less** than 1 pound?
Circle **more** or **less**.

Word Bank

pound

1. pencil

more

(less)

2. backpack

more

less

3. chalk

more

less

4. globe

more

less

California Content Standards *Measurement and Geometry 1.1 Compare the weight of two or more objects by using direct comparison or a nonstandard unit. Also Mathematical Reasoning 1.2.*

three hundred fifty-five **355**

5. Circle the things that weigh
   less than 1 pound.
   Put an X on things that weigh
   more than 1 pound.

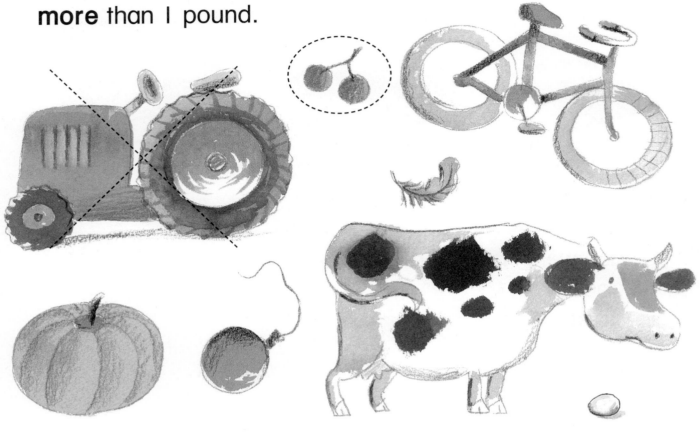

6. Find objects in your classroom.
   Do they weigh **more** or **less** than 1 pound?

more	less
	pencil

356 three hundred fifty-six

Home Activity Help your child find food products in your home that are less than, more than, and about 1 pound.
Homework Workbook 11-6

Name_____ **Kilograms**

less than 1 kilogram   about 1 kilogram   more than 1 kilogram

Does each thing measure **more** or **less** than 1 kilogram?
Circle **more** or **less**.

Word Bank

kilogram

1. plant

more

(less)

2. 3 books

more

less

3. folder

more

less

4. shoe

more

less

California Content Standards *Measurement and Geometry 1.0 Students use direct comparison and nonstandard units to describe the measurements of objects. Also Mathematical Reasoning 2.0, 2.1.*

three hundred fifty-seven **357**

Circle the things that measure
more than 1 kilogram.

5.

Problem Solving

Solve.

6. Tara's pet measures 2 kilograms.
   Ricardo's pet measures 3 kilograms.
   Color Ricardo's pet. Tell how you know.

358 three hundred fifty-eight

🏠 **Home Activity** Practice measuring 1-kilogram amounts
(about 2.2 pounds) of dry materials, such as beans, pebbles, or
marbles, on a household scale. Homework Workbook 11-7

Name_____

1. Circle the longer object.

2. Use cubes and an inch ruler to measure. Write how long.

about _____ cubes

about _____ inches

3. Circle the animals that weigh less than 1 pound.

4. Circle the heavier object.

5. Circle the lighter object.

Name_____

1.

15 ◯ 16

>	<	=	NH
◯	◯	◯	◯

2.

90 ◯ 89

>	<	=	NH
◯	◯	◯	◯

3.

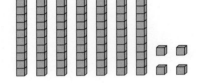

75	47	74	NH
◯	◯	◯	◯

4.

59

58	60	69	49
◯	◯	◯	◯

5.

59

60	69	49	58
◯	◯	◯	◯

6.

16 − 7 = ☐

7 + 9 = 16	7 + 8 = 15	16 − 9 = 7	NH
◯	◯	◯	◯

7.

18  9

18 − 9 = 9	18 + 9 = 27	9 − 9 = 0	NH
◯	◯	◯	◯

Oral Directions *Mark the correct answer. NH means "Not here." Mark it whenever the answer is not given.*

#1–2. Mark the symbol that makes the statement true.
#3. Which number tells how many?

#4. Which number is one more than the number in the circle?
#5. Which number is ten less than the number in the circle?
#6. Mark the addition fact you could use to help you subtract sixteen minus seven.
#7. Molly has eighteen crayons. She lost nine of them. Mark the number sentence that tells how many are left.

Name_____ **Capacity**

Some things hold **more**.   ## Some things hold **less**.

more

less

Circle the container that holds more.

1.

2.

3.

4.

5.

6.

California Content Standards *Measurement and Geometry 1.1 Compare the volume of two or more objects by using direct comparison or a nonstandard unit. Also Mathematical Reasoning 2.0, 2.1.*

three hundred sixty-one **361**

Circle the container that holds the most.
Order the containers from most to least.

7.

2

1

3

8.

___

___

___

9.

___

___

___

 Math Reasoning

Estimation

10. You can fill the smaller can
with 10 cubes.
About how many cubes do you
think would fill the bigger can?
Tell why you think as you do.

🏠 **Home Activity** Give your child pairs of empty household
containers. Ask your child to identify which container holds
more and which holds less. Use water to check if your child's
answers are correct. Homework Workbook 11-8

Name_____

Cups, Pints, and Quarts

2 cups fill 1 pint.   2 pints fill 1 quart.

How many can you fill?
Circle to show how many.

Word Bank
cup
pint
quart

1.    

2.    

3.    

4.    

California Content Standards *Measurement and Geometry 1.1 Compare the volume of two or more objects by using direct comparison or a nonstandard unit. Also Mathematical Reasoning 2.0, 2.1.*

Remember,
2 cups fill 1 pint.
2 pints fill 1 quart.

Circle the two that hold the same amount.

5.

6.

7.

Problem Solving

8. Is there enough juice to make the fruit punch?
   Circle **yes** or **no.**
   Tell why or why not.

Fruit Punch

1 cup orange juice

1 quart pineapple juice

1 pint cranberry juice

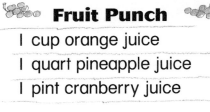

yes   no

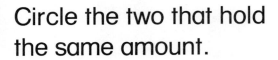

Home Activity On a trip to the grocery store, have your child identify containers and compare the quantities each holds.
Homework Workbook 11-9

Name_____ **Liters**

less than 1 liter

1 liter

more than 1 liter

1. Circle the things that hold more than 1 liter.

Word Bank

liter

California Content Standards *Measurement and Geometry 1.1 Compare the volume of two or more objects by using direct comparison or a nonstandard unit. Also Number Sense 6.1, Grade 2, Mathematical Reasoning 1.2.*

2. Circle the things that hold less than 1 liter.

I liter

Problem Solving

Estimation

Solve.

3. Each jar holds 4 liters.
About how many more liters do
you need to fill each jar?

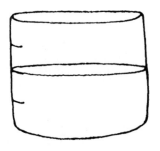 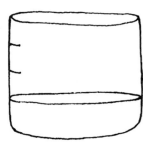 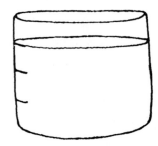

about ____ liters   about ____ liters   about ____ liters

366 three hundred sixty-six

 Home Activity Display a 1-liter bottle at home and help your child find containers that hold more than, less than, and about 1 liter. Homework Workbook 11-10

Name_____

Use the right tool to measure.
Think: What do you need to find out?

How long is it?   How much does it hold?   How heavy is it?

Circle the tool you would use.

1. How long is it?

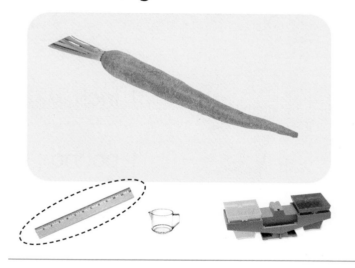

2. How heavy is it?

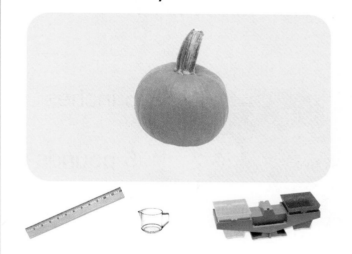

3. How much does it hold?

4. How tall is it?

California Content Standards *Measurement and Geometry 1.1, Grade 3, Choose the appropriate tools and units and estimate the length, liquid volume, and weight/mass of given objects. Mathematical Reasoning 2.0. Also Mathematical Reasoning 2.1.*

Circle the correct measurement.
Tell why you think as you do.

5. How long is it?

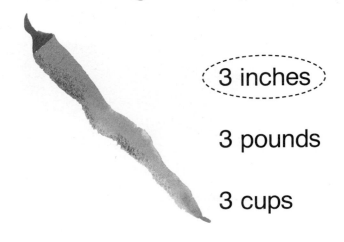

(3 inches)

3 pounds

3 cups

6. How much does it hold?

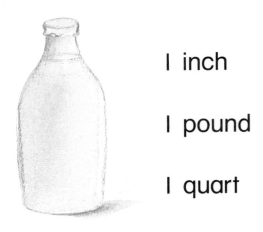

1 inch

1 pound

1 quart

7. How heavy is it?

5 inches

5 pounds

5 pints

8. How much does it hold?

1 inch

1 pound

1 cup

9. How tall is it?

2 inches

2 pounds

2 cups

10. How heavy is it?

4 inches

4 pounds

4 cups

Home Activity Ask your child to name things in your home that can be measured with a ruler, a measuring cup, and a scale. Homework Workbook 11-11

Name_____ **Temperature**

A thermometer measures the **temperature.**

Circle the thermometer that
shows a colder temperature.

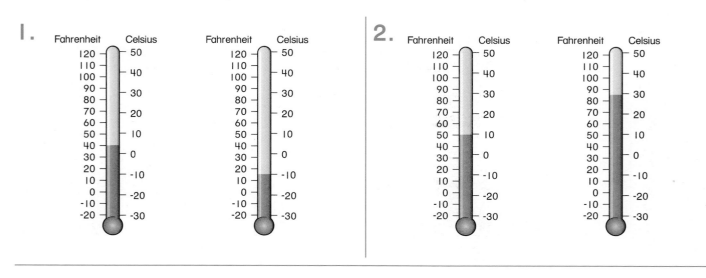

1.

2.

Circle the thermometer that
shows a hotter temperature.

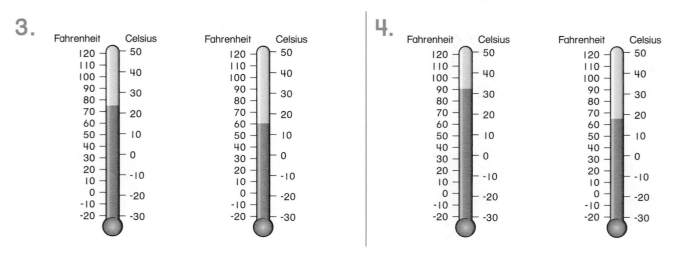

3.

4.

California Content Standards *Measurement and Geometry*
1.0 Students use direct comparison and nonstandard units to
describe the measurement of objects.

Draw a line from the thermometer to the correct picture.

5.

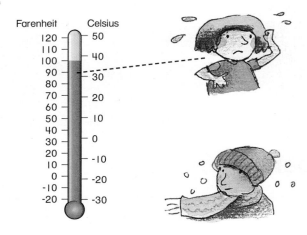

6.

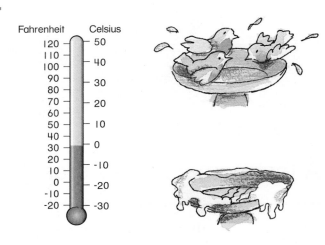

7.

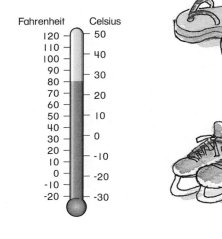

8.

9.

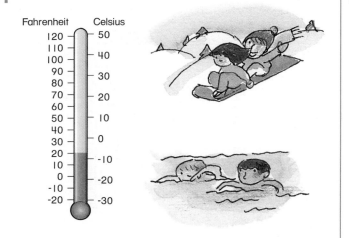

10.

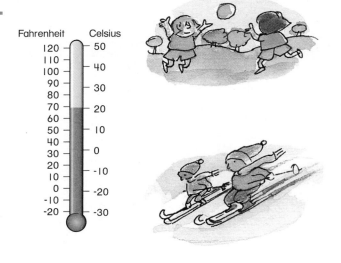

Home Activity Help your child record the temperature at different times of the day or at the same time on different days.
Homework Workbook 11-12

Name_____

Circle the container that holds the most.
Order the containers from most to least.

1.

_____   _____   _____

Circle the containers that hold less than 1 liter.

2.

How long is it?
Circle the tool you would use.

3.

Circle the thermometer that shows a colder temperature.

4.
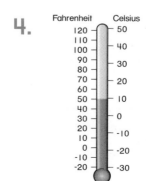   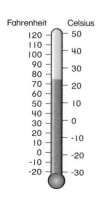   5.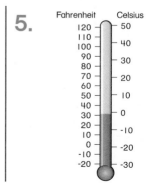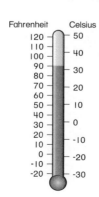

Name_____

1.

7:30   8:30   8:00   9:30

○   ○   ○   ○

2.      

           ○   ○   ○   ○

3.

Pets We Own

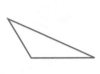

birds	dogs	cats	fish
꞉꞉꞉꞉	꞉꞉꞉꞉꞉꞉	꞉꞉꞉꞉	꞉꞉

birds   dogs   cats   fish

○   ○   ○   ○

4.

○   ○   ○   ○

5.

○   ○   ○   ○

Oral Directions *Mark the correct answer. NH means "Not here." Mark it whenever the answer is not given.*

#1. Mark the time.
#2. Mark the matching shape.

#3. Look at the chart. It tells the kind of pets children have. What kind of pet do most children have?
#4. Which flower is above the square rectangle?
#5. Mark the item that holds the most.

1. Circle the longer bug.

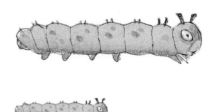

2. Circle the thermometer that shows the colder temperature.

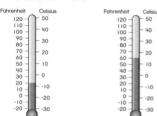

3. Circle the container that holds more.

4. Circle the container that holds more than 1 liter.

5. Does it weigh more or less than 1 pound?
Circle **more** or **less.**

more   **less**

6. Does it measure more or less than 1 kilogram?
Circle **more** or **less.**

more   **less**

7. How much does it hold?
Circle the tool you would use.

8. Circle the lighter object.

9. How many cups can you fill with ?

10. Measure the crayon with paper clips, cubes, and with an inch ruler. Complete the list.

Crayon		
about _____	clips
about _____	cubes
about _____	inches

11. About how long is this pen? Use cubes to measure. Then use a centimeter ruler to measure.

about _____ cubes   about _____ centimeters

374 three hundred seventy-four

1.

○   ○   ○   ○

2.

2 clips   **7 cubes**   **4 cubes**   **10 clips**

○   ○   ○   ○

3.

6 cubes   **5 cubes**   **4 cubes**   **3 cubes**

○   ○   ○   ○

4.

4 inches   **4 pounds**   **4 cups**   **4 cubes**

○   ○   ○   ○

5.

○   ○   ○   ○

Oral Directions *Mark the correct answer. NH means "Not here." Mark it whenever the answer is not given.*

#1. Mark under the item that is taller than you.
#2. Mark under the measurement that is correct.

#3. About how many cubes long is the ribbon?
#4. How heavy are the books? Mark the correct measurement.
#5. Mark under the answer that holds the same amount as one quart.

6.

○   ○   ○   ○

7.

○   ○   ○   ○

8.

○   ○   ○   ○

9.

○   ○   ○   ○

10.

4 centimeters
○

3 centimeters
○

2 centimeters
○

1 centimeter
○

Oral Directions *Mark the correct answer. NH means "Not here." Mark it whenever the answer is not given.*

#6. Which object is the heaviest?

#7. Mark under the item that holds the least.
#8. Mark under the object that weighs more than one pound.
#9. Which container holds more than one liter?
#10. About how many centimeters tall is the plant and the flower pot?

CHAPTER 12
Two-Digit Addition and Subtraction

Diagnosing Readiness
for Chapter 12

Write the missing numbers.

1. $10 + 4 = $ _____

2. $9 + 9 = $ _____

3. $13 - 6 = $ _____

4. $8 - 0 = $ _____

17
8 9

5. _____ $+$ _____ $=$ _____

_____ $+$ _____ $=$ _____

_____ $-$ _____ $=$ _____

_____ $-$ _____ $=$ _____

To the Family

Looking Back	Chapter 12	Looking Ahead
In Chapters 2, 3, 4, 7, and 8 children learned addition and subtraction facts to 20 and learned addition and subtraction strategies.	**Two-Digit Addition and Subtraction** Children learn to add and subtract two-digit numbers with regrouping. Also, they are introduced to rounding numbers and estimating to check answers.	In Grade 2 children add and subtract two- and three-digit numbers with regrouping and apply their knowledge of addition and subtraction when learning multiplication and division.

Page 377 Your child solved problems that review math skills from previous chapters and will help your child with the skills in Chapter 12.

Math at Home Help your child practice adding and subtracting two-digit numbers without regrouping. For example, adding costs of two items such as 22¢ and 35¢.

Math Literature Read stories and do activities with your child relating to addition and subtraction. Look for the following books in your local library.
Hold Tight, Bear! by Ron Maris (Harcourt Brace, 1993)
Sea Sums by Joy N. Hulme (Hyperion Books for Children, 1996)

California Content Standards in Chapter 12 Lessons*

	Teach and Practice	Practice		Teach and Practice	Practice
Number Sense			**Statistics, Data Analysis, and Probability**		
1.3 Represent equivalent forms of the same number through the use of physical models and number expressions.		1, 2, 4, 6, 7, 9	2.0 Sort objects and create and describe patterns by numbers or colors.	5	1, 6
1.4 Count and group objects in ones and tens.		2, 4, 7, 9	**Mathematical Reasoning**		
2.6 Solve addition and subtraction problems with one- and two-digit numbers.	1–4, 6–10	12	1.0 Make decisions about how to set up a problem.	10	5
3.0 Use estimation strategies in computation and problem solving that involve numbers that use the ones and tens.	11	12	1.1 Determine the approach, materials, and strategies to be used.		2–4, 8–10
3.1 Make reasonable estimates when comparing larger or smaller numbers.	11	12	1.2 Use tools, such as manipulatives or sketches, to model problems.		8, 10, 11
Algebra and Functions			2.0 Solve problems and justify their reasoning.		5, 11
1.1 Write and solve number sentences from problem situations that express relationships involving addition and subtraction.		4, 7, 9	2.1 Explain the reasoning used and justify the procedures selected.		1, 6, 12
			2.2 Make precise calculations and check the validity of the results from the context of the problem.	12	
1.3 Create problem situations that might lead to given number sentences involving addition and subtraction.		3	3.0 Note connections between one problem and another.	5	1, 6, 7

* The symbol (🔑) indicates a key standard as designated in the Mathematics Framework for California Public Schools.
Full statements of the California Content Standards are found at the beginning of this book following the Table of Contents.

Name_____ **Adding Tens and Ones**

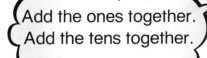

Add the ones together.
Add the tens together.

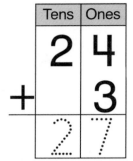

Tens	Ones
2	4
+	3
2	7

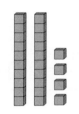

$24 + 3 = 27$

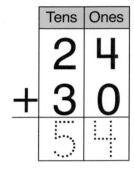

Tens	Ones
2	4
+3	0
5	4

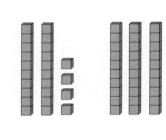

$24 + 30 = 54$

Add.
Use models and Workmat 4.

1.

Tens	Ones
3	1
+	4

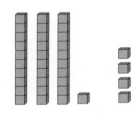

$31 + 4 = $ _____

2.

Tens	Ones
4	8
+2	0

$48 + 20 = $ _____

3.

Tens	Ones
5	5
+3	0

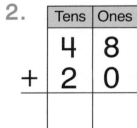

$55 + 30 = $ _____

4.

Tens	Ones
6	2
+	7

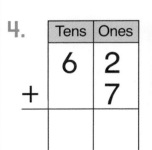

$62 + 7 = $ _____

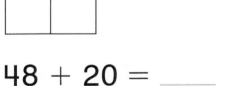

California Content Standards *Number Sense 2.6 Solve addition problems with one- and two-digit numbers. Also Number Sense 1.3, 1.4, Mathematical Reasoning 1.1.*

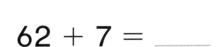

three hundred eighty-one **381**

Find the sum.
Use models if you like.

5.

$$\begin{array}{r} 26 \\ +\ 2 \\ \hline 28 \end{array}$$

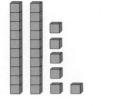

6.

$$\begin{array}{r} 35 \\ +\ 30 \\ \hline \end{array}$$

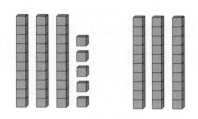

7.

$$\begin{array}{r} 43 \\ +\ 2 \\ \hline \end{array}$$
$$\begin{array}{r} 16 \\ +\ 3 \\ \hline \end{array}$$
$$\begin{array}{r} 69 \\ +\ 10 \\ \hline \end{array}$$
$$\begin{array}{r} 14 \\ +\ 70 \\ \hline \end{array}$$
$$\begin{array}{r} 60 \\ +\ 5 \\ \hline \end{array}$$

8.

$$\begin{array}{r} 10 \\ +\ 27 \\ \hline \end{array}$$
$$\begin{array}{r} 3 \\ +\ 14 \\ \hline \end{array}$$
$$\begin{array}{r} 20 \\ +\ 20 \\ \hline \end{array}$$
$$\begin{array}{r} 13 \\ +\ 10 \\ \hline \end{array}$$
$$\begin{array}{r} 3 \\ +\ 25 \\ \hline \end{array}$$

9.

$$\begin{array}{r} 91 \\ +\ 8 \\ \hline \end{array}$$
$$\begin{array}{r} 20 \\ +\ 36 \\ \hline \end{array}$$
$$\begin{array}{r} 5 \\ +\ 84 \\ \hline \end{array}$$
$$\begin{array}{r} 27 \\ +\ 50 \\ \hline \end{array}$$
$$\begin{array}{r} 40 \\ +\ 40 \\ \hline \end{array}$$

Problem Solving

Solve.

10. Randy has 15 shells.
He finds 2 more.
How many shells
does he have now?

_____ shells

11. Liz has 20 shells.
Randy gives her 19.
How many shells does
she have now?

_____ shells

Home Activity Ask your child to tell you how he or she found each sum on page 382. Homework Workbook 12-2

Name_____

Adding Two-Digit Numbers

How many seeds are there in all?

11

32

① First add the ones.

Tens	Ones
3	2
+ 1	1
	3

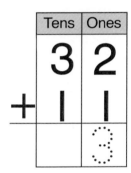

② Then add the tens.

Tens	Ones
3	2
+ 1	1
4	3

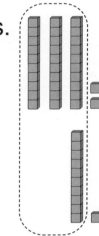

Use models and Workmat 4.
Find each sum.

1.

Tens	Ones
3	5
+ 4	2
7	7

Tens	Ones
2	1
+ 1	3

Tens	Ones
1	3
+	6

Tens	Ones
2	2
+ 6	0

2.

Tens	Ones
3	4
+ 5	2

Tens	Ones
7	9
+ 1	0

Tens	Ones
3	1
+	5

Tens	Ones
2	7
+ 7	2

California Content Standards *Number Sense 2.6 Solve addition problems with one- and two-digit numbers. Also Algebra and Functions 1.3, Mathematical Reasoning 1.1.*

three hundred eighty-three **383**

Find each sum.
Use models if you like.

3.
24	15	32	24	46
+ 30	+ 40	+ 65	+ 23	+ 52
54				

4.
83	10	60	11	65
+ 2	+ 29	+ 30	+ 11	+ 13

5.
82	15	17	54	63
+ 14	+ 74	+ 60	+ 11	+ 1

 **Problem Solving**

Conner made a table to show his card collection.

Trading Cards	
Type of Card	Number
Football	23
Hockey	61
Baseball	21

Solve. Show your work.

6. How many football and hockey cards does Conner have? _____ cards

7. Use the table to write a number story. Ask a classmate to solve it.

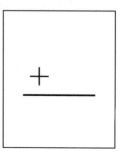

384 three hundred eighty-four

Home Activity Ask your child to add two numbers together without regrouping such as 22 + 17 =. Homework Workbook 12-3

Name_____

Adding with Regrouping

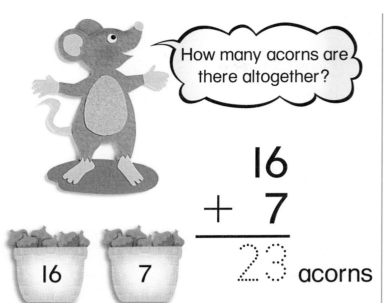

How many acorns are there altogether?

16
+ 7
-----
23 acorns

16   7

① Show 1 ten and 6 ones.
Show 7 ones.

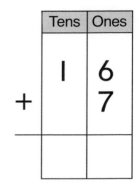

Tens	Ones
1	6
+	7

Tens	Ones

② Add the ones.
Change 10 ones to 1 ten.

Tens	Ones
1	6
+	7
	13

Tens	Ones

③ Add the tens.
Show the answer.

Tens	Ones
1	6
+	7
2	3

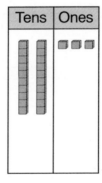

Tens	Ones

Add.
Use models and Workmat 4.

1.

Tens	Ones
1	7
+	8
2	5

Tens	Ones
2	4
+	9

Tens	Ones
4	8
+	6

Tens	Ones
7	6
+	5

California Content Standards Number Sense 2.6 Solve addition problems with one- and two-digit numbers. Also Number Sense 1.3, 1.4, Algebra and Functions 1.1, Mathematical Reasoning 1.1.

Add.
Use models and Workmat 4 if you like.

2.

Tens	Ones
1	9
+	3
2	2

Tens	Ones
3	3
+	8

Tens	Ones
5	6
+	7

Tens	Ones
8	9
+	5

3.

Tens	Ones
2	7
+	7

Tens	Ones
8	8
+	1

Tens	Ones
7	9
+	8

Tens	Ones
4	2
+	8

4.

Tens	Ones
6	6
+	6

Tens	Ones
5	9
+ 3	0

Tens	Ones
6	5
+	7

Tens	Ones
3	8
+	7

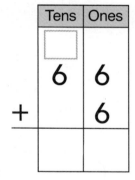

Math Reasoning

Algebra

5. Write the numbers to make the number sentence true.

$$28 + 4 = \underline{\hspace{1cm}} + \underline{\hspace{1cm}}$$

 **Home Activity** Ask your child to add two numbers together with regrouping such as 34 + 7 =. Homework Workbook 12-4

Name_____ **Problem-Solving Strategy**

Find a Pattern

On Monday, James picks up 4 shells.
On Tuesday he picks up 8 shells.
On Wednesday he picks up 12 shells.
If James continues the pattern, how
many shells will he pick up on Friday?

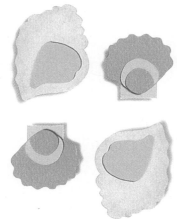

Understand

You need to find out how many shells
James will pick up on Friday.

Plan

Look for the pattern. Then continue it.

4 + 4 = 8 and
8 + 4 = 12

Solve

The pattern is to add ___4___ more shells each day.

Monday	Tuesday	Wednesday	Thursday	Friday
4	8	12	16	20

James will pick up 20 shells on Friday.

Look Back

Did you answer the question?

Find a pattern.

1. Eva collects 5 baseball cards in March.
   She collects 10 cards in April. She collects
   15 cards in May. What is the pattern?

   The pattern is to add _____ more cards each month.

California Content Standards *Statistics, Data Analysis, and Probability 2.0 Students create and describe patterns. Mathematical Reasoning 3.0. Also Mathematical Reasoning 1.0, 2.0.*

Find the pattern. Solve.

2. Dan finds 8 leaves in 1 hour.
   He finds 16 leaves after 2 hours.
   He finds 24 leaves after 3 hours.
   What is the pattern?

   The pattern is to add _____ more leaves
   each hour.

3. What if Dan continues this pattern?
   How many leaves will he find after 5 hours?

1 hour	2 hours	3 hours	4 hours	5 hours
8	16	24		

   Dan will find _____ leaves after 5 hours.

4. Tina is making a banner with green
   and blue triangles.
   She puts the triangles in this pattern.

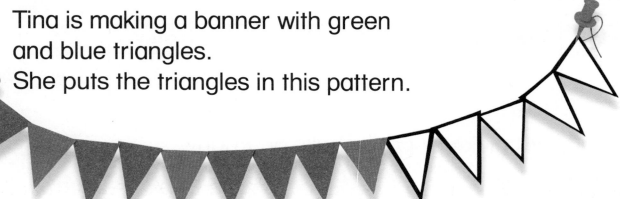

What is the pattern? _____

_____

5. Color to continue Tina's pattern.
   How many blue and green triangles
   will she need for the banner?

 _____

Home Activity Ask your child to tell you about each pattern
on this page and then tell what would come next. Homework
Workbook 12-5

Write the numbers.
Add.

1.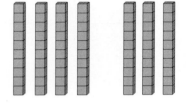

_____ + _____ = _____

2.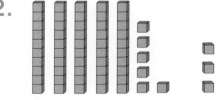

_____ + _____ = _____

Add.

3.

Tens	Ones
2	7
+	2

Tens	Ones
3	2
+ 5	4

Tens	Ones
6	4
+	7

Tens	Ones
7	8
+	6

Find the pattern.

4. Ann reads 5 books in March. She reads 10 books in April. She reads 15 books in May.

The pattern is to add _____ more books each month.

Use the table to solve.

5. How many apples did Joe and Don eat?

_____ apples

Tens	Ones
+	

Apples	
Name	Number
Joe	15
Ann	11
Don	7

1.

9:30   10:00   10:30   11:00

○   ○   ○   ○

2.

$6 + 3$ $12 - 3$

○   ○

$11 - 3$ $4 + 5$

○   ○

3.

○   ○   ○   NH

                                         ○

4. $7 + 6 = \Box$

1   11   13   14

○   ○   ○   ○

5. $\begin{array}{r} 18 \\ -\ 9 \\ \hline \end{array}$

9   10   8   11

○   ○   ○   ○

6.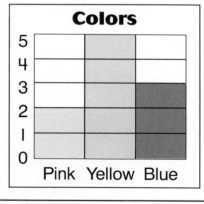

$3 - 1 = 2$ $2 + 3 = 5$

○   ○

$5 - 2 = 3$ $5 - 3 = 2$

○   ○

Oral Directions *Mark the correct answer. NH means "Not here." Mark it whenever the answer is not given.*

#1. Mark the time shown on the clock.
#2. Which is not another name for nine?

#3. Count the coins. Mark the set of coins that shows the same value.
#4–5. Add or subtract.
#6. Look at the graph. Choose the number sentence that shows the difference between yellow and blue.

Name_____ **Subtracting Tens**

Subtracting tens is like subtracting ones.

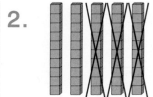

7 ones — 3 ones   7 tens — 3 tens

7 — 3 = 4   70 — 30 = 40

Write the numbers. Subtract.
Use models if you like.

1.

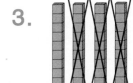

____ tens — ____ ten

____ — ____ = ____

2.

____ tens — ____ tens

____ — ____ = ____

3.

____ tens — ____ tens

____ — ____ = ____

4.

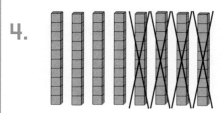

____ tens — ____ tens

____ — ____ = ____

California Content Standards *Number Sense 2.6 Solve subtraction problems with one- and two-digit numbers. Also Number Sense 1.3, Statistics, Data Analysis, and Probability 2.0, Mathematical Reasoning 2.1, 3.0.*

Write the numbers. Subtract.
Use models if you like.

5.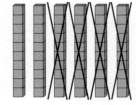

___6___ tens – ___4___ tens

___60___ – ___40___ = ___20___

6.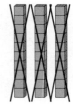

_____ tens – _____ tens

_____ – _____ = _____

7.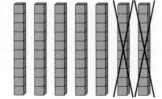

_____ tens – _____ tens

_____ – _____ = _____

8.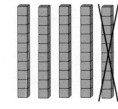

_____ tens – _____ ten

_____ – _____ = _____

 Math Reasoning

Number Sense

9. Look for a pattern. Subtract.

10. Tell how you found each difference.

8 – 3 = _____

80 – 30 = _____

800 – 300 = _____

Home Activity Ask your child to subtract numbers that are multiples of ten. Homework Workbook 12-6

Name_____

Subtracting Tens and Ones

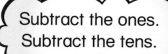
Subtract the ones.
Subtract the tens.

Tens	Ones
3	6
−	4
3	2

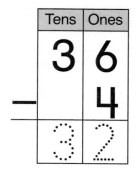

$36 - 4 = 32$

Tens	Ones
5	7
− 3	0
2	7

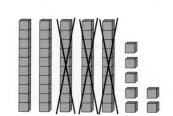

$57 - 30 = 27$

Subtract.
Use models and Workmat 4.

1.

Tens	Ones
2	5
−	3

$25 - 3 = $ _____

2.

Tens	Ones
4	9
− 3	0

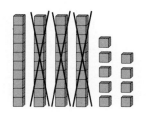

$49 - 30 = $ _____

3.

Tens	Ones
6	7
−	5

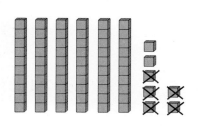

$67 - 5 = $ _____

4.

Tens	Ones
8	4
− 5	0

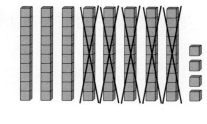

$84 - 50 = $ _____

California Content Standards Number Sense 2.6 (🔑)
Solve subtraction problems with one- and two-digit numbers.
Also Number Sense 1.3, 1.4, Algebra and Functions 1.1,
Mathematical Reasoning 3.0.

Subtract.
Use models if you like.

5.
```
   36
 -  4
 ───
   32
```
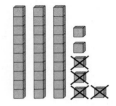

6.
```
   74
 - 60
```
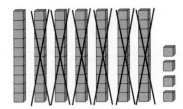

7.
```
   28        15        60        59        88
 -  6      -  1      - 20      -  4      - 40
 ────      ────      ────      ────      ────
```

8.
```
   91        37        25        47        95
 - 60      -  3      -  2      - 20      - 20
 ────      ────      ────      ────      ────
```

9.
```
   60        99        78        36        89
 - 30      -  5      -  3      - 20      -  3
 ────      ────      ────      ────      ────
```

 **Problem Solving**

Find each rule.
Use models if you like.

10. Subtract ___2___

59	57
46	44
37	35

11. Subtract _____

34	33
89	88
76	75

12. Subtract _____

77	57
46	26
89	69

394 three hundred ninety-four

Home Activity Ask your child to subtract two numbers without regrouping such as 25 − 10 =. Homework Workbook 12-7

Name_____ **Subtracting Two-Digit Numbers**

59
Rosie

24
Nathan

How many more shells does Rosie have?

① First subtract the ones.

② Then subtract the tens.

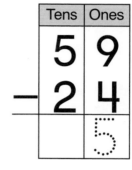

Tens	Ones
5	9
− 2	4
	5

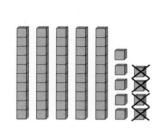

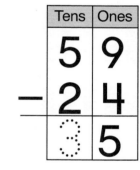

Tens	Ones
5	9
− 2	4
3	5

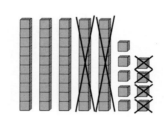

Use models and Workmat 4.
Find each difference.

1.

Tens	Ones
6	9
− 3	5
3	4

Tens	Ones
5	8
− 2	1

Tens	Ones
9	6
− 7	4

Tens	Ones
7	4
− 5	3

2.

Tens	Ones
3	4
− 2	0

Tens	Ones
8	9
− 2	3

Tens	Ones
6	7
−	3

Tens	Ones
3	9
− 1	2

California Content Standards *Number Sense 2.6 (⟿) Solve subtraction problems with one- and two-digit numbers. Also Mathematical Reasoning 1.1, 1.2.*

Remember, subtract the ones first.

Cross out to subtract.

3.

Tens	Ones
6	5
− 2	3
4	2

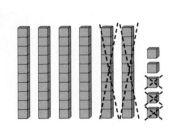

4.

Tens	Ones
7	3
− 4	0

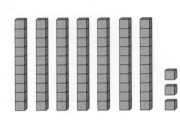

5.

Tens	Ones
5	5
−	4

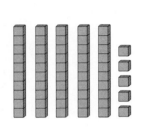

6.

Tens	Ones
2	7
− 1	2

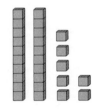

7.

Tens	Ones
4	8
− 2	3

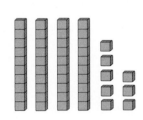

8.

Tens	Ones
8	1
−	1

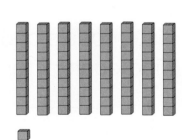

Problem Solving

Solve.

9. Ben has 27 feathers.
He finds 10 more.
Then he loses 3.
How many feathers does he have now? _____ feathers

Home Activity Ask your child to tell you how he or she found each difference on page 396. Homework Workbook 12-8

Name_____

Subtracting with Regrouping

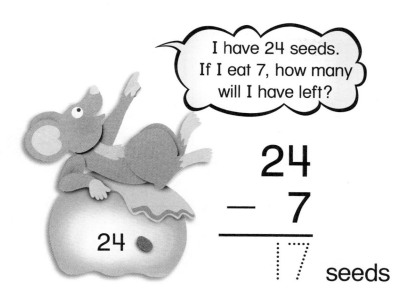

I have 24 seeds. If I eat 7, how many will I have left?

24

$$24 - 7 = \underset{\text{seeds}}{17}$$

① **Show 2 tens and 4 ones.**

Tens	Ones
2	4

Tens	Ones

---

② To subtract 7 ones, change 1 ten to 10 ones.

Tens	Ones
1 2̸	14 4̸
−	7

Tens	Ones

③ Subtract 7 ones.
Subtract 0 tens.

Tens	Ones
1 2̸	14 4̸
−	7
	17

Tens	Ones

Subtract.
Use models and Workmat 4.

1.

Tens	Ones
1 2̸	11 1̸
−	6
1	5

Tens	Ones
3	2
−	7

Tens	Ones
5	6
−	9

Tens	Ones
4	3
−	6

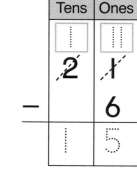 **California Content Standards** *Number Sense 2.6 (🔑) Solve subtraction problems with one- and two-digit numbers. Also Number Sense 1.3, 1.4, Algebra and Functions 1.1, Mathematical Reasoning 1.1.*

Subtract.
Use models and Workmat 4 if you like.

2.

Tens	Ones
1	15
2	5
–	7
1	8

Tens	Ones
4	8
–	9

Tens	Ones
7	4
–	7

Tens	Ones
6	3
–	8

3.

Tens	Ones
8	1
–	5

Tens	Ones
3	7
–	8

Tens	Ones
9	6
–	8

Tens	Ones
4	8
–	5

4.

Tens	Ones
7	5
–	8

Tens	Ones
6	2
–	4

Tens	Ones
9	1
–	7

Tens	Ones
8	3
–	4

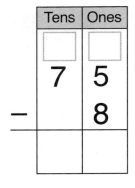

Math Reasoning   **Algebra**

5. Write the numbers to make the number sentence true.

$$36 - 8 = \underline{\hspace{1cm}} + \underline{\hspace{1cm}}$$

398   three hundred ninety-eight

Home Activity Ask your child to subtract two numbers with regrouping such as 42 − 6 =. Homework Workbook 12-9

Name_____

Use the picture to solve.
Think: Do you need to add or subtract?

1. Jesse has 56¢.
He buys a bag of marbles.
How much money does he have now?

$$\begin{array}{r} 56\ ¢ \\ -35\ ¢ \\ \hline 21\ ¢ \end{array}$$

2. Alice buys a trading card.
Then she buys a book.
How much money does she spend?

_____ ¢
_____ ¢
_____ ¢

3. Paco buys a box of shells.
He also buys a car.
How much money does he spend?

_____ ¢
_____ ¢
_____ ¢

4. Beth has 98¢.
She buys an airplane.
How much money does she have now?

_____ ¢
_____ ¢
_____ ¢

California Content Standards *Mathematical Reasoning 1.0 Students make decisions about how to set up a problem. Number Sense 2.6. Also Mathematical Reasoning 1.1, 1.2.*

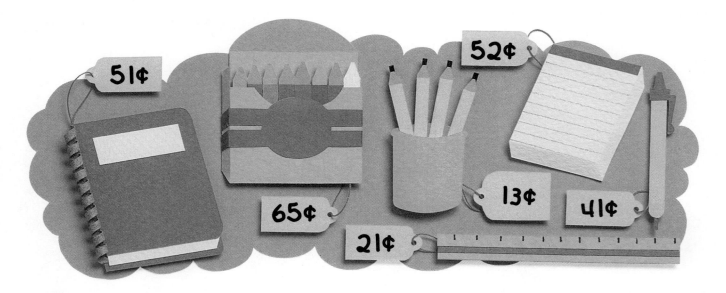

Use the picture. Add or subtract to solve.

5. Luis has 69¢.
   He buys a pencil.
   How much money does he have now?

   _____ ¢
   _____ ¢
   _____ ¢

6. Molly buys a notebook.
   She also buys a ruler.
   How much does she spend?

   _____ ¢
   _____ ¢
   _____ ¢

7. Tal has 77¢.
   He buys a pad.
   How much money does he have now?

   _____ ¢
   _____ ¢
   _____ ¢

8. Choose 2 things to buy. Then solve.

   I buy a _____ .

   Then I buy a _____ .

   How much do I spend?

   _____ ¢
   _____ ¢
   _____ ¢

Home Activity Put price tags up to 50¢ on several toys. "Go shopping" with your child to practice adding and subtracting. Homework Workbook 12-10

Name_____

Rounding to the Nearest Ten

Is 12 closer to 10 or 20?

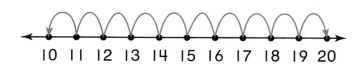

10 11 12 13 14 15 16 17 18 19 20

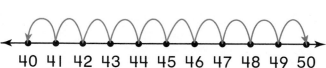

12 is closer to 10.
We round 12 to 10.

Is 47 closer to 40 or 50?

47 is closer to 50.
We round 47 to 50.

40 41 42 43 44 45 46 47 48 49 50

Show the hops to each ten.
Write the number.

1. Is 17 closer to 10 or 20?

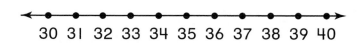

10 11 12 13 14 15 16 17 18 19 20

20

2. Is 33 closer to 30 or 40?

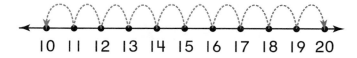

30 31 32 33 34 35 36 37 38 39 40

_____

3. Is 68 closer to 60 or 70?

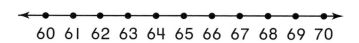

60 61 62 63 64 65 66 67 68 69 70

_____

California Content Standards *Number Sense 3.0 Students use estimation strategies in computation and problem solving that involve numbers that use the ones and tens places. Number Sense 3.1. Also Mathematical Reasoning 1.2, 2.0.*

Write the ten that is closest
to the number shown.

4.

  ____   ____ 27 ____

5.

33 ____ 56 ____ 48 ____

6.

62 ____ 69 ____ 77 ____

7.

39 ____ 51 ____ 83 ____

8.

66 ____ 94 ____ 27 ____

 **Math Reasoning**

9. Jack's number is closest
   to 20.

   What numbers could it be?

   _____

   _____

10. Sue's number is closest
    to 50.

    What number could it be?

    _____

    _____

 Home Activity Say a number between 1 and 100. Ask your child to round the number to the nearest ten. (Avoid numbers with 5 ones.) Homework Workbook 12-11

Name_____

Solve the problem.

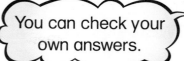

You can check your own answers.

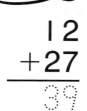

① Dana picked 12 apples.
Rico picked 27 apples.
How many apples did they pick altogether?

$$\begin{array}{r} 12 \\ +27 \\ \hline 39 \end{array}$$

② Estimate to check your answer.
12 is closer to 10.
27 is closer to 30.

39 is close to 40!

$$\begin{array}{r} 10 \\ +30 \\ \hline 40 \end{array}$$

③ Write the answer.

_39_ apples

Solve the problem.
Estimate to check your answer.
Write the answer.

1. Terry sent 16 cards.
Andy sent 21 cards.
How many cards did they send altogether?

_37_ cards

Solve	Check
$\begin{array}{r} 16 \\ +21 \\ \hline 37 \end{array}$	$\begin{array}{r} 20 \\ +20 \\ \hline 40 \end{array}$

2. Sam made 47 cupcakes.
Mia made 26 cupcakes.
How many more cupcakes did Sam make?

_____ cupcakes

Solve	Check

California Content Standards *Mathematical Reasoning 2.2 Make precise calculations and check the validity of the results from the context of the problem. Also Number Sense 2.6, 3.0, 3.1, Mathematical Reasoning 2.1.*

four hundred three **403**

Solve the problem.
Estimate to check your answer.
Write the answer.

3. Karen found 36 shells.
   Josh found 23 shells.
   How many shells did they
   find in all?

   _____ shells

   Solve

   _____

   Check

   _____

4. Pat put 64 blocks in the box.
   Tom put 31 blocks away.
   How many more blocks did
   Pat put away?

   _____ blocks

   Solve

   _____

   Check

   _____

5. Matt has 78¢.
   He buys a book for 46¢.
   How much does
   he have now?

   _____ ¢

   Solve

   ¢

   ¢
   _____
   ¢

   Check

   ¢

   ¢
   _____
   ¢

Home Activity Give your child everyday problems to solve
and check using estimation. For example, there are 46 paper
clips in the box; I take 22 paperclips, how many are left? (Avoid
numbers with 5 ones.) Homework Workbook 12-12

Name _____

Cross out to subtract.

1.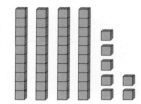
$$\begin{array}{r} 50 \\ -20 \\ \hline \end{array}$$

2.
$$\begin{array}{r} 47 \\ -\ 2 \\ \hline \end{array}$$

Subtract.

3.
$$\begin{array}{r} 26 \\ -\ 3 \\ \hline \end{array}$$
$$\begin{array}{r} 60 \\ -40 \\ \hline \end{array}$$

$$\begin{array}{r} 89 \\ -26 \\ \hline \end{array}$$
$$\begin{array}{r} 97 \\ -\ 5 \\ \hline \end{array}$$

4.

Tens	Ones
4	5
−	8

Tens	Ones
7	2
−	9

Write the closest ten.

5.  (12) ____ (63) ____ (79) ____

Solve the problem.
Estimate to check your answer.
Write the answer.

6. Jane has 88¢.
   She buys a kite for 46¢.
   How much money does
   she have now?

   _____ ¢

   Solve

   _____ ¢
   _____ ¢
   _____ ¢

   Check

   _____ ¢
   _____ ¢
   _____ ¢

Name_____

1. ⭕   NH

    ○   ○   ○   ○

---

2.   **32**
    + 27

    $30 + 30 = 60$ $30 + 20 = 50$
          ○   ○

    $30 - 30 = 0$ NH
          ○   ○

---

3.   **44**
    + 32

    76   13   44   NH
    ○   ○   ○   ○

---

4. 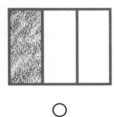   NH

    ○   ○   ○   ○

5.

    $7 - 2 = 5$ $5 + 2 = 7$ $5 - 2 = 3$ NH
    ○   ○   ○   ○

---

6.   1 2 3 2 1 2 3 2 1 2 3 _____

    1   2   3   NH
    ○   ○   ○   ○

Oral Directions *Mark the correct answer. NH means "Not here." Mark it whenever the answer is not given.*

#1. Mark the object with a face that matches the circle.
#2. Which number sentence would you use to estimate and check the answer for thirty-two plus twenty-seven?

#3. Solve.
#4. Mark the shape with one-fourth shaded.
#5. Mark the number sentence that matches the picture.
#6. Mark the number that is most likely to come next in the pattern.

406 four hundred six

Name_____

Add or subtract.

1. 15 − 3 = _____

2. 24 + 4 = _____

3. 36 − 2 = _____

4. 45 + 4 = _____

Write each number sentence.

5.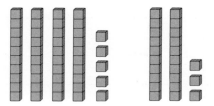

_____ + _____ = _____

6.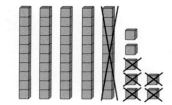

_____ − _____ = _____

Add or subtract.

7.
$$\begin{array}{cccccc} 15 & 29 & 58 & 60 & 76 & 48 \\ +\ 2 & +30 & -\ 6 & -30 & +13 & -24 \end{array}$$

Find the pattern.

8. Mike runs 1 mile in 8 minutes.
He runs 2 miles in 16 minutes.
He runs 3 miles in 24 minutes.

1 mile	2 miles	3 miles
8	16	24

The pattern is to add _____ minutes
for each mile.

Cross out to subtract.

9.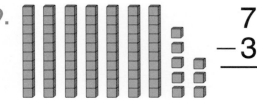
$$\begin{array}{r} 78 \\ -33 \\ \hline \end{array}$$

10.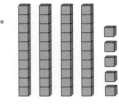
$$\begin{array}{r} 45 \\ -\ 4 \\ \hline \end{array}$$

Write the closest ten.

11.

(27) _____ | (52) _____ | (84) _____

Add or subtract.

12.

Tens	Ones
□	
2	4
+	7

Tens	Ones
□	□
9	5
−	8

Tens	Ones
□	
3	9
+	8

Tens	Ones
□	□
6	2
−	6

Solve the problem.
Estimate to check your answer.
Write the answer.

13. Tony has 69¢.
    He buys a bag of grapes
    for 56¢.
    How much money does
    he have now?

    _____ ¢

Solve	Check
¢	¢
¢	¢
¢	¢

1. $41 + 5 = \square$ | 36 ○   46 ○   47 ○   NH ○

2. $29 - 7 = \square$ | 26 ○   21 ○   22 ○   NH ○

3.   12 | 10 ○   20 ○   30 ○   NH ○

4.   67 | 60 ○   50 ○   40 ○   NH ○

5.

Monday	Tuesday	Wednesday	Thursday
4	8	12	

16 ○   18 ○   20 ○   NH ○

6.

 47¢    32¢

15¢ ○   89¢ ○   79¢ ○   NH ○

Oral Directions *Mark the correct answer. NH means "Not here." Mark it whenever the answer is not given.*

#1–2. Add or subtract.
#3–4. Look at the number in the circle. Mark the closest ten.

#5. Emily saw four butterflies on Monday, eight butterflies on Tuesday, and twelve butterflies on Wednesday. Using the pattern, how many butterflies did she see on Thursday?
#6. Jacob bought a bag of dog treats for forty-seven cents and a bag of cat treats for thirty-two cents. How much money did he spend?

7. $68 - 37 = \square$

$60 - 30 = 30$ ○

$70 - 40 = 30$ ○

$70 - 30 = 40$ ○

NH ○

8.
$$\begin{array}{r} 16 \\ + 6 \\ \hline \end{array}$$

10 ○　　22 ○　　24 ○　　NH ○

9.
$$\begin{array}{r} 75 \\ - 23 \\ \hline \end{array}$$

72 ○　　50 ○　　52 ○　　NH ○

10.
$$\begin{array}{r} 43 \\ + 25 \\ \hline \end{array}$$

78 ○　　69 ○　　18 ○　　NH ○

11.
$$\begin{array}{r} 31 \\ - 5 \\ \hline \end{array}$$

36 ○　　25 ○　　26 ○　　NH ○

12.

Crayons	
Color	Number
Red	49
Blue	34
Yellow	23

16 ○　　72 ○　　26 ○　　NH ○

Oral Directions *Mark the correct answer. NH means "Not here." Mark it whenever the answer is not given.*

#7. Mark the number sentence you would use to estimate to check the answer of sixty-eight minus thirty-seven.

#8–11. Add or subtract. Mark the answer.
#12. The table shows the number of red, blue, and yellow crayons in the classroom. How many more red crayons are there than yellow crayons?

410 four hundred ten

add

2 + 3 = 5

addition sentence

4 + 2 = 6

after

7, 8

8 is just after 7.

altogether

3   and   1

4 altogether

before

5, 6

5 is just before 6.

between

6, 7, 8

7 is between 6 and 8.

calendar

June						
S	M	T	W	T	F	S
			1	2	3	4
5	6	7	8	9	10	11
12	13	14	15	16	17	18
19	20	21	22	23	24	25
26	27	28	29	30		

centimeter

circle

cone

Picture Glossary

corner

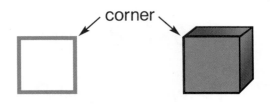

curves

count back

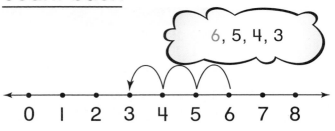

cylinder

count on

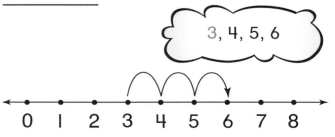

difference

$$5 - 2 = 3$$

$$\begin{array}{r} 5 \\ -\ 2 \\ \hline 3 \end{array}$$

difference

cube

A cube is a rectangular prism with 6 equal faces.

dime

or

10¢   10 cents

cup

double

$$2 + 2 = 4$$

equal parts

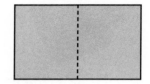

2 equal parts

fact family

$$4 + 2 = 6 \qquad 6 - 2 = 4$$
$$2 + 4 = 6 \qquad 6 - 4 = 2$$

equals

$$2 \overset{\downarrow}{=} 2$$
$$3 + 2 = 5$$
$$1 + 2 = 6 - 3$$

fewer

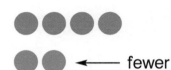

← fewer

estimate

solve: 12   estimate: 10
          + 27   + 30
          ───   ───
           39   40

fraction

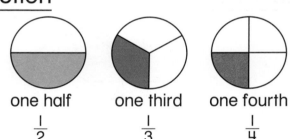

one half   one third   one fourth
$\frac{1}{2}$ $\frac{1}{3}$ $\frac{1}{4}$

even numbers

2, 4, 6, 8, 10

graph

Favorite Foods

0   1   2   3   4   5

face

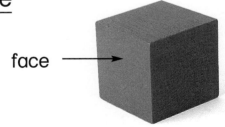

face →

greater than

3 is greater than 2.

$$3 > 2$$

Picture Glossary

heavier

heavier→

kilogram

5 peaches measure about 1 kilogram.

hour

It takes about 1 hour.

left

5 minus 2
3 left

hour hand

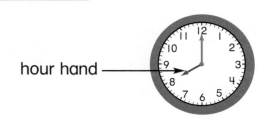

hour hand →

less than

2 is less than 3.
2 < 3

in all

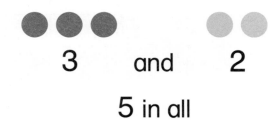

3   and   2

5 in all

lighter

← lighter

inch

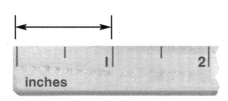

inches

liter

longer

 ←longer

nickel

 or

5¢   5 cents

minus

$$9 - 7 = 2$$

↑
minus

number line

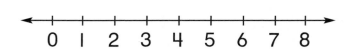

minute

I can count to 60.

It takes about a minute.

o'clock

9 o'clock

minute hand

minute hand →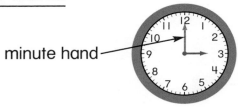

odd numbers

1, 3, 5, 7, 9

more

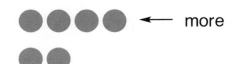 ← more

one fourth

$\frac{1}{4}$	$\frac{1}{4}$	$\frac{1}{4}$	$\frac{1}{4}$

Picture Glossary

one half

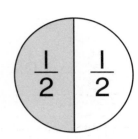

one third

ones

4 ones

pattern

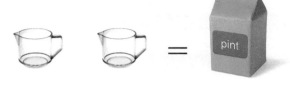

penny

 or

1¢   1 cent

pint

plus

$$5 + 4 = 9$$

↑
plus

pound

 3 apples weigh about 1 pound.

quart

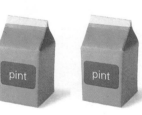 

quarter

 or

25¢   25 cents

416 four hundred sixteen

rectangle

shorter

← shorter

rectangular prism

sides

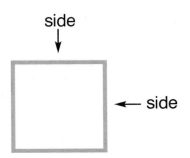

side ↓

side ←

regroup

10 ones = 1 ten

skip count

2   4   6   8

related facts

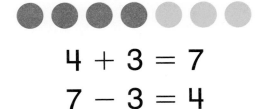

4 + 3 = 7
7 − 3 = 4

sphere

rounding

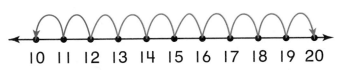

10 11 12 13 14 15 16 17 18 19 20

12 is closer to 10 than to 20.
12 rounds to 10.

square

A square is a rectangle
with 4 equal sides.

Picture Glossary

subtract  $4 - 3 = 1$	taller  taller →
subtraction sentence $7 - 3 = 4$	tally 
sum $4 + 4 = 8$ $\begin{array}{r} 4 \\ + 4 \\ \hline 8 \end{array}$ ↑ ↗ sum	tens 2 tens 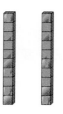
take away  3 take away 1	triangle 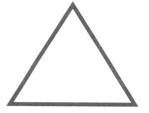

1	one	
2	two	
3	three	
4	four	
5	five	
6	six	

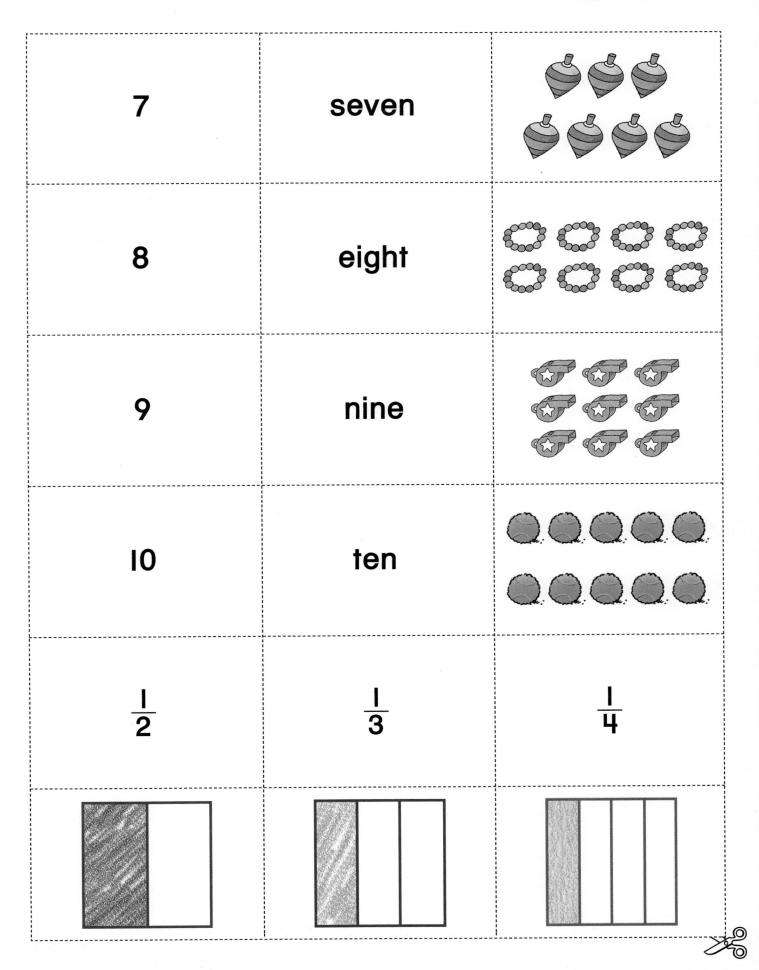

7	seven	
8	eight	
9	nine	
10	ten	
$\frac{1}{2}$	$\frac{1}{3}$	$\frac{1}{4}$

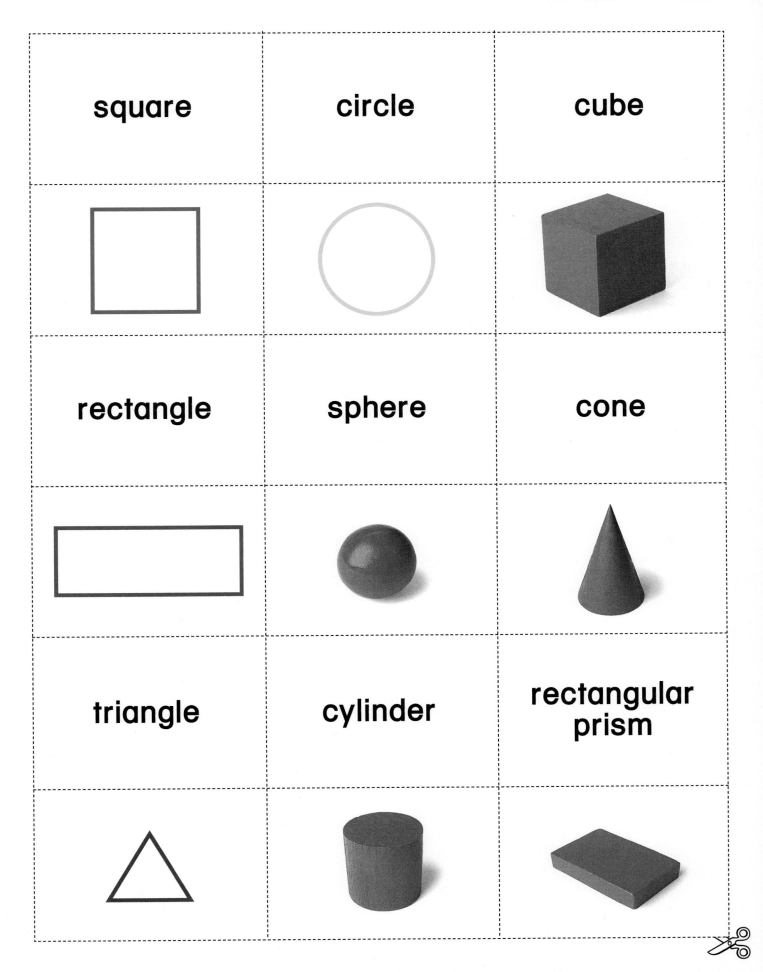

square

circle

cube

rectangle

sphere

cone

triangle

cylinder

rectangular prism

+	−	=
add	subtract	equals
		penny
5:00	10:30	or
nickel	dime	quarter
or	or	or

Credits